Arts Graduates, Their Skills and Their Employment:

To Sir Raymond Rickett CBE
Chairman, Council for National Academic Awards

Arts Graduates, Their Skills and Their Employment:
Perspectives for Change

Edited by

Heather Eggins

The Falmer Press

(A member of the Taylor & Francis Group)
London • Washington, D.C.

UK The Falmer Press, 4 John St., London, WC1N 2ET
USA The Falmer Press, Taylor & Francis Inc., 1900 Frost Road, 101, Bristol,
PA 19007

First published 1992

Library of Congress Cataloging-in-Publication data are available on request

A catalogue record for this book is available from the British Library

ISBN 0 75070 062 9
ISBN 0 75070 063 7

Set in 10/11pt Bembo by
Graphicraft Typesetters Ltd., Hong Kong

Printed in Great Britain by Burgess Science Press, Basingstoke on paper which has a specified pH value on final paper manufacture of not less than 7.5 and is therefore 'acid free'.

Contents

Contents

Preface

This book has been put together in order to make a contribution to the pressing debate which affects all of us in higher education and in industry, commerce and the public sector. The question that confronts us is how we can best prepare the high number of graduates that we shall be producing in arts subjects so that they can develop their skills to the utmost and thus contribute as effectively as possible to the development of the United Kingdom, and, in the context of the free movement of labour that is to come, to the development of the European Community.

We are unique in Europe in producing such a high percentage of arts graduates, and unique in that employers in the UK, recognizing this, have as many as 40–50 per cent of their vacancies available for 'any discipline' graduates.

This book surveys, first, the views of employers ranging from manufacturing industries to the financial services. It then presents the findings of significant research work on arts graduates and their employment, and on transferable skills, drawing on international initiatives. Included are the views of a recent graduate, and student perceptions of what skills they acquire during their courses, and what they would like to acquire. Finally it explores, in a series of chapters, what institutions are doing to meet student needs.

The title refers deliberately to 'Arts' graduates in the belief that this book will be of as much interest to those in the present 'university' sector as to those in the polytechnics and colleges of higher education. Although, under the terms of reference of the Council for National Academic Awards, the initiative principally involved the polytechnics and colleges, universities did participate, particularly in the final conference. The term 'Humanities' commonly used in polytechnics and colleges of higher education is virtually synonymous with the 'Arts'. The range of subjects generally referred to in this book are history, English, philosophy, theology and related studies, languages and combined and general arts. The views expressed by the authors are those held personally by them and are not necessarily those of the CNAA.

The book as a whole presents an image of an alert, responsive higher education system which can and does work closely with those who employ the graduates they produce. These images are not yet perhaps seen throughout the system, but they are present; it is hoped that this book might be a vehicle for further dissemination of them.

The contents of this book have been gathered together over a number of years. Some contributions are in the form of speeches, delivered at the seminars hosted by the Council for National Academic Awards during the period 1987–89 when the initiative on 'Humanities and Employment' took the form of nationwide seminars and conferences. Other contributions refer to research work undertaken during the years 1987–91. Yet others are up-to-date pieces commenting on the situation as it is now. However, although the economic context shifts during this period, the central questions for discussion remain the same: arts graduates, their skills and their employment. Indeed, the issue has, if anything, become more pressing in that the shift to a mass system of higher education is led in the universities by demand for humanities degrees. How we can best equip our graduates to enable them to develop their maximum potential must remain high on any higher education agenda.

Heather Eggins
London
January 1992

Acknowledgments

This book owes its being to the prescience of the Committee for Humanities of the CNAA, chaired by Professor Andrew Hook, Professor of English Literature, University of Glasgow, who conceived the original idea.

The programme for the initiative on 'Humanities and Employment' was planned by, first, a Working Party, and later by a Steering Group, both of which were chaired by Professor Channon, Head of Humanities at Bristol Polytechnic. We are indebted to the inspiration and leadership offered by both chairmen, and also to the huge amount of creative energy and effort put into the initiative by those many specialist advisors to CNAA who gave generously and freely of their time.

A special thanks go to the many employers who supported the initiative, as well as to those whose chapters are included, to David Bradshaw whose extensive research findings form a pivotal node of the book, and to all who were persuaded to contribute, and so willingly did.

Particular thanks are due to Patricia Pearce with whom I batted around ideas, to my colleagues at CNAA, to my husband, and to Joanne Reading, my secretary, who worked long and hard on preparing the manuscript.

Chairman of the Steering Group

Geoffrey Channon

The context of the CNAA's Humanities and Employment initiative, begun in 1987, was one in which the traditional policy assumption that there was a natural match between what graduates wanted to do, what employers needed, and what was best for the economy, was being rapidly eroded. Ministers in successive administrations from 1979 onwards wanted to reorder the object-ives of institutions so that in future higher education would better serve the needs of a strong enterprise economy. Changes in the system of funding, governance and control would promote this change of emphasis, and would lead to a system of higher education in which educational objectives, tradi-tionally set by the institutions themselves, would be encouraged to recognize this agenda. These changes in public perceptions and public policy, reinforced by the popular belief that higher education in general, and the humanities in particular, had for more than a century been hostile to industry and com-merce, and had 'failed' the economy, suggested an uncertain future for the humanities. They were seen as being not so obviously 'relevant' as some other disciplines in preparing students for the world of work. The signals that the polytechnics and colleges received from outside were unambiguous and for teachers of humanities (and social sciences) quite chilling. The National Ad-visory Body (NAB), which was responsible for allocating resources to the public sector at that time, developed a funding methodology whose main feature was differential weightings wich encouraged institutions to shift the balance of their work towards the higher weighted 'preferred areas' and away from the humanities (and the social sciences).

It was in order to meet the challenges posed by these environmental changes that the CNAA's Committee for Humanities decided to plan the series of regional seminars and conferences which led to the present collection of essays. The initiative was always intended to be ongoing. Its primary aim was, and is, to create a climate in which employers, teachers and students can communicate directly with each other to bring about a better understanding and to promote action at the appropriate levels. It complements other related projects such as the Training Agency's 'Enterprise in Higher Education' and the Royal Society of Arts 'Higher Education for Capability' which have sought to raise the level of work-related skills and opportunities among students in all types of courses. It would be misleading to suggest that the seminars provided clear guidance on the ways forward nor perhaps should they have done. What they did do, however, was perhaps more important: they brought the major parties together, defined the areas of debate, articulated various models of response within institutions and above all, raised levels of consciousness. Much of the flavour of what was discussed is captured in the essays.

The stimulus for the initiative came at a particular moment in the planning of higher education when it seemed that a growing gap was being created between the student demand for humanities courses and the provision of places. Over the last few years, however, institutional priorities in the polytechnics and colleges have changed dramatically, and now such courses are being used to promote institutional growth, not least by widening access to mature applicants and to those with limited formal qualifications. The widespread availability in the humanities of access courses, flexible undergraduate programmes, modular schemes and credit transfer have all helped to facilitate access. Indeed, the humanities are well placed to play a full part in the change towards the system of open, mass higher education presaged in the recent White Paper *Higher Education: A New Framework* (May, 1991). Subjects such as engineering and the applied sciences may be 'preferred' subjects in Whitehall and may offer better financial rewards to those so qualified but students still show a strong preference for the humanities and social sciences. There is, though, a warning note to be sounded: as the recent experience of fees-only recruitment demonstrates, the humanities may be used for expansion by competitive price-cutting, cost-reduction and the cumulative transformation of what is being offered to students and through them to society.

The present economic recession, the worst since the 1930s, presents a more immediate, grim prospect, especially for the increased numbers of humanities graduates who are seeking jobs. With the notable exception of defence, much of the cutting back has been focussed on the service sector rather than manufacturing, in contrast to the previous recession in early 1980s. Not surprisingly humanities graduates are the most affected. Firms that recruit engineers and scientists have not cut back nearly so much. It is perhaps understandable, however, that for a brief time in the mid-1980s, when the general demand for graduates was rising, that providers of humanities courses could believe that they had discovered a panacea which would reconcile their commitment to traditional academic values with the needs of employers and the new vocationalism. The panacea was, of course, personal transferable skills. The humanities and employment seminars provided a window on what was being done in this area and raised a number of important issues. For example, were employers and academics using the same language to describe different things? How were skills to be developed and assessed? How far down the skills and competences route was it possible to go without losing sight of subject content? Could any one set of disciplines supply a full panoply of skills, habits of mind and attitudes? Or would a broader-based, perhaps negotiated curriculum supply what was needed? The experience of the current recession does not negate the importance of these questions nor indeed does it demonstrate that the responses in the institutions are misguided. What is at issue here is the conflict between the short-term imperatives of the economic cycle, over which educationalists have little or no influence, and the long-term needs of an economy whose growth requires a much larger 'output' of 'suitable' graduates. As David Bradshaw shows in his perceptive chapter it may just be possible in the longer term for educationalists, and perhaps for those in the polytechnics and colleges in particular, to find a solution which is acceptable to them, to the main actors in the external environment and which serves the personal needs of their students and of the economy.

Heather Eggins played a major role in bringing together the contributors to the present volume at the time of the seminars and through her energy and commitment has done much to maintain the momentum of the debate and to promote the diffusion of new ideas and practices. The volume itself represents a most unusual, if not unique, collection of perspectives. As such it should serve as a valuable source of information and ideas — and perhaps of inspiration — for those who wish to learn more about how the humanities and the world of work already interact and how the relationship between them might be shaped in the future as the United Kingdom moves rapidly to a system of mass higher education.

Part A
Employers' Requirements and Expectations

Chapter 1

Prudential Corporation PLC

Sir Brian Corby

In his address to delegates Dr Channon, Chairman of the Steering Committee, stated that one of the main aims was to consider how employers perceive humanities graduates and what skills, qualities and attributes we, as employers, require. I hope to spread some light on the first of these questions by concentrating my comments on the second.

We are all aware of the changes that have taken, and continue to take, place in the UK economy. Arguably, nowhere have these changes been more marked than in the area of financial services. Competition is growing and graduates are increasingly in demand, both to act as agents of that change and to manage it successfully to ensure continuing business prosperity.

It is probably fair to say that from the employers' view point, competition for graduates, especially for those with that special something, 'quality', has never been greater. I am sure that few of us need reminding that the number of 18-year-olds has been declining now for some years and is not projected to begin increasing again till around 1995.

Modern undergraduates are already exhibiting new characteristics. The most obvious consequence of all this is that it is a good time to be a graduate. Encouragingly they are placing increasing importance on the quality and quantity of training that they are likely to receive. Similarly, well thought-out career planning is now expected, with some clear indication of likely progression in the short to mid-term.

Secondly, and perhaps more significantly, has been the need for employers to review more critically their reason for recruiting graduates. They have begun to realize there are no such things as 'graduate jobs'. Graduates are sought for many different reasons and to fill many different roles. It is not sufficient now to say that we recruit graduates because 'everyone else does'.

Amongst the larger-scale recruiters in particular, much time is being given and effort concentrated on determining precisely what skills and attributes graduates need in order to perform effectively within that organization. Given the increased competition, it is not sufficient, nor is it cost-effective, to enforce some rigid selection criteria, (such as, for example, possession of a particular degree or study at a particular institution) without being sure of its necessity. Not only does this unnecessarily restrict the number of potential applicants, but it may also deter specific individuals who would be more than capable of meeting the demands of the position.

We at the Prudential are going through a process of examining our recruitment procedures. Not only are individual business units within the Corporation questioning their own reasons for recruiting graduates, but over the past eighteen months all have been identifying the skills and aptitudes necessary for effective performance within that business, and establishing the most appropriate mechanisms for training and development.

This trend towards the breaking down of unrealistic selection criteria does of course have a direct bearing on the employment prospects of humanities graduates.

Certain professions, such as actuaries, place highly technical or specialized demands upon trainees. Entry requirements and training programmes are thus strongly influenced by the requirements of relevant institutes. Trainee actuaries, for example must, in all but exceptional cases possess a minimum grade 'B' at 'A' level maths, whilst our potential surveyors must have obtained a degree giving maximum exemption from RICS examinations.

These requirements are clearly intended to restrict employment to a particular group of students. However, such prescriptions are increasingly being concentrated in demonstrably technical or scientific work. With half of all graduate jobs now open to students of any discipline there is plenty of scope for the individual with motivation and determination to succeed.

In addition, technical proficiency alone, even in areas such as those I have just described, is now unlikely to be sufficient for effective performance. Employers are increasingly looking to their graduates and other young professionals to become tomorrow's managers. To do this, they need additional skills to those acquired through the education system.

Appreciation of this has led the Prudential to examine closely the issue of 'transferable' or 'common' skills. Through systematic analysis of all types of work likely to be undertaken by graduate and other trainees in their first year or two with the organization, we have identified thirteen key attributes, around which a Corporate Development Programme for young professionals has been based, (these are reproduced at the end of this chapter). There is a strong emphasis on communication skills; both 'listening' (the ability to pick out important information when people are speaking), and 'oral' communication, (the effective expression in individual or group situations). No less surprisingly, a cluster of motivational factors have also been found to be important, including 'work standards' (the setting of high goals or standards for one's self, others and the organization) and 'teamworking' (the willingness to participate as a full member of a team of which an individual is not leader). In this environment, the way is surely open for humanities students to take pride in their academic achievements, and, ensuring that they can demonstrate the additional qualities that employers are seeking, make a significant impact in the recruitment market place.

Let me illustrate by once more talking about actuaries, my own profession. For almost all candidates, the application form or CV determines whether or not they are to be interviewed. In the Corporation, no less than six separate factors are considered under the heading of 'work experience' alone. These include the relevance of holiday jobs, the type of contacts with other people, the amount of figure work or statistical work. On the social side, the degree of involvement in non-academic activities is examined, as is the presentation of the application form itself; its legibility, use of grammar and spelling. In other words, the short-listing process consists of much, much more than mechanically searching for degree discipline and expected classification. This is typical of the approach taken by the Prudential in all areas of graduate recruitment. Equally, I suspect, it is typical of the approach adopted by many employers. Before closing, however, let me sound of a word of warning. The reality of today's graduate recruitment process is that most candidates must go under the microscope of the selection assessment board, whose aims, it must be said, include minimizing the risks of expensive recruitment mistakes. I wonder what experience the English or history undergraduate has of writing one-page business reports or of making five minute presentations with little time to prepare? No matter how academically gifted a participant on a selection board, employers will be looking for ability at, or genuine understanding of, the demands of the job under consideration. Unless this is demonstrated, participants are going to be at a disadvantage.

I am not in a position to comment on whether or not the degree discipline of humanities students means they are more or less likely to possess the requisite skills. Their 'non-business' focus might suggest that the answer is 'less'. Rather than leave this to chance though, would not it be better for candidates, through their studies or the help of their careers service, to be provided the opportunities to develop those other skills which will ultimately have a strong bearing on long-term career progress?

In summary, let me return to one of my opening statements where I hoped to spread light on the question of how humanities graduates are perceived, by concentrating on the skills, qualities and attributes that we as employers require. Degree discipline is probably less important now than at any time in the recent past. Increasingly, employers are looking for broadly-based young people. I see no reason why the humanities graduates should not be able to meet this short, but comprehensive criteria. Where they do, their future looks assured.

Appendix

Key Criteria for Effective Performance of Graduate Recruits and Young Professionals in the Prudential Corporation

The following performance criteria have been identified as related to successful job performance for graduates/young professionals in the Prudential Corporation.

(A) COMMUNICATION

Listening — Ability to pick out important information in oral communication. Questioning and general reactions indicate 'active' listening for example

— appears to listen carefully to what is being said before responding;
— is a responsive, active listener who appears to think through what is being said;

— asks questions to ensure has gained thorough, understanding of what has been said.

Oral Communication — Effective expression in individual or group situations (includes gestures and non-verbal communication) for example

— expresses ideas and views in a clear, confident and logical manner, in language the listener can understand;
— responses to questions, explaining how ideas/suggestions were thought out;
— checks that the listener(s) have understood what has been said;
— speaks out clearly and concisely at meetings;
— uses humour to good effect when working with others.

(B) MOTIVATIONAL

Job Motivation — The extent to which activities and responsibilities available in the job overlap with activities and responsibilities that result in personal satisfaction, for example

— appears enthusiastic, self-confident and self-motivated;
— demonstrates inquisitiveness and an interest in what is going on around them;
— appears to enjoy and actively seek out new and 'stretching' work.

Work Standards — Setting high goals or standards of performance for self, others and organization. Dissatisfied with average performance, for example

— takes an obvious pride in own work;
— consistently produces work which supervisor/manager considers of a high standard;
— will seek advice from others when unable to proceed, rather than produce sub-standard work as a result of having inadequate knowledge/ experience etc.

Commitment — Belief in own job or role and its value to the organization, makes the extra effort for the organization though may not always be in own self interest, for example

— takes responsibility for own work;
— actively seeks out additional work; does not sit back and wait to be asked to do something;
— works long hours where necessary to complete a large volume of work or meet deadlines;
— flexible with personal arrangements if circumstances require this;
— readily accepts extra work over and above normal workload.

(C) PERSONAL

Attention to Detail — Total task accomplishment through concern for all areas involved no matter how small, for example

— is conscientious, precise and accurate with own work;
— persists with all tasks, even routine ones, until satisfactory solutions are found;
— displays tolerance for routine administrative matters when necessary, for example, answering the phone, recording information, etc.
— accurately documents all work in progress.

Practical Learning — Assimilating and applying new, job-related information, taking into consideration rate and complexity, for example

— takes on board new ideas quickly and sees opportunities to use knowledge gained as soon as it is learned;
— appears to learn quickly from previous experience or advice given by others;
— clearly uses past experience to help resolve problems.

(D) INTERPERSONAL

Impact — Creating a good first impression, commanding attention and respect, showing an air of confidence, for example

— gives the impression of being confident in own ability, with a clear idea of what is expected of them;
— is assertive without being aggressive;
— will make the first approach to speak to others, displaying few inhibitions;
— appears confident when making formal presentations or otherwise speaking to others.

Tenacity — Staying with a position or plan of action until the described objective is achieved or is no longer reasonably attainable, for example

— appears prepared to attempt all realistic alternatives to solve a problem; does not give up after the first few attempts;
— will attempt to solve problems beyond current knowledge or experience (but will seek help/guidance when absolutely necessary);
— displays a preference for finding own way through a task, to achieve the work target unaided.

Independence — Taking action in which the dominant influence is one's own convictions rather than the influence of others' opinions, for example

— expresses own views openly and convincingly;
— puts forward own views strongly and with authority;
— displays an independence of thought and will stand by own views, however willing to accept suggestions/direction from others where appropriate.

Teamwork — Willingness to participate as a full member of a team of which he/she is not necessarily leader; effective contributor even when team is working on something of no direct personal interest, for example

— participates in team activities by sharing ideas and knowledge to help solve problems;
— appears to identify personally with team objectives (becomes actively involved);
— other people seem keen to turn to him or her to become a team member.

(E) DECISION MAKING

Oral fact-finding — Gather information for decision-making through questioning, for example

— asks probing questions of others to help resolve problems;
— extracts information from a variety of sources by research and questioning;
— challenges points of view expressed by others and seeks additional information, if doubt exists in own mind.

(F) MANAGEMENT

Self-Organization — Ability to schedule own time and activities efficiently, for example

— consciously prioritizes tasks and prepares in advance for situations that may arise;
— regularly completes tasks within prescribed timescales;
— does not allow routine work to get in the way of high priority work;
— prepares for meetings and other important events well in advance;
— appears to keep a balance between work and study.

Chapter 2

British Rail

Colin Wheeler

Looking at the respective backgrounds of two people involved in graduate recruitment it is difficult to imagine two more different than Helen Perkins from British Steel and myself. I have been recruiting graduates for six years. I am a practising chartered engineer, she is a personnel professional. I once made the mistake of criticizing the graduate intake one year to which, of course, the reply was — 'If you can do any better, you had better try.' That was six years ago and I have been doing it ever since. I get a lot of enjoyment from it, and in fact it is British Rail's policy to use ex-graduate recruits from any discipline as contact officers with given higher education institutions for recruiting for all functions. Contact officers maintain contact with College Careers Services and conduct the preliminary interviews before successful candidates go forward to central selection. I recruit for personnel, finance, general management etc., in fact for all our graduate management schemes, despite the fact I am a civil engineer. Or perhaps because I am a civil engineer; I am never quite certain.

It was suggested that I should comment on transferable skills, but being a non-humanities graduate myself I have decided not to do so. I think it is better for me to specify what I look for from an employer's viewpoint and outline the kinds of personality skills I am seeking. I shall then leave you to judge the value of transferable skills in relation to the person specifications.

As I understand it you are all course leaders and lecturers, career advisers etc. and you are therefore, probably better equipped than I to make the assessment as to which of the requisite skills I am more likely to find in humanities graduates than elsewhere. We are really talking about what I look for in the 'milk round'. Because it is still the 'milk round' at present, even if it does seem to be changing a little. Basically how does an employer go into the milk round?

As British Rail Contact Officer, I go in to the 'milk round' along with my colleagues, with a target against which to recruit something like 110–120 graduates each year within a budget. Now if this early reference to cost surprises somebody, if finding it is as commercial as that hurts, I make no apology. I suggest it is something you ought to know. I estimate we spend between £35,000–£40,000 per person recruited, by the time we have put them through various courses and the relevant in-house training schemes, so that we are being repaid by their skills. That amount is made up of the salary we are paying them, the overheads, the cost of training courses etc. The lower the failure rate of those whom I recruit, the cheaper will be the cost to the industry of procuring the full number of people to fill future middle management and senior management vacancies. Now that is a totally commercial and business-like viewpoint — but I submit that it is totally valid.

The advantage which humanities graduates should have relates to good communication skills but before going into the skills I should tell you about the range of British Rail recruitment into management.

All contact officers for British Rail have a book containing a set of person specifications from our different functions, against which we have to recruit. I have person specifications that I actually recruit against, so that I can judge, measure and evaluate suitability by comparison with the relevant functional requirements.

In 1987 we were looking for 117 graduates in total and 107 in 1988. Again, it is up to each function to decide on a year by year basis how many graduates they wish to recruit. The spread over the last three years has been as follows:

Table 2.1: British Rail Graduate Management Recruitment Targets

	1987	1988	1989
*General management	35	30	27
*Personnel	10	11	15
*Marketing	6	6	—
*Supplies	4	4	4
Finance	16	8	8
Engineers-civil	10	15	30
Engineers-mechanical/electrical	10	10	10
Engineers-telecoms/signalling	8	6	10
Operational research	4	5	4
Research and development	14	12	13
TOTALS	117	107	121

Humanities graduates are particularly suitable for schemes marked *. This works out on average to 45 per cent of all graduate vacancies.

Now obviously humanities graduates are in general not suitable for schemes like research and development or operational research where we are looking for a very high level of scientific and mathematical skills. Nor are they suitable for engineering, including civil engineering, where specific degrees are needed. However, finance is a possibility and humanities people who go into finance, complete the training and obtain a professional qualification in accountancy or finance, do make some of the very best finance people as far as we are concerned, because of their other skills.

I accept, of course, that it may be more difficult for a humanities graduate to become qualified in finance than for a graduate with a relevant or semi-relevant degree. The first four on the list are the main functions where I believe that humanities people probably have an advantage.

Of course these schemes are open to people with any form of degree so long as it is an honours degree. Interestingly I am told that 40 per cent of graduate opportunities basically are open to humanities people. You will note that we are heavily into the management of people and consequently our percentage works out to about 45 per cent; so a little bit more perhaps than the average.

That is the 'shopping list', that is what we are looking for each year. As I said earlier we work from person specifications from each function. These are updated annually. They are broken down into seven headings. I believe it will assist if I say something about each of the seven headings, against which we award a mark and against which we make comments. The secondary interviews are based on the same seven headings. The headings which I shall briefly mention are as follows:

1 Intellect

Here we are not talking specifically and only about the class of degree, the class of 'A' level, the results and range of 'O' levels, there is much more to it than that. Academic standards do matter. So do the standard of a graduate's leisure interests and the standards they attain in pursuance of their leisure interests, and that is something that we always probe at interview. We are also looking for people who are able to argue from first principles on say current affairs or a matter of their own interest. We look for people who are able to justify their opinions and views on whatever subject. Normally I can pick something up to probe from the application form.

Judgment is the other very important one which goes with intellect. Judgment I would define as the ability to make a realistic assessment of both people and situations. Now again I use current affairs for that at interview. I also use a case history, drawn from the function for which I am interviewing, to see how, given a set of circumstances, that person thinks they will react (a technique known as situational interviewing). I do not expect candidates to know BR's rules and regulations or how we do things. What I am looking for is somebody who will in fact think something through on their feet, there and then, and come up with a reasonable working solution.

2 Creativity

Creativity does not appear in the person specifications for many of the schemes. It obviously, as you would imagine, appears very high on the list for marketing. I think of creativity in terms of original thinking and imagination, the ability to think laterally, a breadth of vision, possession of good interpretative skills. This normally goes along with an assessment, that I try to make at interview, of what use that person has made of any opportunities that they have already had to use their initiative, to use their originality of thought, be it at college, be it before college, or in their leisure interests, and that again is something which I try to assess. We try to put a mark on and comments about the evidence which has been found. Novel view points and novel solutions are obviously important, but they have to be practical.

3 Social Skills

Now we are getting as far as I am concerned to the core of management. Is the applicant a loner or do they mix well? Do they mix well with different social groups? To quote from Rudyard Kipling's poem *If* — 'If you can talk with crowds and keep your virtue or walk with kings nor lose the common touch.' These are the sorts of qualities in people which we need in our management posts. Has that person not only mixed well but if they have had a problem mixing in a social group how did they overcome it? Did they overcome it fully and what were the circumstances that pertained afterwards? Questions like that often produce the answer I am looking for in terms of social skills.

4 Interpersonal Skills

This one, as far as I am concerned, is perhaps the very essence of what I am looking for in potential managers. A person has to be willing to take responsibility, wanting to take responsibility. They have to have an ability to organize and lead. They must not be the sort of person who dictates in any way, and yet ideally they should have what I can only describe as a 'presence'. They should be the person, who when they join the group everybody automatically looks to because he/she is the person who always makes 'it' happen and will organize and will achieve if we go along with them. I can only call it a presence. It is a sort of confidence that commands respect which some people have and some people do not. When I meet somebody who has a 'presence' then that is a great plus point.

They must be very good written and verbal communicators and that comes back to the humanities skills perhaps, because a lot of people from the science and engineering side, I shall say it myself, are not necessarily good communicators. They must be self-assured and independently minded. I said they must not dictate, they must also be prepared to listen as well as speak, be good listeners who take other views into account. Again with ambitious people who want to take responsibility, that is not always there. We also want somebody who is prepared to discuss things and win people over so that in fact employees want to do whatever is asked of them. Nonetheless, having a 'bottom line' is equally important as well.

5 Adjustment

This is very important for our line managers dealing with emergency situations at any time. Emotional maturity and self knowledge is essential plus a knowledge of a person's own strengths and weaknesses. I expect to find stability, a balanced perspective, a consistency, an ability to cope with stressful situations. One of the sets of circumstances I use in situational interviewing reveals perhaps more clearly what I mean. For example, in general management terms, if you were the person with two trains stopped, a suicide victim in front of a train, and various other things happening, what would you do about it? Perhaps that is an unfair question to put to someone about to graduate. But what I am trying to find is the right sort of non-panic thought process and then a reasoned and practical solution to the problem. It is surprising some of the answers I get.

6 Motivation

This is drive, determination, ambition and not least, the commitment to achieve. Often evidenced, as far as I am concerned by the standard set and achieved in that person's leisure interests. That is why the leisure interest section together with the part-time employment section of the application form are so very important to me. I expect to find evidence of motivation there. It has been said that 'positive motivation is the best prognosis for prolonged high achievement'. I cannot improve on that statement. Positive motivation, together with interpersonal skills, are the two most important skills for a manager in my opinion.

7 Commitment

We try to retain at least three-quarters of our graduates and I think that is about the level we achieve. I do not rate commitment as highly as the other six. We expect a certain commitment to BR, we look for people who want to work for BR. We also look, these days, for people whose image of BR is similar to the image which BR either has now or is hoping to achieve. One gorgeous in-house phrase which you can work out for yourself is 'Above all — beware puffer nutter'. I leave that without further comment.

So those are the seven criteria. How do we mark the people under these headings? We have a marking system. It is a subjective assessment which starts off by saying the middle 40 per cent are the middle 40 per cent and they are average. Perhaps not scientifically rigorous but as good as any other system I would contend. Against the listed seven criteria I submit a report on a form awarding As, Bs, Cs, Ds, and Es against the seven criteria and I use pluses or minuses where I need them.

We do not get many As — they really are exceptional. If I have somebody with more than one 'A' in the seven then I shall consider recommending them forward as exceptional. Equally the chances are that if they are in the bottom 10 per cent they will not get recommended forward anyway, unless it is one of the criteria which is not so essential in the specification.

But what is critical in the specifications? We now need to examine more closely the variations in specification between functions. Ratings per heading are used at our second interview stage together with comments that I have made on the evidence that has caused me to award the markings. It is the principle rather than the detail I will explain in a simplified way because there are three or four sheets of specifications for each function. What I have tried to do is to pick out the most important ones. As you would expect for marketing, creativity must score a B+ or A. No Es and a maximum of two Ds are allowed. Personnel management is very high on social and interpersonal skills, similarly general management.

InterCity on Board Services, our train catering department, are trying to improve service and quality and efficiency. They are consequently specifying top grades in social and interpersonal skills. Remember these specifications do get revised annually. The other thing to say is that our schemes are not generally oversubscribed. Against the trend I think this year, although we had far fewer total applicants, we have had a much better success rate than in some years and have virtually filled all our vacancies for 1988 graduates. We did not do so well in 1987 in respect of general management particularly. Yet general management is one where I would have expected that humanities skills would be most important. So the idea that humanities graduates are not getting the jobs, because the jobs are not there, is not true as far as BR is concerned. It has more to do with the way in which people apply and the way in which they present themselves at interview, I would suggest.

When I talk to undergraduates about how they should 'market' themselves, and I make no apologies for using the work 'market'. I often quote the following:

Table 2.2: *Graduate Recruitment: Ratio of Job Offers to Applications*

	1986	1987
General management	1:10	1:20
Personnel	1:63*	1:71*
Supplies	1:7	1:5
Finance	1:28	1:52
Engineering — (civil mechanical)	1:20	1:23
electrical	1:18	1:21
Operational research	1:14	1:22

How should undergraduates market themselves when they come to apply to work in industry? I do not have time to answer that question but I would draw your attention to the fact that in the engineering disciplines we make one job offer for every twenty applications.

Many of the people to whom we offer jobs also receive offers from a number of other firms, so the ratio is not as bad as it appears. In 1987 many people applied for finance and then withdrew, hence the strange statistic. Supplies and purchasing management is a young scheme which has only been going for three or four years. A very interesting scheme, in a little known field where due to the importance of negotiating skills humanities people ought to be able to do well. One of the easiest schemes appears to be for general management. Nonetheless in 1987 and 1986 we had difficulty in filling the vacancies with competent people.

Personnel — I am always concerned about this scheme. Hopefully everybody here who is in a careers advisory service knows why. I have starred up the ratios for this scheme due to the ongoing difficulty of convincing people of exactly what the job of a personnel manager is all about.

We are not running an aid group to the local DHSS. We need professionals to advise line managers on personnel for the system, to come up with the salaries we need to pay, to come up with the skills that we want for specific jobs. Unfortunately, despite all our efforts I would estimate that 50 per cent of the applicants who apply for personnel do not really understand what the job involves.

Before I conclude may I add a little plea from me as a recruiter. I preselect out about 50 per cent of the applications submitted to me; I wish it was more difficult to do so. The 50 per cent I pre-select out are the application forms which it is not worth my time and trouble to pursue. Applications from people who have not specified the scheme they wish to apply for, or they have not filled the form in properly, or they have applied for a scheme for which they are clearly unqualified. I told the story last night, which was received with surprise bordering on disbelief, of the very good history graduate who applied to become a chartered mechanical engineer. It is a true story, it is the first time it has ever happened to me, but it happened this year. That is an extreme case but that is why it is so easy to pre-select out 50 per cent. Many of the people who apply clearly do not understand the scheme they have applied for; they may not even have seen the brochure and have definitely done no background reading on that type of employment apart from the brochure.

If humanities graduates are going to succeed, they must submit good applications. I know there are a large number of Careers Advisory Services who will say 'yes I know'.

Suffice it for me to say that I would be very grateful if in future it became much more difficult for me to pre-select out so many.

In some of the long established traditional universities there is even an active discouragement by Heads of Departments of Humanities to people going into industry at all. I find that sad and almost unbelievable but I am still, so far, finding it to be true.

There is also, a growing 'Micawber' like attitude 'I need not bother chasing for a job, something will turn up'. The better jobs are unlikely to do so. Undergraduates still have to market themselves to me in the same way I have got to seek them, if they want to be recruited into the best posts with high potential for advancement.

Chapter 3

IBM UK Ltd

Peter McManus

I suppose the reason I have been invited to address you is because I am a classicist, nowadays something of a rare bird; but classicists in IBM are something of a protected species, and pop up in unusual places, as you will see later.

To start on a personal note, my interest in computing goes back to 1962, at the start of my last year at Oxford. At that time, there was just one computer in the University of Oxford, and it filled a whole house in the science area, along with its acolytes. I used to pass it on my way from college to my fiancee's rooms, and became curious as to what computing was all about. Needless to say, no-one in the Classics Faculty could shed any light on this, but a friendly mathematics Fellow encouraged me to enrol on an 'Introduction to Computing' course. I discovered too late that this was intended for postgraduate physicists, and after the first ten minutes ceased to understand a word being said: but fortunately (for me) my curiosity persisted, and I applied to several computer companies for employment.

IBM offered me a job, and here, twenty-five years later, I find myself in one of the most technical parts of IBM, with a humanities background. My fellow-classicists at college embarked on more traditional careers — two went into the Foreign Office, one became a solicitor, and one still teaches classics as a schoolmaster. But our present Chief Executive in IBM UK was a contemporary at Oxford reading classics, and there are several more of us scattered around the company.

It is true that IBM recruits from a variety of backgrounds, especially into its field sales force, which is where I started as a systems engineer. Equally, IBM makes it more than usually straightforward to move from one part of the company to another, and so after six years or so my interest in programming languages led me to move from London down here to Hursley, near Winchester. Hursley at that time was the leading laboratory working on an advanced language known as PL/I, developing 'compilers' and 'interpreters' (programs which translate other programs into a form directly executable by the computer) for IBM customers to use, and before too long I found myself managing a team of programmers, producing a new version of one of these compilers.

Hursley's role is to develop successful products, both hardware and software, for IBM, and I have been fortunate during my career here to gain experience on both sides of the house. Since early 1982, I have been involved mainly in projects associated with the IBM personal computer, and was one of the small group which was put together to launch the PC in Europe. I am currently responsible for most of IBM's hardware and software product development for personal computers done in Europe, both for European and for worldwide markets.

In this sort of job, which sounds very technical, the business and people aspects overshadow the technical challenges. A major part of any senior manager's job in a large corporation is concerned with fighting for resources. We are in an intensely competitive industry, and the competition inside IBM is at least as fierce as the competition outside. There are two IBM laboratories in the USA engaged in personal computer development, and another in Japan, populated by both colleagues and competitors for development resources. So effective selling of Hursley's excellence is a most important part of the job.

Equally important is the need to motivate our people. The sort of people that we want to employ are very marketable, and if they don't like the environment and the work that Hursley has to offer, they have absolutely no problem in getting a comparable job elsewhere. Part of motivating people is developing them. Many of our people will spend their whole working lives in IBM — at least, that's been our history to date, though it may be starting to change. The technical skills that they need will change over time — twenty years ago Hursley was designing large (at the time) processors and programming languages, today it is engaged in graphics and transaction processing. Some of our people will also want to move from technical into managerial careers (and vice versa), and thus need to acquire different skills.

Both technical and managerial types need to learn to communicate effectively if they are to make good career progress. As I mentioned earlier, we have several sister laboratories working in related product areas, and keeping in step with colleagues many time zones away presents some tough challenges: plenty of travel, together with lots of telephone calls and electronic mail messages. Those with humanities backgrounds start with an advantage here, as frequently these subjects provide a good grounding in the art of communication.

The force of strong competition also requires our people to be outward-looking. We measure a product proposal in terms of how well it stands up as 'best-of-breed' versus its anticipated competitors. In other words, we must be able to say that what we are proposing to develop will have the best function for its class on the market, and will be very price competitive. Only if our people are aware of the world about them, and avoid the temptation to become obsessed with what they are doing themselves, will they be able to answer such challenges confidently.

The successful product developer also needs to understand something about marketing. The first question we have to answer about a product is 'Who is going to buy it?' The second question, coming close behind these days, is 'Who is going to sell it, and why?' Products that are very technically attractive have often failed because the incentive to sell them was completely lacking. And so I hope you can begin to appreciate, from these few observations, that the obvious technical background appropriate for computer development is by no means sufficient, and that the skills acquired in a humanities-based education are just as appropriate.

It is curious, after all, that I label myself as a classicist. Certainly, I spent four years at Oxford studying the classics, but I have spent the following twenty-five years in IBM working with computers, and spending far more time acquiring technical skills than I ever did reading Greek authors. Given the accessibility of personal computers these days, I would hesitate to hire someone with as little knowledge of computing as I had when I joined IBM, but it is certainly true that we in IBM look at far more than the specifics of a degree course when making our hiring decisons. We are looking for people with analytical skills. They may need these in order to solve technical problems, but also to address business problems as well. For example, in managing a large laboratory, we have to ask ourselves constantly: what are our key strengths? How can we be seen to offer special skills to the company, unmatched by other laboratories? What are our demographics problems? Our strengths? How can we overcome the problems of geography, in a company that looks primarily to the US business performance in making investment decisions affecting product development?

The sort of person that can succeed in an environment like this may well come from a scientific background, but equally well can have a humanities training. Some people (exceptionally) acquire both as part of their degree course — one of our most promising young managers read a degree in music and computer science! I wish there were more such degrees on offer, and even more, that there were more such people able to cope with their demands!

Success in a business career often requires one to understand people's motivations. What makes him tick? Why did she do that? History, and classical courses including history, can give an excellent grounding in this kind of life skill. 'The proper study of mankind is man', wrote Pope. Gaining an insight into politics via history, or again subjects such as philosophy, politics and economics (PPE) will equip the student well for many sorts of career, even one as technical as computing. And if this skill is not acquired at the university or polytechnic, it must be acquired later, somehow. In this respect, the well-known interest of the employer in the applicant's college or university societies has an obvious basis — and a wide range of interests might be a good indicator of the ability of the applicant to deal with the multiplicity of crises that will be encountered in a senior job in industry.

Besides analytical skills, one is looking for the ability to synthesize as well. One needs, for example, to be able to construct a potential range of competitive threats to one's own strategy, and to devise effective counter-measures. Subjects like history, geography and the classics offer opportunities to develop such skills, properly taught. The challenge to yourselves, as practising teachers in these and similar subjects, is to look beyond the subjects themselves and to think about how the way you teach them will enhance the student's ability to extend the subject-related skills to apply to situations frequently encountered in careers of various sorts. Much of what I have said applies to many kinds of career in industry, and little is specific to computing as such.

Postscript

Since delivering this short talk, I have moved on to a new job in IBM concerned with developing a new business area for the company, and the Hursley Laboratory has gone through a major evolutionary change, now focusing exclusively on software rather than hardware, and almost entirely on products relating to communications applications. This merely serves to show that flexibility of individuals remains a primary requirement in the 1990s, and that a humanities degree will often serve a person well in coping with such types of change.

Chapter 4

National Westminster Bank plc

Kelvin Moore

I wear two hats in my address to you. One is that I am responsible for graduate recruitment and staff development in Nat West Bank, and the other is that I am a geography graduate from Portsmouth Polytechnic. So I am really a local boy coming home here and the debate on degree subjects is very close to my heart, as are the various recruitment issues from polytechnics which I think that many employers have rather ignored in years gone past.

I joined Nat West Bank in 1970, straight from the polytechnic and I followed the branches route which meant working locally as well as in Head Office jobs in the Midlands and the South West. I came to London about ten years ago to branch banking and then moved into a research environment in our Business Development Division dealing with the future planning of our network — whether we need more or fewer branches, whether we need to knock some down or build some more. I went back into a lending role three years ago, and then to my surprise, I went into a management development job at Head Office, looking after our fast track staff. The fast track staff comprised, at that stage, about 50 per cent graduates and 50 per cent non-graduates, and I became very interested in the development and eventually the recruitment of these employees. We want to recruit people to meet the challenges that our Group is likely to face now and in the future.

You may be aware that Nat West has been a consistent recruiter of graduates for over twenty years, usually recruiting about 150 graduates per annum. May I just set the scene by stating what I believe guides our graduate policy in Nat West. Firstly, we have a great need for high calibre people. We are an equal opportunities employer so we have designed our selection process very carefully to be non-discriminating. We also continue to be a recruiter of any degree subject. Very importantly, our whole selection procedure is based on managerial competence potential.

As I have said, Nat West has a great appetite for bright staff and that is nothing unusual. We have rapidly increased the use of technology. We continue to operate on a global scale so we need people that can look further than just within the UK in terms of their future management careers. We are now a very diversified organization, so the traditional view of our staff all being branch managers is very far from being the case and we now, of course, face very stiff and growing competition from many quarters.

We recognize that graduates are individuals and have different aptitudes, preferences and skills and are all looking for different things in their lives. We have therefore introduced three schemes of entry to try to recognize the difference in people's managerial potential and also take account of their preferences. Firstly we have Scheme A which is quite revolutionary for our organization. This is for people whom we wish to bring into the organization at assistant manager status from day one. So gone are the days of being a cashier.

We have Scheme B which is for those people we hope will reach assistant manager status within two years of joining our organization, and finally, we have Scheme C which is a new scheme for Nat West Bank and is really for those graduates that we see reaching management jobs but not necessarily at middle and senior level.

So what are we looking for when we see a graduate? Well I can assure you it is not just based on academic achievement or degree subject — if it was, I probably would not be here today! We have undertaken a great deal of research in Nat West, looking at what differentiates good and average managers at all levels in our organization. For our graduate recruitment, we have really homed in on front line management. We have found that there are competencies which do actually distinguish between average and high performing managers. There are a great many skills that one may need to be effective in Nat West. If you are in lending, for example, you need to be able to read a balance sheet. But reading a balance sheet extremely well will not necessarily make you an effective manager.

We have therefore identified those competencies which we believe distinguish very high performing people from average. We obviously have an appetite for those people who are above average. The competencies that we test for in our selection process include:

Information Gathering — the ability to get information from a wide range of sources and in some depth.

Problem Solving — what happens when all this information is gathered, what do they do with it.

Decisiveness — if you can't make a decision, life can be pretty tough!

Leadership Skills — ability to get other people's motivation working with you.

Team Skills — because we are very much a team-orientated company. Working in groups and teams in branches is very important. If you cannot get on with your colleagues, well, you may just as well pack up and go home!

Personal Impact — which is the ability to persuade other people to accept your ideas and to forge links and networks with other people.

Giving Information — which is the other side of the communication equation, the clarity with which people get their messages across.

Motivation — we are looking for people who want to do things extremely well, want to set high standards, want to push, want to go into new areas and motivate a team alongside them.

Commitment — we are very interested in people who really want to work in financial services. Otherwise they could have all those previous qualities but be very miserable in the financial environment.

So how do we test for these? Our selection procedure includes our own application form which we have designed to try to tease out this potential for management in people. We then have an initial interview which is on a structured basis. Here we have been very careful in devising a range of questions which we want our interviewers to ask and a great deal of guidance is given on what sort of responses we feel indicate high, medium or low performance.

We receive about 5500 application forms and offer a first interview to about 1800. We then put a successful 700 to 800 people through a one-day assessment centre in London. At the assessment centre the candidates undertake a group exercise, a couple of individual written exercises, a numerical and verbal reasoning test and an individual interview. At the end of the day we have a very clear picture, or so we believe, of the person's aptitude for management and also hunger and preference for working in the kind of environment that we offer. Because we regard our recruitment as very much a two-way process, we tell the graduates very clearly that they should be looking at us during the day as much as we are looking at them.

The entrants that join us, on whatever Scheme, quickly compete with other members of staff who in many cases are not graduates. So we make it very clear to them that once they join us, the graduate tag only lasts for about a year or so and very soon they have to be competing with other staff on the basis of sheer merit in terms of performance and demonstrated potential. Having defined the future for graduate recruitment, we definitely see that Nat West will continue to recruit from any degree discipline. We have found no correlation between subjects and potential for middle and senior management.

I would like to conclude by saying that Nat West, alongside many other major employers, will remain highly committed to the graduate market. There are fairly static graduate numbers being produced by the education system each year and with demand for graduates increasing at 5, 6, 7 per cent per annum, together with significantly less 'A' level people available for employment particularly in the South-East of the country, competition for graduates of all degree disciplines will be intense.

Chapter 5

Association of Graduate Recruiters

Helen Perkins

Given the immense diversity in academic backgrounds of colleagues, friends and associates in an array of different occupations it still sometimes strikes me as curious that I should so often be asked to give an employer's view on employability and employment opportunities for arts graduates. However, discussions with careers advisors and students in arts and humanities disciplines soon remind me that there remains a fairly confused picture about the availability of graduate employment for these groups, particularly in the broadest fields of business. Also, focusing on the employment opportunities for this group actually provides an interesting insight into the reasons why employers seek graduates at all, what skills they look for, how they seek to measure and judge such skills and how these in turn relate to the challenges and demands of graduate jobs.

Whilst there are no truly accurate figures which relate graduate vacancies to academic discipline, it is commonly accepted that at least 40 per cent of all graduate opportunities are open to 'any discipline' graduates and it is my belief that this figure is probably more like 50 per cent and perhaps even greater than that. So there is no reason at all why arts graduates should feel that they are non-vocational and thus limited in their career choice. Industry, commerce and business, industry obviously most particularly, certainly do look for a significant proportion of their graduate intake from science and technology-related disciplines in order to provide their essential technological base. Such graduates have been in short supply for some time and the shortage in these areas is set to continue but student choice is still showing heavy favoritism towards arts and humanities in spite of a job market for scientists and engineers that remains extremely buoyant. Beyond these roles, where such technical academic knowledge is regarded as essential, it is often the case that employers may specify a preference for certain supposedly vocational disciplines, whilst in actual fact being prepared to consider arts and humanities graduates so long as they demonstrate the requisite composite of broader personal skills. Everyone is looking for the best person for the job, everyone is looking for the best and what the best tends to mean for most graduate employers is a reasonable level of academic ability and then the personal skills and personality that are likely to make the individual a successful recruit and potential successful senior manager. The equation seems to work quite simply;

the better the personal skills the less degree discipline seems to matter. So the whole debate about personal transferable skills, as they are commonly referred to, is a very important one, although at times still rather dismissed by some academics and careers advisors who remain sceptical about the true skills requirements for many graduate jobs.

Before going any further it is worth elaborating on this issue of personal transferable skills because it lies at the root of assessing employment opportunities for arts and humanities graduates. The Association of Graduate Recruiters certainly makes no claim to having invented the concept but the term 'personal transferable skills' was first coined in a major report produced for the AGR by Peter Dutton, then the Head of Graduate Recruitment for Proctor & Gamble and a leading figure in AGR which formed part of the Association's response to the government's 1985 green paper on the *Development of Higher Education into the 1990s*. Each employer now tends to have an individual list and categorization of such skills, attaching different weights to certain aspects, according to the nature of their business and requirements but broadly we are talking about the sort of skills covered by the following list:

> communication skills
> presentation skills
> conceptual ability
> problem analysis and solution
> team working
> leadership
> numeracy
> verbal reasoning

These are in no particular order of priority, although employers still report that communication skills are those most noticeably lacking in graduate applicants. Ability in these areas, no matter what the occupation, does sort 'the wheat from the chaff' and ability in all of these areas turns an average graduate employee into a contributor and someone likely to make the best of development opportunities leading towards a senior career in their chosen field. Once in the world of work graduates will often find that they are not surrounded by like-minded people, they need to communicate and carry conviction and credibility with a range of different people and be able to communicate their specialist ideas and knowledge to others without that background. Good communication skills tend to be at the top of most employers' lists. All of these skills are of course trainable and many of the early induction and development programmes for young graduates focus on these areas. However it has long been the view of employers that graduates would be better equipped for their early roles and responsibilities if they had achieved as an undergraduate some understanding of what these skills mean, how they can be further developed and perhaps most importantly, some appreciation of their level of competency at the time at which they graduate.

Given that these skills are clearly trainable it is reasonable that there should be a debate about who should provide training in them and there certainly has been a view within higher education that these areas should remain the preserve of graduate employers. Not surprisingly this is not the view held by many students. There is an increasing realization amongst many graduates, especially during their first year of employment as they undergo induction programmes and initial introduction to management training, that there are many ways in which their undergraduate experience could have prepared them better and at a time when they would have had the opportunity to practise and develop their skills in a relaxed and learning environment without some of the pressures and the need to succeed which inevitable intrude in workplace training.

One of the key determinants of early success in a graduate career and indeed for that matter, throughout a career, is confidence. It is not expected that every student will graduate fully fledged and fully developed in all areas of personal competency spoken about here. As much as anything what is needed is an early introduction to these areas and a degree of assessment and self-assessment of the extent to which these skills have been acquired and refined. Much of the developments on the enterprise and higher education initiative (EHE) has been directed towards these areas initially as well as, equally importantly, to aspects of staff development. This latter emphasis rightly responds to the view expressed by many academics that they cannot be expected to inculcate skills in their students if they do not possess them themselves. There is also now much thought being given to the concept of assessment of these competencies and, of course, to issues of assessment generally where the nature of learning and study lends itself less to trial by examination.

There is growing interest in higher education and amongst employers in the concept of students graduating, not just with their degree certificate, which provides a measure of their academic and intellectual ability, but also graduating with some assessment of their competency in the personal skills area. It is not expected that this assessment will need to be of the same order of rigour as that applied to academic ability. Indeed there is probably a preference amongst employers for retaining the degree of rigour in academic and intellectual assessment. The most valuable step forward would be for the students to develop a better idea of their own personal skills competency. This will help them present themselves better at interview and during the selection processes where probably many graduates underestimate or fail to make enough of their abilities. It would also give them the confidence and the direction to make the best use of the training and development opportunities that are open to them once in employment. From the employers' point of view more undergraduate training in these areas will in no way decrease their training needs.

They will, though, be able to target their graduate training better and to operate at a more advanced level, helping graduates move faster to positions of challenge and responsibility, all of which is right for the individual and right for the business. It should also not be forgotten that much of the most recent demand for graduates has come from smaller businesses, with far less extensive training provision in all these areas.

It is again too simple to argue that arts and humanities graduates tend to have better developed skills in these areas than their engineering and science colleagues but there is some truth in this and some obvious reasons why this should be so. Style of teaching and undergraduate research in arts and humanities areas provides an environment in which these skills can be both acquired and practised. There is perhaps in these areas rather less to learn in a factual way and much to be discovered, explored, opened to critical analysis. Smaller tutorial groups, individual or group preparation leading to a presentation of a particular researched line of argument, open to challenge by other members of the course, all provide such opportunities. For the scientists there is much to learn, not previously covered in secondary education, and there is, perhaps, more work of an investigative nature that leaves slightly less scope for challenging ideas and concepts or being required to defend one's own analysis of a particular issue or problem. There is also another simple problem for the scientists and engineers. Their courses are very content intensive, often requiring much time spent in laboratory work and other associated course activities. Consequently there is less time available to get involved in those curriculum vitae enhancing activities of involvement in societies, sports activities or other social, leisure and personal pursuits that are so often the focus of interview questions as a means of getting a broader perspective on an individual. All of this is very much a changing scene and much is going on in higher education to broaden the undergraduate experience in a way that offers more opportunity to all students to participate in a more constructive, participative and less didactic experience.

It would be naive and unrealistic in the extreme to assume that these changes have evolved naturally and without any pain or resistance. To some extent this evolution has been hampered rather than enhanced through a government policy focus on making higher education more relevant to the world of work and introducing the concept of enterprise skills, a term which for many understandable reasons is destined to raise the hackles of a large number of academics dedicated to the learning process. For the employers' part this has meant that we have had to work harder in building partnerships and understanding with academics. Many employers share the view of many professionals in higher education, that the purpose of undergraduate learning is not simply and solely to produce people for the world of work or, as it is sometimes more unkindly put, cannon fodder for industry.

It is the belief of many of us that what we are talking about when we are talking about personal transferable skills are life enhancing skills which happen to be, as a happy coincidence of purpose, also job relevant skills.

In the early days of this debate, in the early 1980s, I was often asked to speak to groups of academics around the country at universities and polytechnics about personal transferable skills. The invitation often came from heads of careers services who could themselves see some of the difficulties that their students were facing in the transition from student to employee and were keen professionally to help see their students better prepared for the career routes that they were choosing. Such invitations were often accompanied by warnings that my reception might not necessarily be warm and that I might face some severe critics. Working in my favour is the fact that I have always personally been strongly anti-vocationalist.

I do believe that people should have the right to choose a course of study that appeals to them without feeling that they have to make a choice between a subject that will lead them to a good job rather than a subject that interests and excites them. Developing a broader base of skills in all undergraduate courses seems to enhance rather than detract from this goal. It always seemed best to meet this challenge head on and to recognize that I would not appreciate being told by a group of academics how to run my business just as there is no reason why they should appreciate a group of employers telling them how to run higher education. There is though still so much that can be learnt through a dialogue between the two parties. I know that some people think that the association of personal transferable skills with life skills seems to be a convenient reworking of the facts but having spent many years recruiting graduates and helping them through the process of transition, watching their careers develop and take off, or not, I remain convinced that this is so. I sometimes used to start the presentations to academic departments with something akin to an encounter group exercise, taking a series of life situations some of which are encountered by graduates in their early years, others later in life: buying a house, getting a mortgage, coping with personal tragedy, getting married, getting divorced, getting a job, losing a job — and then drawing out the personal skills and personal characteristics that were likely to help people cope best with these events. It will not be difficult to see that this list bears a remarkable similarity to the list that employers give for personal transferable skills.

The debate about personal transferable skills is one of a number of issues currently open to question which lie at the heart of business and education partnerships, a term which is broadly taken to mean employers and higher education academics working more closely together to achieve some common goals.

Some employers, although by no means all, have worked hard to forge these partnerships and have been more than met halfway by higher education, perhaps initially mainly by the polytechnic rather than the university sector although this is now also a changing and developing scene. All remain uneasy, at least on occasion, about whether the nature of the relationships thus established are truly partnerships in the best sense. With issues of funding ever present it is difficult for parties to feel they are in the business of partnership when one has the cheque book (although rarely the balance of a scale expected by some parties) and the other does not. Perhaps the most commonly forgotten fact is that employers, in the main, have considerable respect for the professionalism of their partners in higher education and expect a genuine dialogue not capitulation to a list of demands. This is an extremely important point especially in guarding against the short-termism that is unavoidably present in formulating certain immediate employer needs and interests. What may seem important and essential today may be different tomorrow and will certainly be different further down the track. A degree of balance is essential. Once courses have been changed to suit the needs of one particular employer group it is a long way back, and a disaster for the students, if this potential employer group has changed its expectations radically or is perhaps no longer in the market. The personal transferable skills debate transcends this difficulty given the breadth and depth of employer support for these ideas and the obvious benefits for the students. Whilst not wishing in any way to detract from the strength of this argument, it seems only fair to make the point that not every bright idea has quite such broad currency.

There is one further point relevant to all this debate about personal skills that it is worth making before looking at some of the other issues for arts and humanities graduates, and that relates to the interview and selection processes for graduates. The focus of graduate selection is far more on personal competencies than on academic ability, other than in certain extremes where high level academic and technical ability is a prerequisite. There is much research to indicate that broadly employers do not pay much attention to degree class and that a first class honours degree is no more or less of a passport to a good job than a good second or indeed a third class degree. Inevitably some employers might dispute this and undoubtedly some do focus their recruitment on the highest academic achievers with some perceptible benefits. However for the majority of graduate jobs I believe this to be true.

This is sometimes taken as depressing news both for the high achieving students and for their tutors and lecturers. I do not believe that this in anyway detracts from the value of such an academic achievement, it is simply the case that employers who recruit graduates expect that in doing so they are guaranteed a sufficient high level of intellectual and academic ability and then look for other skills and abilities in addition.

It is worth a note in passing that this previously supposed guarantee is less certain than it perhaps has been and there is an emergence of greater emphasis on testing intellectual ability. The graduate selection process however still rarely provides much test of academic or intellectual skills and focuses more on personal achievements. The growing use of assessment centres by employers particularly underlines this. Assessment centres take a variety of forms from a fairly simple approach to group selection to a full-blown two day assessment centre where individuals are involved in a number of different exercises, in groups and individually, as well as ability and personality tests. The purpose of all this sophistication in selection is to try and provide some more objective information on a range of personal skills and competencies. So to some extent developments in graduate selection, methodology and techniques may favour the arts and humanities graduates who tend to react well to these approaches.

So if all these things are positive for arts and humanities graduates what are the negatives? There seem to be two main areas here, one of perception and one of fact. On the question of perception I am very aware that many arts and humanities graduates have a fairly limited view of the scope of employment opportunities open to them and are often reluctant to be directed into different areas. I do not believe that academic discipline should be, or needs to be, a barrier to pursuing any career. Where there is a will there is a way, even if in some cases this could involve substantial extra training and qualification if a real switch of direction is desired. I still believe that the best careers advice I ever had was to think carefully about what it was that I enjoyed doing, the type of environment I wanted to be in and then try and find a way of being paid to do it. I am not sure I have achieved this ambition but I have certainly always kept it in mind as a 'weather vane' on whether I am doing what I want to do and enjoying it. I was recently told the story by a senior careers adviser about an English graduate struggling to enter what the student regarded as the traditional and best career route open to them in the creative media world. After a succession of fruitless applications the graduate was eventually persuaded, with very great reluctance, to attend an information day with an IT consultant and returned inspired and astonished at the degree of creativity required by such an occupation. I believe that this individual was ultimately not sufficiently inspired to go down this route but it is a good illustration of the need to encourage less prejudice and more openness about the challenge which many careers in business and industry can offer.

During my time in manufacturing industry I recruited many arts graduates into the supplies and distribution area which was a career route they had never considered and many felt was either beneath their dignity or wholly inappropriate to their skills and aspirations. A few years later they were waxing lyrical about the breadth and scope of their jobs when interviewed as pen portraits for the graduate brochure, showing as much enthusiasm for having successfully negotiated a good contract on basic electrical equipment as for moving hundreds and thousands of tonnes of iron ore through the Canadian lakes to its ultimate destination at a UK terminal. Without a substantial amount of career counselling included in the interview process many arts and humanities graduates would end up unemployed through channelling their job search into a very limited number of options. This passing reference to the careers guidance element of the early part of the selection process should not be taken lightly.

Many students believe that they should not enter the recruitment fray until they have robust and committed ideas on their preferred career route. This can be especially tough for arts and humanities graduates who may feel that the extent of research needed to explore possible career options is too onerous or time consuming to be undertaken before finals are out of the way. Few employers would support this approach. They would say instead that the time for students to evaluate and firm up ideas is before graduation and the opportunity to explore and revise career direction is via the 'milkround' process. This exposure to job hunting and perceived employer evaluations of an individual's strengths and weaknesses for diverse applications is a valuable experience towards finding the right career choice.

Few employers expect potential recruits to have fixed or dedicated views on career choice and fully expect to be involved in a dialogue about career possibilities. An organization of any quality or vision trains its undergraduate interviewers to undertake this role and must particularly counsel strongly against regarding fixed career choice as any evidence of relevant motivation or commitment.

The other barrier for many arts graduates can be a lack of some essential technical skills, most especially numeracy and computer skills. Just as I have argued for greater breadth in science and technology courses to provide more scope for the development of personal skills so I would argue for more attention to these technical skills areas for arts and humanities graduates. The over specialization of our secondary education system leaves too many of our arts graduates either without the necessary numeric skills or without the confidence that they both possess and can use them. The confidence issue is just as much a barrier as the lack of the skill itself.

I cannot count the number of times I have been told by arts graduates that they are innumerate and cannot get on with computers and yet there is now rarely an occupation, however artistic the career route, where such skills are not really truly essential to successful performance for themselves and for the world in which they are operating. Whilst there are some genuinely innumerate people, in the main the problem is one of confidence because they have not been exposed to the need to use such skills and are fearful of either proving themselves incompetent or demonstrating a lack of ability in these areas. There is a real need for some learning in both these areas for all undergraduates. There remains a perception that there are some career opportunities, particularly in business, that are good routes for innumerate arts graduates but this is a myth that needs to be dispelled. It is most particularly the case with personnel opportunities which are always hugely over subscribed. I would not advise anybody entering a union negotiation on pay or productivity, planning a recruitment budget or assessing training costs, all integral parts of a personnel role, to attempt to do so if wholly innumerate. In fact in the personnel area numerate skills are more in demand than in some other areas. There is therefore a world of opportunity for arts and humanities graduates and I think it is probably the case that employers have a broader view of the roles which such graduates can enter than the graduates have themselves.

Exploiting this breadth of opportunity is fortunately not that difficult. We probably have the most sophisticated graduate recruitment processes in all of Europe with close partnerships, growing ever closer, between business and education, with our professional graduate careers advisory services and campus milkrounds and all the infrastructure by which graduate opportunities are put in front of our students. Indeed the whole concept of any discipline recruitment is somewhat unique to the UK and this is only recently being discovered as some of our students look with broader horizons to careers in Europe. In most other European countries graduate employment is strongly vocationally driven and industry, business and commerce recruit few non-relevant disciplines. Accountancy is a classic case in point. In the UK this is a career route for students of all and every discipline whereas in most of Europe, partly driven by the demands of professional qualification which are different at present to those in the UK, such careers are open only to relevant students. So we already have a very attractive base of employment opportunities for arts and humanities graduates which needs to be exploited even further.

It would be inadequate to conclude a piece on opportunities for arts and humanities students without touching on the issue of mature graduates since so many of the mature students in higher education who are entering higher education in ever increasing numbers tend largely, if not almost exclusively, to study subjects in these areas.

It is no secret that the employment market is less attractive, less open to this group than to their younger colleagues. There are many reasons for this and it is not simply just a case of prejudice or ageism on the part of employers. Demand for graduates in science and technology areas remains high and it is in this area where there is the greatest problem of undersupply to growing demand. This is not the place to debate these issues but there is much to be done in this area by higher education, by employers and by secondary education in trying to encourage more students to take these subjects. The mature graduates in humanities therefore are entering a fairly intensely competitive jobs market. Our graduate recruitment in this country is very much based on the traditional 21/22-year-old intake, recruited for their future potential in senior manager roles as much as for their immediate value. There are some myths to dispel about the development and trainability of mature graduates but nonetheless there are other problems more difficult to resolve. Many mature graduates have entered higher education as much as a way out of where they have been before than as a way on. This is a perfectly reasonable and proper use of higher education but if at the same time the degree route is also seen as providing a passport into a better, graduate status career than they had before it does become more difficult, especially where there are expectations that age and experience will lead to higher salaries, faster career development and earlier levels of responsibilities.

Because such graduates are looking for change they rarely wish to re-enter a world where they have had previous experience and therefore cannot rely on past experience as, necessarily, making them a different employment prospect to younger colleagues. There are not insurmountable barriers. On the basis that nothing sells like success the Association of Graduate Recruiters and the Association of Graduate Career Advisory Services are working to-gether to dispel some of the myths that surround the employment of mature humanities graduates and aim to do this by exploring and publicizing some of the success stories. Indeed there are already a number of employers who feel that they have had considerable success in recruiting and developing mature graduates and who can see that they do bring a different range of skills and abilities all of which can be harnessed to good effect for the individuals and for their employers.

Finally in the current climate it is worth some comment on whether this fairly rosy picture for arts and humanities graduates will continue in a climate of some recession and economic uncertainty. The high demand for graduates certainly fell away to an extent in 1989 and again in 1990 in the face particularly of the economic recession.

There has been much speculation that this will lead to reducing demand for any discipline graduates and an increasing focus on science and technology recruitment which could in turn, if such a picture were to continue for any number of years, lead to students feeling it necessary to redirect their subject choice to the areas of higher employment. Whilst some redirection in these areas would not be unwelcome from the employers' point of view there seems very little likelihood that the market for any discipline graduates will decline dramatically although it may contract for a while. Many of the reasons already cited here underline this; there is long established tradition of any discipline recruitment and it has proved a successful formula. Overall graduates are going to have to work slightly harder than they have in recent years to secure the opportunity of their choice and they will certainly have to be open to a broader range of careers than they might initially have considered. The need for well developed personal skills will only be further underlined by this position, as will the particular need for numeracy skills, but there is no evidence whatsoever that in a period of reduced demand employers will wish to turn away from employing arts and humanities graduates. They are and will re-main a rich source of talent and ability.

Part B

The Skills Dimension

Chatper 6

Classifications and Models of Transferable Skills

David Bradshaw

For most of this century the education services have enjoyed widespread public support and firm belief in their value. In the past fifteen years or so this has changed and the purpose of the education and the policies of institutions and educators have come under deep scrutiny. From the questioning has emerged a belief that British education is insufficiently attuned to the needs of employment. Schools, colleges and universities have all been subject to scrutiny and their failure to be 'relevant', so popular perception has it, has contributed to national economic decline. The shortcomings of higher education, and the universities in particular, have attracted special attention. Martin Wiener's *English Culture and the Decline of the Industrial Spirit 1850–1980* (1981) in particular developed this theme and attracted substantial attention when it appeared. Correlli Barnett's *Audit of War* (1986) took up the same theme. Both works are still widely read and quoted and both give specific attention to the assumptions, courses, and processes of the universities and find them wanting.

As to the public perception, Peter Hennesey (1989) recently observed:

> By the end of the 70s, people had a picture of unattractive, unappetising students, complacent dons, and a university system in particular which had become so entirely bound up with state support as to be irrelevant to the concerns of other people out there in the system. . . That's the reason why, when the troubles came, the dogs didn't bark. (p. 338, quoting Robert Jackson in 'Grey Matters', BBC Radio 4's Analysis, 14 October 1987)

Yet the centrally important place of higher education in the development of people able to contribute to the national economic effort has been recognized for decades. What is new is the increasingly explicit response expected of higher education institutions. Robbins stated a principle for access that 'Courses of higher education should be available for all those who are qualified by ability and attainment to pursue them and wish to do so'. (DES, 1963, p. 8) and defined four aims for higher education of which the first has a direct bearing on employment:

> While emphasizing that there is no betrayal of values when institutions of higher education teach what will be of some practical use, we must postulate that what is taught should be taught in such a way as to promote the general powers of the mind (*ibid*, pp. 6–7)

Robbins' other aims for higher education were the advancement of learning and the transmission of a common culture and common standards of citizenship. Much recent discussion of higher education has endorsed Robbins' aims. In particular the University Grants Committee (UGC) and the National Advisory Body (NAB) in their joint statement of 1984 and the Government in the White Paper *Higher Education: Meeting the Challenge* in 1987 (DES, 1987) all reaffirmed their validity for the 1990s; but they also looked for more explicit treatment of skills development. The UGC and NAB did so in this way:

> Providing instruction in skills and promoting the powers of the mind remain the main teaching purpose of higher education. . .[1]

The Government made its endorsement in these terms:

> The Government takes a wide view of the aims and purposes of higher education. It adheres to the Robbins Committee's definition: instruction in skills, the promotion of the general powers of the mind, the advancement of learning, and the transmission of a common culture and common standards of citizenship. (DES, 1987, para 1.2)

Other authoritative voices have spoken in similar terms. The Council for Industry and Higher Education, for example, state their position:

> . . . Employers will increasingly expect higher education to give a grounding in personal skills; communication, problem-solving, team-work, leadership. In many instances this will be achieved by changing the learning process from passive absorption to active participation. (CIHE, 1987)

The Council for National Academic Awards has been equally clear:

> The aims (of courses) will also include the Council's general educational aims, the development of students' intellectual and imaginative powers; their understanding and judgement; their problem solving skills; their ability to communicate; their ability to see relationships within what they have learned and to perceive their field of study in a broader perspective. Each student's programme of study must stimulate an enquiring, analytical and creative approach, encouraging independent judgment and critical self-awareness.
>   The objective will specify in more detail the knowledge and skills developed by the course and evaluated in the assessment. (CNAA, 1988, p. 18)

There is then some consensus that Robbins was right but that development of skills must be more carefully and explicitly undertaken.

Employers' Requirements

Employers continue to recruit graduates in large numbers, but the way in which employers value and use their skills is changing. Reappraisals often include some of the following elements. Employers are very conscious of the demographic trend which is likely to reduce the number of young graduates available for employment over the next few years. Combined with a decline in the number of graduates in technological disciplines they see a need both to use employees with a technological background only where their special knowledge is essential, and also to utilize people for their general intellectual competence and their ability to learn rather than their immediate background of knowledge. This is reflected in the increasing number of posts advertised on an 'any discipline' basis. An analysis of entries in the Central Services Unit *Bulletin* of current vacancies shows that whereas 31.4 per cent of vacancies were advertised on an any discipline basis in 1980 there were 52.0 per cent in 1989 (quoted in Green, 1989).

Employers need to obtain the maximum benefit from every person recruited and to develop them in post over a long period. And as employers establish staff development programmes with greater care so they also define the prerequisites for such development, and these in turn inform the process of defining what kinds of people should be recruited in the first place. All of these factors lead to a growing interest in defining the general intellectual and personal qualities required in employment and a willingness to state such requirements in advertisements and job specifications. When the Personal Skills Unit at the University of Sheffield analyzed 10,000 job advertisements which appeared in the 'quality press' in June 1989 they found the 50 per cent of their sample specified a requirement for personal skills mentioning a total of 220 different skills in the process.[2]

This book includes five statements made by employers, and two more are quoted here. These are a brief statement by Procter and Gamble and the other by the Polymers Group of ICI.

The Procter and Gamble statement is included because it is brief and also typical. The ICI statement adds the dimension, not opened up in the five chapters, of different expectations for different levels of responsibility.

Procter and Gamble identify five groups of qualities:

   (i)   Setting and achieving objectives — sets demanding objectives, maintains high standards, shows perseverance and resourcefulness, overcomes obstacles, competes, achieves excellent result.

   (ii)   Communicating with and influencing others — organizes thoughts and presents ideas clearly and convincingly, wins support and cooperation from other people, generates enthusiasm.

  (iii)   Solving problems and setting priorities — analyzes problems, identifies key elements, establishes priorities, overcomes obstacles, allocates resources and implements solutions effectively.

  (iv)   Leadership/working with others — works well with other people, assumes leadership/takes responsibility where appropriate, brings out the best in other people, builds effective team work.

(v) Generating new ideas and better ways — finds, develops, implements and evaluates new and better ways of doing things; shows original/creative thought.[3]

In the case of ICI the Chemicals and Polymers Group (C and P) retained the consultants McBer to analyze the job competencies required in their business. McBer trained interviewers from ICI's own staff to use an interview procedure called the 'Behavioural Event Interview'. ICI staff then formed an overview of the abilities and behaviours that led to successful outcomes, and divided interviewees into sub-groups of superior and competent performers.

The Job Competency Analysis indicated that there were three broad classes of ability, and within them eleven *distinguishing competencies*, three *threshold competencies* and a number of *functional competencies*. They defined these as follows:

Distinguishing Competencies

These are competencies held in common across the three functions (commercial, R and T (Research and Technology) and production) which distinguishes superior and competent performers. They are:

(a) *Getting Results*
Four competencies to do with active pushing to get results:

— initiative (top performers have an eye for opportunity which they seize);
— results orientation (concern to 'do the job right', to know what the goal is and reach it);
— efficiency orientation (trying to do things better);
— tenacity (perseverance and determination, continues to act despite frustrations).

(b) *Thinking Styles*
Three competencies which involve different kinds of thinking:

— conceptual thinking;
— analytical thinking;
— strategic orientation.

(c) *Working with others*
Four competencies which involve working effectively with others:

— interpersonal awareness (an ability to sense and take account of other people's concerns);
— concern with impact upon other people;
— assertiveness: ability to take strong positions in ways that did not alienate people whose cooperation would be needed;
— concern to influence strategic thinking.

Threshold Competencies

These are competencies held in common across the three functions which did not distinguish superior and incompetent performers, but which occurred within a frequency sufficient to suggest that they functioned as minimum requirements of effective performance:

(a) rational persuasion;
(b) critical information seeking;
(c) thoroughness.

Functional Competencies

These are competencies which appear in all the functions surveyed. Specific competencies appear to be particularly important in some functions:

For the R & T Manager:
— initiative;
— conceptual thinking;
— analytical thinking;
— interpersonal awareness.

For the Operations Manager
— results orientation;
— thoroughness;
— concern with impact;
— strategic influencing.

For the Business Manager
— initiative;
— efficiency;
— conceptual thinking;
— strategic orientation;
— strategic influence;

Overall the Chemical and Polymer Group believe that the set of competencies which have broad relevance for professional and managerial roles can be summarised as:

Achievement
Initiative
Results orientation
Efficiency orientation
Critical information seeking
Critical information thinking

Thinking Style
Analytical thinking
Conceptual thinking
Strategic orientation

Positive Self-management
Assertiveness
Tenacity
Thoroughness

Influencing
Interpersonal awareness
Concern with impact
The rational persuasion
Strategic influencing

(Note: Working effectively with others is seen through results.)
(Chemical and Polymers Group of ICI, 1988)

A most marked feature of the seven statements used here (five in chapter form and two quoted above) is that employers do not detach competences from the circumstances of their use; they measure them only by the results they produce. Employers are less concerned to analyze and compartmentalize than to see skills and personal qualities in effective combinations, and how these affect performance. The skills themselves are latent or even inert until personal qualities harness them to produce results which, good or bad, are the measure of usefulness. So communication skills are judged as they influence other people, problem-solving skills in the usefulness of the solution produced and team work in the successful pursuit of corporate objectives. Decision-making skills require a will to implement as well as the ability to produce potential courses of action. The specific personal qualities which recur are motivation, the setting and pursuit of high standards, tenacity, drive and determination to achieve. But Helen Perkins makes the point that these are not just skills needed in employment, they are life skills which affect almost all the things we do. But if personal qualities appear to be sought before specific intellectual skills high intellectual ability is assumed and the skills emerge even if they are not structured systematically. Kelvin Moore emphasizes Nat West's 'appetite for bright people' and Peter McManus also refers to 'brightness as an important quality': the intellectual skills still emerge even if they are not structured systematically. Employers constantly list communication skills as a basic requirement. British Rail include written and oral communication among the interpersonal skills sought, the Prudential Corporation go into detail as to the listening and oral skills they require and IBM also place some emphasis on the ability to speak effectively to a group. All three statements either include communication skills among personal skills or tie them to aspects of personal interaction. ICI also makes thinking style one of its four major requirements and describes what it means in these terms:

C and P employs people who are good at seeing reality, breaking it down into component parts, recognizing logical sequences and getting to what it is really about. We call this analytical thinking.

C and P also employs people who can assemble disparate pieces of data; they join things together, see patterns and themes and organize concepts bringing to reality what might just seem a set of unconnected elements. This we call 'Conceptual thinking'.

When both conceptual and analytical thinking are applied to the tasks of developing long-term organizational goals, the result is strategic orientation, the third of the thinking competencies. (*ibid*)

Two of ICI's thinking styles (analytical thinking and conceptual thinking) are close to the 'analyzing and synthesizing skills' listed by IBM. Strategic orientation, however, is probably more an attitude of mind and a way of thinking, and further illustrates the employer's need to combine skills with corporate purpose.

Among the abilities not mentioned generally but which some employers list as important is creative imagination. Colin Wheeler includes 'creativity and original thought' as a significant area, one which British Rail attempts to assess in its appointment procedure, and this appears in other formulations if not quite as strongly. Another mentioned only once (by Nat West and not by other contributors) is that of information gathering from a wide variety of sources, It may be that others assume this. But it raises two important issues. The first is that skills are put to work on information which has to be supplied and so it is necessary to know where information can be obtained. This in turn opens up questions of the breadth of the curriculum and we shall return to both issues.

Employers make increasing use of assessment centres and management consultants in the selection of staff, especially those who will carry important management responsibility. The models used by these advisers provide a different source about the expectations of employers. Their models are more sophisticated than those previously examined in this chapter and are more securely based in current psychological interpretations of human behaviour. One example usefully illustrates the approach of many. Saville and Holdsworth, a company established 1977 'to provide better methods for the objective assessment of human resources and for developing potential' uses a model of personality in which three broad areas (relationship with people, thinking style and feelings and emotions) are divided into nine sub-sections and further divided into thirty job-relevant aspects of personality. Their classification runs:

Relationships with People

Assertive

Persuasive — enjoys selling, changes opinions of others, convincing with arguments, negotiates.

Controlling — takes charge, directs, manages, organises, supervises others.

Independent — has strong views on things, difficult to manage, speaks up, argues, dislikes ties.

Gregarious

Outgoing — fun loving, humorous, sociable, vibrant, talkative, jovial.

Affiliative — has many friends, enjoys being in groups, likes companionship, shares things with friends.

Socially confident — puts people at ease, knows what to say, good with words.

Empathy

Modest — reserved about achievements, avoids talking about self, accepts others, avoids trappings of status.

Democratic — encourages others to contribute, consults, listens and refers to others.

Caring — considerate to others, helps those in need, sympathetic, tolerant.

Thinking Style

Fields of Use

Practical — down to earth, likes repairing and mending things, better with the concrete.

Data Rational — good with data, operates on facts, enjoys assessing and measuring.

Artistic — appreciates culture, shows artistic flair, sensitive to visual arts and music.

Behavioural — analyses thoughts and behaviour, psychologically minded, likes to understand people.

Abstract

Traditional — preserves well proven methods, prefers the orthodox, disciplined, conventional.

Change orientated — enjoys doing new things, seeks variety, prefers novelty to routine, accepts changes.

Conceptual — theoretical, intellectually curious, enjoys the complex and abstract.

Innovative — generates ideas, shows ingenuity, thinks up solutions.

Structure

Forward planning — prepares well in advance, enjoys target setting, forecasts, plans projects.

Detail conscious — methodical, keeps things neat and tidy, precise, accurate.

Conscientious — sticks to deadlines, completes jobs, perseveres with routine, likes fixed schedules.

Feelings and Emotions

Anxieties:

Relaxed — calm, relaxed, cool under pressure, free from anxiety, can switch off.

Worrying — worry when things go wrong, keyed-up before important events, anxious to do well.

Controls:

Tough minded — difficult to hurt or upset, can brush off insults, unaffected by unfair remarks.

Emotional control — restrained in showing emotions, keeps feelings back, avoids outbursts.

Optimistic — cheerful, happy, keeps spirits up despite setbacks.

Critical — good at probing the facts, sees the disadvantages, challenges assumptions.

Energies:

Active — has energy, moves quickly, enjoys physical exercise, doesn't sit still.

Competitive — plays to win, determined to beat others, poor loser.

Achieving — ambitious, sets sights high, career centred, results orientated.

Decisive — quick at conclusions, weighs things up rapidly, may be hasty, takes risks. (Saville and Holdsworth, 1988).

Although sophisticated and comprehensive this model is far from neutral. It is heavily charged with values and qualities which make for managerial success as currently recognized. In some cases the classification includes two forms of behaviour normally regarded as opposite ends of a continuum. Thinking styles for example includes both 'traditional' and 'change oriented' perhaps because employers need both styles to make balanced decisions. But in other cases it includes one quality and omits its counterpart; so 'tough-mindedness' appears within the sub-group 'feelings and emotions', but not 'tender-mindedness'. The assumptions behind these stereotypes of desirable business can be (and are) challenged. Even more doubts surround these qualities as a basis for life in general; not everyone accepts tough-mindedness as a 'better' outlook on life and its problems than tender-mindedness, and there are still those who believe playing 'fairly' is better than 'playing to win'. It is doubtful whether it's possible to construct a value-free model. Finally, the model accepts and values the attributes of some personality styles and ignores or, by implication, rejects the attributes of others. This aspect is discussed further below.

This model is a good example and representative of many; but just as individual statements by employers show differences of emphasis and definition so do those of assessment centres. A similar problem exists in the United States. One analysis of the 'Knowledge Skills and Attributes' (KSAs) of people tested in a number of centres found that:

— titles were frequently the same, but the operational definitions were partially or entirely different;
— definitions were similar, or even identical, but the titles were different;
— some assessment centres merely used a dimension title without an operational definition;
— each operational definition consisted of one or more elements. Identifying each element simplified the ability to compare the similarities and differences of each dimension, regardless of title or definition. (Maher, 1983)

Because most employers recruit to many jobs on an any-discipline basis, the characteristic ways of thinking developed by many disciplines seldom surface. One appreciation of how one discipline develops ways of thinking comes from a source outside those so far quoted.

In an article entitled 'History and employability: History is in business' Roy Harrison, then Director of Staff Education Training and Development at British Coal, listed some of the historian's attributes: the realization that there is no one way of looking at things, and that problems may have more than one answer; the development of healthy scepticism in challenging assumptions, and policies inherited from the past; an ability to break outside of the received views of the organization in which they work and an ability to discard information corrupted by much retelling, and to go back to original sources. (Harrison, 1986).[4] This insight into the way historians think and its usefulness in employment has a general point to make. Employers need not only specific skills but habits of mind and attitude.

Employers emphasize the need for personal qualities and accord a high place to commitment. Although this is found in a number of countries it is particularly strong in Britain and should be tempered with a reservation in the British context. Chris Hayes (1989) recently emphasized the need for a better balance in British practice pointing out that '. . .commitment on its own is not sufficient in order to create high quality delivery, you also need competence, you also need understanding, you also need knowledge'. This emphasis has deep roots in British (and especially English) culture. It is part of what John Wellens thirty years ago called the 'anti-intellectual tradition in the west' and within which he saw two main strands in Britain. One was the dependence of the Industrial Revolution on pragmatists and artisans struggling to make progress in an exciting but harsh world. The virtues of these 'hard way men' and their successors were always preferred to those of 'men with paper qualifications'. The second was the 'public school colonial ethic' where courage, endurance, initiative and loyalty, the qualities needed in the establishment of the British Empire, were sought above academic learning (Wellens, 1959).[5] Both aspects of the tradition persist and do damage, not because the positive qualities are undesirable (on the contrary they are to be prized), but because they are valued in an exclusive way, shutting out rather than harnessed to the pursuit of learning and the acquisition of high level skill. Here too may lie one of the roots of the failure to develop skills for any but the immediately perceived task which has been a recurring aspect of national policies for education and training over the last fifteen years or so.

The conduct of war illustrates even more strikingly the danger of over-reliance on commitment.

Some battles are won by surprise and soldiers need courage, commitment and fighting spirit. But they also need weapons and training; and success in battle rests on these plus logistics planning and leadership. Military success and disaster may be more spectacular than the activities of the world of work, but some of the same principles apply.[6]

The Response of Higher Education in Britain

Within institutions of higher education there is a real awareness of the changes in public attitudes and the strictures of the 'Wiener-Barnett' school. Indeed much of the literature of economic decline and educational culpability comes from within the universities. Martin Wiener and Corelli Barnet are both dons, and there have been other studies by university teachers too (for example, Roderick and Stephens, 1978). And within institutions there is widespread understanding of what kinds of skills are required. In 1985 and 1986 a team based at Brunel University examined the broad question of how undergraduate teaching in higher education institutions on both sides of the binary divide respond to the labour market. It is a study of nine institutions: four universities, three polytechnics and two colleges of higher education. The findings of the Brunel Study are now being published in a series of books which is one of these *Higher Education and the Preparation for Work* (Boys *et al*, 1988).

Weiner examines the way in which preparation for work is handled in six disciplines: history, English, physics, electrical engineering, economics and business studies. It also examines students' perceptions of careers advisory services, the changing role of higher education institutions and the theoretical perspective to responsiveness. Finally it discusses the policy implications of all of these.

The book makes two statements which come close to 'models' of skills. One, listed among the policy implications, is the hope that,

Each subject of the curriculum. . .could well benefit from institutional scrutiny of the extent to which teachers ensure that all students can:

- express themselves adequately both orally and in writing;
- work in groups, seminars, workshops and laboratories (where appropriate as teams, as well as individually);
- have at least a working knowledge of elementary information technology which should go beyond an ability to use a wordprocessor and show some familiarity with the use of computers for display and computation;
- have some awareness of the relationship of their subject, whatever it is, to wider concerns of the economy and society. (*ibid*, p. 221)

The second is one of the conclusions of the study that 'Many courses. . . recognize the generic value of communication skills (verbal and written ability) numeracy and computer literacy and social skills (teamwork and self-presentation)' and these recur in a number of the chapters on specific disciplines or vocational subjects. To these the course team found they could add imagination and creativity, two qualities which are additions to the consensus view of the range of generic skills (*ibid*, pp. 203 and 41). The belief that this represents a generic consensus is strengthened by the way it was derived. For it was inferred by the project team through many interviews, rather than being offered to the institutions for comment or interrogation. Nonetheless although this understanding existed within the sample institutions the Brunel group felt that institutions were not systematically raising the two questions of which skills were thought to be transferred from academic to other situations and whether courses of higher education should develop them in a specific way. There was then some understanding of the issues but no marked will to act upon them.[7] This is not an unusual phenomenon, for universities and polytechnics are not always good at applying the findings of their own research; theoretical awareness is often not accompanied by practical responses. But there has been some change since this research was carried out. An increasing number of course teams have made the development of named skills an explicit aim of their courses and, more recently institutions as such have begun to develop and implement policies to develop transferable skills across a wide range of courses. One college recently wrote:

> The success of the programme implies the development of appropriate transferable skills and the team is currently beginning to explore the possibility of understanding this development by the use of models. Work is ongoing, but it seems likely to include two sets of factors which may or may not have a clear causal relationship. The first set of factors is that concerned with the skills of the student: general and communication skills, problem solving, interactional and interpersonal skills, clarifying values, analytical skills, synthesizing skills, quantification skills and specific knowledge of course content. The second set of factors, which we believe have a facilitating influence on the first, are those relating to the programme: the nature of the intake, course structure, course content, teaching process, teaching team and the physical environment.
>
> The course in seeking to encourage the development of transferable skills is constantly trying to make these skills more explicit. If theoretical frameworks emerge and are validated then it should be possible to consider the balance and range of skills and to identify any necessary actions to modify these.[8]

Other not dissimilar courses are referred to elsewhere in this volume.

Returning to the institutional level polytechnics have, on the whole, been quicker to respond than universities and some are now moving towards the formation of institutional policies. At Sheffield City Polytechnic, for example, a 'Personal Skills and Qualities Project' began in May 1987 following an initiative from the Polytechnic Careers Service. This is considered in detail in chapter 9.

Of the universities which have begun to take action the most notable is the University of Sheffield. Here, following wide consultation within the University over several years, the Senate established a Personal Skills Unit in 1988, initially for a three-year period. This works with academic staff to make them aware of the way in which the process of teaching and learning can develop generic skills. This service is available to all departments, but departmental initiatives are needed to invite the Unit's staff in to help. After nine months of consultation with staff and students in many academic departments, the members of the Sheffield unit identified some 110 skills 'considered to be desirable attributes of any higher education programme'. The team then grouped these under eight headings. These, together with examples were:

Personal Skills	**Examples**
Social	working in a team, networking, sharing responsibilities
Intellectual	identifying and solving problems, analyzing and evaluating data
Self-managing	being organized, responsibly planning own workload
Communication and linguistic	active listening, ability to communicate to a variety of audiences
Technical	keyboard skills
Adaptive	dealing with ambiguity, adopting concepts, skills, materials to new situations
Creative	ability to think laterally
General	setting priorities, working to deadlines

The Sheffield team next applied their understanding of several schools of psychological interpretation to develop a conceptual model which it offered as 'guidance for practice' within the University. Essentially a derivative model it was 'drawn from a wide range of skills considered to be desirable attributes of any higher education programme'. The model, reproduced as figure 6.1 is built on the concept of three phases or zones which 'form a sequence of increasingly complex behaviours moving from an assembly of core skills which may be practised in one-to-one situations, through those needed in group situations to those required in an organizational setting'. There are four of these styled 'orienting areas' namely communication, teamwork, managing and organizing and problem solving which are defined in the following ways:

Communication includes the skills required to receive, transmit and act upon information and to integrate activities. Teamwork includes the skills required to work harmoniously and productively in a group of people to a goal; with explicit recognition of the contributions, positive and negative, of each team member.

Table 6.1: Transferable personal skills — A developmental model

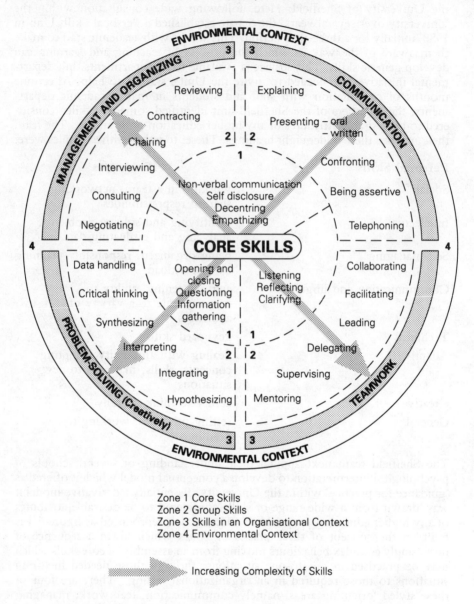

Zone 1 Core Skills
Zone 2 Group Skills
Zone 3 Skills in an Organisational Context
Zone 4 Environmental Context

Increasing Complexity of Skills

(Reproduced with permission from the *Personal Skills Unit, University of Sheffield*)

Managing and Organising includes the skills to set agenda for action and then establish and maintain networks to implement those agenda.

Problem solving includes the skills required to identify a problem, to generate alternative solutions, to choose between alternatives and to implement an appropriate course of action. Activity in each of these areas draws upon skills from the two preceding inner zones so that teamwork, for example, draws upon such core skills as listening and questioning and such group skills as delegating and collaborating. The model attempts to 'formalize the skills required to engage in tasks appropriate to a given organizational culture'. So, for example, 'students studying law will be influenced by professional norms and expecting goals'. In its diagrammatic form this is shown in the model as 'the environmental context'. (University of Sheffield Personal Skills Unit, 1990a)

Most models are altered in the light of experience; it is only when they cease to be used that they cease to be changed. So although the Sheffield model is now being used within the University it is still open to criticism and subject to amendment. The definition of problem-solving for example may well be extended to make the detail of the purely intellectual skills more apparent. One of its immediate successes is that it has been derived from internal perceptions of what are the desirable achievements of a higher education programme as such. As a result the Sheffield model commands wide support within the University. Yet it succeeds at another level at the same time, for the skills and attributes appear to be those which employers also say that they need. The staff of the Unit increasingly use this model in consultancy activities with other institutions.

The Manpower Services Commission (now the Training Agency) added a powerful stimulus to institutional action when in 1987 it announced its Enterprise in Higher Education (EHE) initiative. The initiative set out to 'encourage the development of qualities of enterprise amongst those seeking higher education qualifications'.[9] For the purpose of the initiative the MSC adopted the joint UGC and NAB statement as defining the transferable skills and qualities it wished to develop. Institutions which secured funding in the early stages of this initiative used this statement as their starting point. It is reflected in institutional statements though there are some modifications. These usually make them more employment oriented.

At the University of Durham for instance the project:

aims to enhance the University's drive to produce high quality graduates in the 1990s and beyond. The University will employ the resources made available through the EHE to enhance the development in undergraduates of the academic-related qualities that form the hallmark of the good graduate, whatever their discipline, whatever job they specialize in and whatever path they follow in their personal and social lives.

These academic related qualities have been defined (for this project) as

(a) Analytical and — critical thinking
    personal   — communication and presentation
                  — personal and social
(b) Knowledge   — computer literacy
    specific   — numeracy
                  — economic awareness
                  — foreign languages

The broader applicability of the skills to other aspects of life is an interesting feature of the Durham statement which makes in practice the point made by Helen Perkins that transferable skills are more than skills for employment. A very different response to the demand for 'relevance' has been to draw attention to the skills which are already developed through the process of higher education. Among these at a general level is the influential Lady Warnock who recently argued against the narrowing influence of some attempts to make higher education more responsive to the needs of employment (Warnock, 1989, pp. 35–6).

At the level of single disciplines there have been a number of studies identifying the development of transferable skills. The anthropologist M.G. Whisson, for example, identifies the development of the literacy, analysis and synthesis, oral communication, numeracy fieldwork by which he means observation and information gathering and statistics as the transferable skills gained by studying anthropology (Whisson, 1986, pp. 23–4).

Few British teaching institutions have developed their own models of transferable skills (the University of Sheffield is a notable exception), but validating bodies and development agencies have been hard at work to do so. Outside of higher education they are usually called 'core skills' but these have much in common with the transferable intellectual and personal skills referred to in the literature of higher education. The Youth Training Scheme (YTS), the Technical and Vocational Education Initiative (TVEI) and the Certificate of Pre-Vocational Education (CPVE) all developed checklists of desirable skills. At a more general, but very influential level Mr Kenneth Baker, when Secretary of State for Education and Science, and the CBI have pressed the importance of developing core skills and have outlined their content. More recently the National Council for Vocational Qualifications (NCVQ) has published a report, 'primarily to inform those who are involved in developing National Vocational Qualifications' (Jessup, 1990) which proposes a potential framework for dealing with core skills. This places skills in three groups: group 1 consists of three broad areas — problem solving, communication and personal autonomy; group 2 also consists of three areas — the application of mathematics, information technology and foreign language competence; group 3 includes five — economic and industrial understanding, environmental education, education for citizenship, career education and guidance and health education. This deeply thoughtful and carefully researched document both takes account of the earlier work referred to above and also of parallel studies undertaken by the National Curriculum Council (NCC). Although intended primarily at the incorporation of core skills in NVQs the document is aimed also at the development of skills in A and A/S level courses and already a number of schools and sixth-form colleges have developed processes to audit the acquisition of skills by their A and A/S students. This is a particularly encouraging development. With the enormous influence now exerted by the NCVQ this model is likely to be one of the main focal points first for implementation then for further development.

The Business and Technology Education Council validate courses which cross the further/higher education divide. Since the divide is administrative and financial rather than educational it is to be expected that their document sees courses as a continuum.[10] Because it applies across such a wide range the BTEC model is quoted here. The BTEC document makes the point, 'The term skill is not limited to purely technical manipulative abilities, but encompasses abilities to cope with problems of an unpredictable character, and to acquire new knowledge' (BTEC, 1986a, p. 2). The same guidelines also provide a list of possible skills, but with the caveat that these are 'just one convenient way of grouping core skills. They are not a definitive list. . .' (*ibid*, p. 7). It goes on to offer *a Specimen Skills Statement* which shows 'one possible approach to more detailed specifications of skills' (1986b). The purpose of this is to:

— exemplify one alternative approach to grouping skills;
— suggest the kinds of student activity and assignment task needed to ensure the development of common skills;
— provide a resource for designing common skills specifications.

Although the flexibility of BTEC's approach suggests wide applicability it seems to have had little influence on course design and content outside of the courses validated by BTEC itself.

Developments in the United States of America

In contrast to Britain, the academic world in the United States has produced a number of models of generic skills. But the starting point has been substantially different. The pressures on American institutions have been four-fold: the need to give a stronger and more specific purpose to programmes of general education; the need to prepare students enrolled on teacher education programmes for work other than teaching when teaching opportunities were in decline during the institutional reorganization, including the development of teachers' colleges into state colleges and universities; the need to redress to erosion of standards that occurred during the period of 'open admission'; and a general tendency for the expectations of students to decline. Some of these pressures are recent but the first of them (concern to give greater meaning and purpose to programmes of general education) goes back several decades. For example, in the immediate post-war years the Harvard Committee on General Education suggested that the ability 'to think effectively, to communicate thought, to make relevant judgments, to discriminate among values' should be developed through general programmes (Report of the Harvard Committee, 1946).

The closeness of this to contemporary summaries of 'transferable skills' is obvious.

Five American examples of model building illustrate the variety of approach. In the mid-1970s the American College Testing Program established the College Outcomes Measures Project (COMP). This assumed that a college degree did not automatically indicate the ability to function competently as an adult and set about establishing criteria by which such ability could be judged. The COMP staff concluded that higher education could be measured in two dimensions; one of process and one of content, with three major areas in each. The COMP's own summary of these is as follows (Forrest and Steel, 1982):

Content Areas

* Functioning within social institutions: can identify those activities and institutions which constitute the social aspects of a culture (for example, governmental and economic systems, religion, marital and familial institutions, employment and civic volunteer and re-creational organizations); understands the impact that social institutions have on individuals in a culture; analyze one's own and other's personal functioning within social institutions.
* Using science and technology: can identify those activities and products which constitute the scientific/technological aspects of a culture (for example, transportation, housing, energy, processed food, clothing, health maintenance, entertainment and recreation, mood-altering, national defense, communication and data processing); understand the impact of such activities and products on the individuals and the physical environment in a culture; analyze the uses of technological products in a culture and one's personal use of such products.
* Using the arts: can identify those activities and products which constitute the artistic aspects of culture (for example, graphic art, music, drama, literature, dance, sculpture, film, architecture); understands the impact that art, in its various forms, has on individuals in a culture; analyze uses of works of art within a culture and one's personal use of art.

Process Areas

* Communicating: can send and receive information in a variety of modes (written, graphic, oral, numeric and symbolic) within a variety of settings (one-to-one, in small and large groups), and for a variety of purposes (for example, to inform, to understand, to persuade, and to analyze).
* Solving problems: can analyze a variety of problems (for example, scientific, social, personal); select or create solutions to problems; and implement solutions.
* Clarifying values: can identify one's personal values and the personal values of other individuals, understand how personal values develop, and analyze the implications of decisions made on the basis of personality held values.

Several hundred institutions have used the COMP tests and found the results help them to identify courses and teaching where improvement can be made.

Working independently, but at approximately the same time, the American Programme Evaluation Project (APEP) run by the American Association of State Colleges and Universities identified the broad skill areas of communication, quantification, analysis, synthesis and values clarification, within this framework participating institutions had to spell out their own definitions. One, Wayne State College, Nebraska, made the following formulation.

Communication Skills

Competence in communication, in a very broad sense, involves all those procedures that allow an individual to express him/herself effectively. Within this broad range two distinct, though clearly related, types of competence may be identified. The first type is verbal competence. It is ability to speak and write clearly and effectively. The second type is non-verbal competence. Skills in this area are displayed in a variety of non-verbal systems of codification, which range from aesthetic symbols to gesture and digital language systems. From the definition it follows that effective communication is a form of human behaviour that may be exhibited in a variety of media and contexts.

Quantification Skills

Just as college graduates must be able to express themselves in an organized, clear, concise manner using appropriate verbal and non-verbal symbols, they must also be familiar with basic quantitative principles and procedures.

Quantitative competence involves the ability to find solutions to quantitatively-based problems. It also includes the ability to discern limits of quantitative techniques — that is, to determine when these techniques are not suitable for solving a problem.

Analytical Skills

Analytical skill involves identifying the parts of a whole and the relationships of those parts to the whole. It includes the ability to identify the essential components of ideas, events, problems and processes; to draw logical deductions about those components; and to recognize the limitations of these deductions. Since most problems are not isolated from one another, analytical skill includes the ability to establish relationships, where they exist, between problems.

Analytic competence also involves the ability to think critically and to solve problems.

Synthesizing Skills

Synthesizing skills are those which help an individual integrate basic knowledge, feelings, or the like. At all levels of every field of study and work this skill allows individuals to create innovative combinations of ideas, objects, processes and people. Students with highly developed synthesizing skills are adept at putting apparently unrelated facts into a common frame of reference. They are able to find unifying themes or common threads that enable them to deal effectively with diffuse bodies of information.

They not only possess a facility for constructing a general framework to accommodate whatever information they have, but they can move beyond that information, applying its principles to new situations or other bodies of information.

Values Clarification

Values influence the behaviour of people. Valuing means judging benefits, liabilities, effectiveness, strengths, and weaknesses according to certain criteria. Since values play such an important role in life, it is important to be able to identify them and to have some idea of how they are formed. Education can help people to develop the ability to identify their own values and the value system of others. Furthermore, education can help people determine how values influence decisions and how they translate into behaviour that might affect other people (Wayne State College, 1985).

The third American example comes from Alverno College, a small private women's Catholic College in Milwaukee, Wisconsin. It has worked to identify the outcomes of higher education for almost twenty years, and has produced one of the most thorough-going analyses of the relationship between content and process in the curriculum so far developed anywhere. In 1972 the College decided both to remain a women's college, and also to commit itself to the special focus of educating women for professional careers and with it the responsibility of developing competence through the curriculum process. The Alverno Faculty identify eight competencies each stratified into four general levels which are required of every student, and two further specialized levels from which the student makes choices relevant to her chosen area of academic or professional specialisation. In doing so the Alverno Faculty enter a number of caveats of which two are particularly important. Firstly they emphasize that competences are characteristic of individuals; the development of skills or an enumeration of tasks does not require this concern for the wholeness of people and is avoided (Alverno Faculty, 1989, p. 5). Secondly the Alverno position is the product of long and mature experience. But it is dynamic and still changing. So the current statement of the educational aims of Alverno, the fourth to be published under the title *Liberal Learning at Alverno College*, represents the latest in a series of 'still photographs of a moving body' (*ibid*, p. 2).

Alverno's eight competence areas described in the College's own terms are as follows:[11]

(i) *Communication*
Communication as a required competence in the Alverno learning program focuses on sustained presentation of messages by the student

as sender, and on response by the student as receiver of a variety of presentations.

A student develops the ability to make clear and forceful presentations of any message she sends, with and without the aid of graphs data, visual illustrated and electronic media. She also learns to take in such presentations — even if they lack clarity and force — so that she can make meaning from them in relation to her thinking and her life. Preparing students to present an extended message has classically focused on forms. We have tried to focus the Alverno Communications Competence on a process — the process of making connections between a presenter and an audience. . .

The criteria of effectiveness in this process are all based on clarification and involvement. When the student developing her communication ability speaks, writes, creates media, or presents in mixed media, she must clarify her message for an audience and use means to involve them in it. Reading, listening to, or interpreting a presentation, she must clarify the sense of the message for herself and involve herself with it. . .

As audience, she learns to assume the same kind of responsibility. She practices taking in presentations accurately, translating them into her own experience, relating them or her own ideas, confronting them with her own values and convictions, and examining them for limits, implications, and possible applications. . .

At all levels the student demonstrates her developing competence in two distinct roles — initiator/presenter and responder/audience. She does so before an instructor/assessor or a team of assessors, who evaluate her performance using the same criteria she has learned to apply.

(ii) *Analysis*

. . .analytical competence is a major contributing factor to the larger ability we call critical thinking. Analysis is the active process of examining, searching, comparing, dissecting, synthesizing — all in the pursuit of understanding and knowledgeable judgment.

Analysis is at the heart of most disciplines. Mathematicians stress the inherent logic that enables number systems to describe and predict; philosophers rely upon systematic investigation of arguments and issues; physical and behavioral scientists teach the imperatives of careful data analysis and scrupulous verification of hypotheses. Critics of art and literature express judgments that result when analytic minds join with experience to reveal the beauty and pattern of expressive works. . .

A student should leave college equipped to deal with everything from opinion polls to art movements to religious philosophies — and to judge them reasonably. She should be ready to employ the same analytical abilities in making decisions in her personal and professional life.

(iii) *Problem Solving*

Asking a critical question, making an educated guess, proposing alternate solutions — these are generally recognized as distinctive features of human intellect. Getting things done, adapting a plan to the constraints of time and resources, critically evaluating performance in midstream — these, too, are admitted hallmarks of applied intelligence.

At Alverno we have grouped these abilities, readily acknowledged as desirable yet rarely planned as deliberate outcomes of education, under problem solving. We have attempted to design a plan for their development in response to the need — and the opportunity — for the educated person in our society to enter into innumerable processes of planning and change, in both public and private life.

Problem solving is focused on developing a student's ability to get things done through a conscious, organized process. . .

Problem solving, which coordinates many separate abilities, clearly overlaps other competence areas in the Alverno learning program. It draws on abilities fostered in analysis (the habit of trained observation, identifying relationships) and valuing (the ability to apply values at each stage in making a decision). It also involves the ability to formulate a goal and to articulate obstacles, alternate approaches and costs — skills developed in communications and social interaction.

At the same time, however, problem solving calls for its own unique and often difficult-to-assess qualities. One is the imaginative ability to project consequences, and to pursue intuitive 'hunches'. Another is the affective strength to risk implementing a solution, and to persist in the face of drudgery and frustration. A third is the flexibility to adapt to constraints, and to accept and learn from negative results.

(iv) *Valuing*

Alverno College includes valuing at the core of the student's learning process. As educators, we assume that her ability to engage her values in an ongoing dialectic with her world will be crucial to the direction and meaning of her life. Our age of alienation and mass society gives us ample warning, moreover, that valuing abilities are survival tools on which not only the individual but the whole of Western culture may well depend.

Decisions about 'What is the good?' 'What ought to be done?' 'What is worth striving for?' are implicit in every human endeavour. The attempts to make those decisions explicit, to deal consciously and consistently with such questions, is one of the classic enterprises of the educated person. In the spirit of this enterprise, the Alverno Faculty addresses itself directly to developing a student's abilities to discern values, to resolve value conflicts and moral dilemmas through a decision-making process, to evolve and articulate a personal framework for committed living, and to carry that value framework into effective action.

Because valuing is pervasive, the broadest range of disciplines — aesthetic, scientific, political, economic, philosophical, religious, literary — are included as the proper context for the student's development of her abilities. Because values are dynamic, her learning environment attempts to challenge her to a continuous choosing of goals and restructuring of her values.

(v) *Social Interaction*

The ability to deal with others is crucial to personal and professional success. A society that accomplishes the bulk of its work in consultation, discussion and debate, on committees and task forces, must depend heavily upon those members who can be effective in interpersonal situations.

We have depended, as a society, on learning social skills almost totally without formal attention to their development. We learn interaction initially the same way we begin to learn our oral and written language — by being born into a family of persons who speak and interact. Yet we supplement language development with years of elementary and secondary school instruction in reading and writing (with less attention to listening and speaking). College curricula continue the development of writing, but have rarely included the development of interaction skills in their scope — assuming either that students come with these skills or that their growth in effectiveness is somehow a by-product of the total experience.

But we know that not all persons do develop social skills automatically — and few are as effective as they would like to be. The needs of our students, coupled with new work in the behavioural disciplines that has provided tools to describe, assess, and develop social interaction, have encouraged the Alverno Faculty to attempt defining a social interaction competence as an integral part of the learning program. Effective social interaction, as defined at Alverno, is two-fold: interpersonal competence in one-to-one situations; and competence in task-oriented situations. Though the two overlap considerably, certain abilities characteristic of each have been distinguished for the purpose of learning and assessment.

The developmental sequence is guided by a pedagogic rationale similar to that in communication with which it is closely allied. The student is brought to take an active role in the time-honoured education sequence — reflection-performance-critique — by entering at once into the performance phase.

(vi) *Taking Responsibility Towards the Global Environment*

In our highly urbanized and industrialized American society, learning to manage one's life systems effectively within the context of the global environment is perhaps more critical — and more difficult — than ever. In the broadest sense of the term, the global environment is our world: a complex unity of mutually dependent, interrelated parts. We define our place in this world in different ways with dramatically different consequences: harmony or hubris, stewardship or domination. Our personal lifestyles as well as our culture and institutions are expressions of such definitions. In an interdependent world we must develop a mature understanding of our place in it, and apply that understanding, in order to live more compatibly with nature and humankind. These concerns lie at the heart of the global environment ability at Alverno College. A student learns to take responsibility regarding the global environment in a series of learning situations that enable her to better understand herself and to analyze the complexity and ambiguity of the modern environment so that she can act effectively.

As the student develops this ability, she uses frameworks to understand increasingly complex environmental situations. In using these frameworks, she explores and develops diverse perspectives that enable her to formulate and probe alternatives to deal effectively with global concerns.

(vii)   *Effective Citizenship*
The end and essence of liberal education is freedom, and to live in freedom is to develop responsibility for self and society. Many thinkers have observed that, paradoxically, we realize the fullness of our individuality only within the framework of society as a whole. Effective citizenship means developing and acting on a vision of the public good through which both the individual and the community are enriched. Participating this way in the life of society is the essence of how the Alverno Faculty define effective citizenship.

Effective citizenship requires that the student generate definitions of 'the public good' and 'the public sphere', focusing, adapting and extending her abilities to this purpose. Through analysis and valuing, she creates a basis for and commitment to positive social action. Through communication, problem-solving and social interaction, she pursues a path of conduct in an appropriate arena.

(viii) *Aesthetic Response*
Without providing a neat rationale, society has consistently required of the liberally educated adult a degree of aesthetic understanding and sensitivity. The Alverno student, who is required to demonstrate aesthetic responsiveness learns to ask why art is important to society and to probe the question with an ongoing discovery of what can be expressed verbally, and what must be expressed symbolically. She learns to perceive, analyze and evaluate the kinds of patterns that create an aesthetic effect wherever they exist.

As part of that competence, she develops an understanding of the difference the aesthetic dimension makes in those forms of thought and expression which seek to illuminate the human condition.

In developing competence in this area, the student calls on aspects of her analytical, communicative, problem solving and valuing abilities. She develops an educated response that combines cognitive and affective perception to probe how works in the arts and humanities organize meaning.

These statements are general. In practice the Alverno Faculty have identified the skill elements to be developed within each area of competence with great care. The statements which define what students will be able to do at each of the levels of competence show this depth. The following example illustrates it.

Valuing

The first major task to engage the student at Level 1 is *making values* explicit. She works at identifying those beliefs and attitudes by which she understands and organizes her experience. She works at becoming aware of the sources of her values, and the relationships among them.

Through recorded journals and logs, through simulation and role playing, the student examines her own behaviour patterns for the values they express. She looks at her decisions, and the process by which she makes them, and begins developing a vocabulary with which to analyze values and decisions.

At Level 2 the student extends her attention beyond individual values to historical and cultural expressions. *Inferring values* from literary, artistic, historical, philosophical and religious works, she begins to understand the impact of individual and group value choices upon the human community. She also learns to explore the historical origins and impact of ethical systems and norms.

The student at this level establishes a base from which she can distinguish individual from social values and goals. She gains insight into the causal relationships between values and the cultural matrix.

Within the College process has been considered at even greater depth.

The extensive quotations from *Liberal Learning at Alverno College* illustrate both the model of competence developed by the College and also the way their development is integrated within the curriculum. But if the curriculum at Alverno must include process, process without content is totally inaccurate; the two are always bound together. Similarly although skills are developed through process and can be identified, the College sees them only within the total context of learning.

The fourth American example is an initiative to improve standards in baccalaureate degrees taken by the National Commission in Excellence in Education. Our Lady of the Lake University, (OLLU) (1982), San Antonio, Texas, worked within this project to develop a competence-based general education programme. All bachelors degree candidates are assessed in five areas of skill and one 'synoptic competence' in their junior year, and they receive refresher instruction on any parts failed and must pass all parts prior to graduation.

The six competencies are:

Skill Competence 1: can send and receive information in a variety of settings, and a variety of purposes.

Skill Competence 2: can analyze a variety of problems, select or create solutions to problems, and implement solutions.

Skill Competence 3: can interact effectively in a social setting.

Skill Competence 4: can identify one's personal values and the personal values of other individuals, understand how personal values develop, and analyze the implications of decisions made on the basis of personally held values.

Skill Competence 5: can express one's self creatively in an art form.

Synoptic Competence: can integrate liberal knowledge and lifetime skills to produce a reasoned and consistent world view.[12]

The assessment programme thus serves both as a quality control device, making sure that all students whatever their entry level meet defined exit levels of competence before getting a degree, and also a source of feedback on instructional efficacy, showing that OLLU students achieve nearly twice the national average gain in general education competences.

This approach to assessment incorporates something of the thinking which measures the benefits of higher education by asking what value has been added to the student by the experience? Northeast Missouri State University has been prominent among institutions attempting to place this question at the centre of its thinking. The basic tenet is

> that true quality resides in the institution's ability to affect its students favourably, to make a positive difference in their intellectual and personal development. The higher quality institutions, in this view are those that have the greatest impact — add the most value — to the students' knowledge, personality and career development. (Astin, 1981)

Northern Missouri State University describes the value-added programme like this:

Value Added in Operation

In operation, a value-added programme works like this. A set of measurement devices is identified that are appropriate for evaluating a student's standing relative to some desired educational outcome. . .these measures might include standardized tests, performance samples, essays, departmental exams, interviews and surveys. The last, surveys, are particularly useful where student attitudes weigh heavily in outcome goals.

Using these devices, initial measurements are made when a student begins a phase of the educational program (i.e. enters the institution, declares a major, or starts a course). These entering scores provide a profile of each student's strengths and weaknesses. As placement tools, these scores allow the institution to match curriculum alternatives to student needs. As counselling aids, these scores enable students to understand the rationale for the curriculum, and clarify the type and amount of improvement they must make. Most importantly, these initial scores provide a baseline for gauging subsequent performance.

As the students proceed through a course of study, the same or equivalent measures are again used to provide feedback on educational progress for students and institution. Finally, when students complete that phase of their education, the same devices are again used as exit measures. By themselves, these exit measures may be used to certify terminal competency. When compared to each student's entry scores, they establish the 'value added' by that educational experience. (Northeast Missouri State University, 1984, pp. 11–12)

It is immediately apparent that this purposeful approach to measurement implies unusual clarity both in defining the undergraduate curriculum and also in defining the aspects of personality (attitudes in particular) thought to be developed by higher education. Such definitions are models of a kind.

Issues Arising from Models Developed by Academics

Like employers, academics have no agreed vocabulary for the definition and discussion of transferable skills. The same ideas and the same skills appear under different terminology and are grouped in different ways. So Wayne State College, for example includes problem solving skills and critical thinking skills within 'Analytical Thinking' while others show 'Problem Solving Skills' as skills in their own right though without defining them. In other cases the same term carries different meanings. Valuing or values clarification is an example. Some colleges in APEP include values clarification as a specific kind of analysis. Wayne State College, for example, makes it a major area of competence. So also does Alverno College but here, while students begin to develop the competence of valuing by learning to identify and analyze values, it is as a first step towards the ultimate aim to enable students to come to decisions for herself about 'what is the good, what ought to be done, and what is worth striving for'. In both cases there is a concern for intellectual honesty and rigour but in the one case the process remains neutral and dispassionate while in the other it is to enable intelligent and rational commitment. The difference is included here only for the sake of example; but in doing so it inevitably raises other issues about the purpose of education which have been the subject of debate and disagreement for a century and a half. The identification of competences and the development of skill cannot be divorced from the wider issues of the content of the curriculum and, more fundamentally, of the whole purpose of higher education. This lack of an agreed vocabulary and meanings is not unique to the study of transferable skills. A particularly close parallel exists with studies of management where the Institute of Manpower Studies at Sussex University recently examined the anomalies and variations. This showed not only a similar problem but also that discussions of management studies and of transferable skills use many concepts and words in common (Hirsh and Bevan, 1988). Neither is there a consensus on the degree of disaggregation of skills. Graham Hitchcock (1987) has shown how the tasks required in a part of courses in the DipHE programme can be sub-divided into minute sub-skills. Yet at a functional level it is usually necessary to reaggregate the components into useful clusters. The University of Sheffield model is particularly helpful in defining levels of specificity in that it prescribes an aspect of the context within which it is used i.e. one-to-one, group or organization. Some skill areas are more clearly understood and defined than others. So while Alverno includes 'Aesthetic Response', and Our Lady of the Lake University includes 'Can express one's self creatively in an art form', neither attempts to define them in a precise way. Alverno recognizes that aesthetic appreciation is an activity that draws upon a number of skills. Creative thinking as a skill separate from its application in an art form is also very rare. It does appear in some classifications though not in any of the examples quoted here. Overall the activities which are clearly defined are linear, logical, language or mathematically-based activities. This is inevitable for they can of their nature be analyzed, categorized and listed. Holistic activities resist such treatment; but they exist none the less. No matter how precise the definition however, the relationship between skills and knowledge is blurred. At one level skills are knowledge in that they are learned and once acquired they become in part habits of behaving. But skills are also ways of approaching and processing knowledge.

The Alverno model recognizes that skills do not exist in isolation by expecting each student to develop them and apply them both through the variety of the general education programme and also within any specialists major study. Alverno College sees the development of skills within the much wider framework of liberal learning and its primary concern is with the whole person. In consequence Alverno's eight areas of competence are not self-contained, but interdependent. In particular two of the areas of competence use clusters of skills developed in other contexts, and in using them they reinforce their development. So 'taking responsibility for the global environment' and 'effective citizenship' use the skills of analysis, problem solving and valuing. By using these skills in a focused way they require the student to search for, analyze and draw conclusions about knowledge. The COMP model, developed to assist the assessment of competence achieved by people graduating from United States colleges and universities also divides its attention equally between content and process. But even if it is not stated this duality is implicit in other models; skills exist in relation to the acquisition and use of knowledge, data and information.

Comparisons of Models Developed by Employers and by Academics

Classifications and terminology in the models developed by academics differ substantially one from another just as do those of employers. It is not surprising then that it is difficult to bring the approaches together in a coherent overall statement. A further problem is the difference of purpose. Most of the academic models quoted here are from North America and have been developed to improve undergraduate programmes rather than to respond in a specific way to the needs of employers. But comparisons of the two kinds of approach are instructive. Where employers assess skills in the context of such personal qualities as commitment, academics tend to ignore them altogether. Academics work towards the acquisition of skills and measure their deployment in academic programmes; commitment is assumed. The application of skills to complex issues, as at Alverno, is far from usual. It is more usual for them to be applied to narrower pre-defined academic problems. Moreover, although students must complete assignments to time the commitment of students is to the long-term completion of courses of study which thus is far removed from commitment to corporate goals with their pressing deadlines and profit determined imperatives. But above all, even where there appears to be agreement, it is often illusory. Definitions of 'communication' offer a telling example. The following two definitions represent extreme positions but make the point effectively. The Prudential Corporation's definition of communication is broken into two sub-sections, 'listening' and 'oral communication', with listening placed first. These are defined:

Listening: ability to pick out important information in oral communication. . . 'active listening', for example, appears to listen carefully to what is being said before responding.
— asks questions to ensure has gained a thorough understanding.

Oral Communication:
— expresses ideas and views in a clear, confident and logical manner, in language the listener can understand;
— checks that the listeners have understood what has been said.

Wayne State College, Nebraska, defines communication as comprising two types of competence, the first verbal competence (the ability to speak and write clearly and effectively); the second non-verbal competence, with skills in a variety of non-verbal systems ranging from aesthetic symbols to gesture and digital language systems. Thus Wayne State College does not refer to listening skills and the Prudential summary does not include writing skills. But the omission of written skills and the emphasis upon oral skills is widespread. In its analysis of 10,000 job advertisements appearing in June 1989, the Personal Skills Unit at the University of Sheffield found that of those which stated personal skills as a requirement (59 per cent of the sample) 10 per cent specified communication as one of them. Of these 83 per cent referred to oral or verbal skills explicitly and only 17 per cent to written skills (University of Sheffield Personal Skills Unit, 1990b).

Although the discrepancy may be explained because the 'missing' skills are assumed, the reason may be much more fundamental. In an article published in 1976 Henry Mintzberg considered the then recent findings of the way the two hemispheres of the brain operate in the context of managing and planning business. He concluded:

The five Chief Executives I observed strongly favoured the verbal media of communication, especially meetings over the written forms . . .of reading and writing. (The same result has been found in virtually every study of managers.) (They) seem to favour it for two reasons. . . First, verbal communication enables managers to read facial expressions, tones of voice and gestures (which seem to be processed in the right hemisphere). Second, they desire relational simultaneous methods of acquiring information rather than the orderly sequential ones. (Mintzberg, 1976)

Although in omitting written communication altogether the Prudential definition is almost unique, it points forcefully to the differences of emphasis and approach. Other evidence strengthens the view that skills must be seen in conjunction with personality, and it is to theories of personality that we turn next.

David Bradshaw

The Psychological Bases of Differences

Minzberg's observations of the way managers behave point to the way in which the basic structure of personality affects the way we operate as people. The way will and personality combine is well illustrated by Edward Hall who relates

> During World War Two, when great numbers of trained technicians were in demand, it was assumed that those who had mechanical aptitude would make good airplane mechanics. The careful analysis of this assumption proved otherwise. It turned out that a good shoe clerk in civilian life would become a better mechanic for military purposes than someone who had fixed cars most of his life, and learned on a Model T Ford. The critical trait was not mechanical aptitude, but the ability of the trainee to follow instructions. The army then worked out its instructions manual so meticulously that the best recruit turned out to be a mildly obsessional person who could read and follow instructions. The last thing that they wanted was someone with his own ideas on how to fix equipment. (Hall, 1959, p. 94)

The work of four groups of researchers helps to shed light on these connections and their relevance both for preparation for working life and also for the academic process. None of them provides a complete explanation of behaviour and there is danger in applying any of them rigidly. But they do provide a framework of understanding both of the ways skills develop and their relationship to the structure of intellectual ability and also the conversations between skill and patterns of behaving. The first interpretation is that of David Kolb, an American psychologist who conceives learning as a four stage cycle:

> immediate concrete experiences are the basis for observation and reflection. These observations are assimilated into 'theory' from which new implications for action can be deduced. These implications or hypotheses then serve as guides in acting to create new experiences. . . (Kolb, 1983)

Although everyone learns through this cycle it is unusual[13] to develop an equal facility in all four phases. For the four are in effect two dimensions of activity where the extremes of each dimension are opposites. One dimension runs from the concrete experience of events (CE) at one end, to abstract conceptualization (AC) at the other. The second dimension has active experimentation at one end and reflective observation (RO) at the other. Activity in any of the four modes tends to inhibit activity at the other end of its dimension. One can be either active or reflective but not both at the same time. One can be busy experiencing events but while doing so the capacity for reflection is inhibited. In practice people develop preferences for one or two kinds of activity. They may be capable in the less preferred activities, but are less motivated to use them and may suffer some stress when they have to. Working from this basis Kolb and his colleagues developed a Learning Style Inventory, 'a simple self description inventory, designed to measure an individual's strengths and weaknesses as a learner'. The LSI measures an individual's relative emphasis on the four learning abilities: concrete experience (CE), reflective observation (RO), abstract conceptualization (AC) and active experimentation (AE) (Kolb, 1983). David Kolb and his colleagues administered the LSI to 800 practising managers and graduate students to obtain norms for the management population, and from this study they identified four styles which they call, the Converger, the Diverger, the Assimilator and the Accommodator. These they describe as follows

> The *Converger's* dominant learning abilities are abstract conceptualization (AC) and Active Experimentation (AE). His greatest strength lies in the practical application of ideas. We have called this learning style the converger because a person with this style seems to do best in those situations like conventional intelligence tests where there is a single correct answer or solution to a question or problem (cf Torrealba, 1972). His knowledge is organized in such a way that, through hypothetical-deductive reasoning, he can focus it on specific problems. Liam Hudson's (1966) research on this style of learning shows that convergers are relatively unemotional, preferring to deal with things rather than people. They tend to have narrow technical interests, and choose to specialize in the physical sciences. Our research shows that this learning style is characteristic of many engineers.
>
> The *Diverger* has the opposite learning strengths of the converger. He is best at Concrete Experience (CE) and Reflective Observation (RO). His greatest strength lies in his imaginative ability. He excels in the ability to view concrete situations from many perspectives. We have labelled this style 'Diverger' because a person with this style performs better in situations that call for generation of ideas such as a 'brainstorming' idea session. Hudson's (1966) work on this learning style shows that divergers are interested in people and tend to be imaginative and emotional. They have broad cultural interests and tend to specialize in the arts. Our research shows that this style is characteristic of managers from humanities and liberal arts backgrounds. Personnel managers tend to be characterized by this learning style.
>
> The reason that there are four dominant styles is that AC and CE are highly negatively correlated as are RO and AE. Thus individuals who score high on both AC and CE or on both AE and RO occur with less frequency than do the other four combinations of LSI scores.
>
> The *Assimilator's* dominant learning abilities are Abstract Conceptualization (AC) and Reflective Observation (RO). His greatest strength lies in his ability to create theoretical models. He excels in inductive reasoning; in assimilating disparate observations into an integrated explanation. He, like the converger, is less interested in people and more concerned for abstract concepts, but he is less concerned with the practical use of theories. For him it is more important that the theory be logically sound and precise. As a result, this learning style is more characteristic of the basic sciences rather than the

applied sciences. In organizations this learning style is found most often in the research and planning departments.

   The *Accommodator* has the opposite learning strengths of the Assimilator. He is best at Concrete Experience (CE) and Active Experimentation (AE). His greatest strength lies in doing things; in carrying out plans and experiments and involving himself in new experiences. He tends to be more of a risk-taker than people with the other three learning styles. We have labelled this style 'accommodator' because he tends to excel in those situations where he must adapt himself to specific immediate circumstances. In situations where the theory or plan do not fit the 'facts', he will most likely discard the plan or theory. (His opposite style-type, the assimilator, would be more likely to disregard or re-examine the facts.) The accommodator is at ease with people but is sometimes seen as impatient and 'pushy'. His educational background is often in technical or practical fields such as business. In organizations people with this learning style are found in 'action-oriented' jobs often in marketing or sales. (*ibid*)

Kolb's understanding of learning and intellectual style has parallels with interpretations of behaviour that see personality type as the key to understanding human behaviour. Most current theories of personality types derive from the theory and description developed by Isabel Myers who in turn built on the work of Carl Jung (1923) and drew upon substantial observation and testing over many years. Isabel Myers also acknowledged the debt to her mother Katherine Briggs and to her son Peter Myers. The Myers-Briggs theory of personality differences (1980) is in brief, that each individual has four dimensions of personality. The first is the way we become aware of things, and handle information about people, happenings and ideas. There are two contrasting processes. One, usually called 'sensing', is the conscious use of the five senses. The other, called 'intuitive' is much less direct, and here use of the senses, although real, is unconscious and impressions, sometimes quite strong ones, are received and formed without conscious reception of specific data. While we all have the ability to use both our senses and our intuition we show early in life a preference to use one or the other; and the more we use the preferred mode, the more we come to rely upon it. So sensing people come to trust data which can be touched or measured in some way while intuitive people come to rely upon their hunches or intuition.

   The second dimension is the way we come to conclusions. Here one process is by logical thought aimed at reaching impersonal conclusions. The other is by forming views on the basis of subjective feelings. Once again these develop into a preference for one or the other while we retain a capacity for the unpreferred mode. The third dimension is in peoples' attitude to their outer and inner worlds with extroversion and introversion as the two preferences. Extroverts tend to have a primary interest in their outer world, the things and people around them while introverts are mainly interested in an inner world of ideas and concepts. Once again introverts can deal with the outer world of their environment and extroverts do have an inner world of ideas which they can manage. But all other things being equal they will show a preference for and be more comfortable with their basic type.

Fourth and finally there is the dimension that has to do with forming opinions and dealing with the world around us. Here there are the two styles — 'judgmental' and 'perceptive'. People with a judgmental preference reach conclusions in a final way. They make their minds up on the basis of what they know and once made up 'That's it and all about it'; no further evidence is considered. The perceptive preference leaves options open, suspends judgment and looks for more evidence. It is more comfortable with ambiguity. No one operates on a fixed point in any of the four dimensions, indeed we all have a range within not just our four preferred modes but within all eight styles. So, for example, a parent whose basic style is perceptive may suddenly switch to a judgmental mode and decide that the prevailing noise level has gone on long enough and that its time to 'pack it in'. Or a boss who lives comfortably with ambiguity most of the time may decide that the time has come for precise, sharp answers to some pressing questions. But we cannot be both judgmental and perceptive at the same time, we are either one or the other. And we are more comfortable with, have a preference for and therefore commonly operate within either one or the other of all four of the dimensions. This combination of preferences shape our personality style. Within the combination there tends to be one process that is dominant and one that is auxiliary to it and the dominant and the auxiliary processes lead the other two.

Isabel Myers saw how psychological type affected every aspect of life and her insights have been applied to education (especially the education of young children) in a number of school districts in the United States, to occupational counselling through detailed research into the relationship between personality type and job preference and to marriage guidance.[14]

A number of other workers have adopted the Myers-Briggs understanding of personality though with some modification. In particular some of them see that the dominant and auxiliary processes as being less important than do Myers-Briggs and see the combinations of all four as shaping personality style. But these are relatively minor differences. More important are the clear points of overlap between the findings of the Myers-Briggs and David Kolb schools. Charles Margerison and Ralph Lewis (1981) who have, for example, noting the parallels between the work of Myers-Briggs and that of David Kolb, specialized in the appreciation of these insights to managerial performance. They organize the combinations of preferences according to two factors, one of 'reality' with a continuum of preference that runs from hard tangible reality at one end to the intangible and ambiguous at the other, and the factor of 'action' with contrasting preferences for new experience on the one hand and for conserving on the other. Margerison and Lewis see major implications of the types produced by this analysis in the development of teams. This aspect is considered further below but their model is summarized here.

Charles Margerison identifies eight styles of management behaviour:

Creator innovators are good at producing ideas and pressing for their implementation.
They challenge the existing, dislike conformity and like experiment and change but they are better at generating new ideas than at working them out in practical terms.

Explorer promoters look for new ideas and for new ways of doing things. They are alert to what is happening outside the organization, adept at making new contracts, at securing fresh information and at seeking where new ideas can be developed. They find new ideas and enthuse others about them. They are sometimes less good at carrying through their new idea to completion as when a new idea has been introduced they tend to move on to another project.

Assessor developers are practically minded people who look for ways of turning ideas into practice, but they will first of all assure themselves by rigorous criteria that the idea is wanted and will work. They like to use statistical, factual tools and are keen on such things as market research. Once a project is launched, however, they too are more likely to develop another project which they can assess and develop and produce on a regular basis.

Thruster organizers like to get things done. 'They set objectives, establish plans, work out who should do what, and then press hard to get results. . . They will go through obstacles if they cannot get round them.' They are conscious of deadlines and organize people and systems to ensure that they are met.

Concluder producers like regularity and their strengths lie in completing jobs to a high standard. They find satisfaction in maintaining standards over a period of time as opposed to innovating and introducing new things. They are not easily bored by routine.

Controller inspectors have a great capacity for detail, and an ability to pursue things in depth. They are not easily distracted and frequently have considerable powers of concentration. With their eye for detail they find they have a capacity to spot errors and have a liking for improving performance.

Upholder maintainers work from a basis of strong conviction and firm beliefs. They are very team-minded, supporting other members of 'their' team well and defending them against outside criticism. In the development of projects they like to be sure that changes are well consolidated before moving to the next step. They have to be fully persuaded before moving from a position they have adopted, and can be difficult to move unless they are certain it is right to do.

Reporter advisers are good at generating information and gathering it together in such a way that it can be understood. They have a central concern to ensure that jobs are done correctly, but because of their reliance on information gathering they can sometimes put off making decisions for what seems to them lack of full enough information.[15]

Yet another interpretation of behaviour is found in trait theory,where the work of Raymond Cattell provides the fullest exposition. Raymond Cattell identified and listed more than 120 behavioural traits, and by rigorous factual analysis he reduced these to sixteen. These are usually referred to as the 'Sixteen Personality Factors' (16PF). They comprise intellectual capacity, and fifteen aspects of behaviour described in contrasts of behaviour, namely,

reserved	outgoing
emotional	calm
humble	assertive
serious	happy go lucky
expedient	conscientious
shy	bold
tender-minded	tough-minded
trusting	suspicious
meticulous	imaginative
natural	shrewd
confident	apprehensive
conservative	radical
dependent	self-sufficient
uncontrolled	controlled
relaxed	tense

By further factoral analysis Cattell identified anxiety/stability, extroversion/introversion, creative disposition and intellectual ability as the basic factors which organize the other traits, and these are indeed ways of behaving (Cattell, 1965, especially pp. 117–9).

Understanding personality by an analysis of traits or by personality type are not the only possible ways. Other interpretations include the Freudian and Behaviourist schools. These are acknowledged but not discussed here. Nor are any of the interpretations likely to be permanent. Recent advances in our understanding of brain structure and functioning suggest that this will ultimately provide explanations of the phenomena described by psychology, with the evolution of the brain a central part of the theory. Much of the current research effort is concentrated upon the differences of task performed by the left and right hemispheres of the brain and the way in which the two hemispheres pursue specialist roles but at the same time support and relate to one another.[16] Although our understanding of these matters is still incomplete it provides yet another helpful way of understanding generic skills. In brief the two hemispheres tend to process information in a different way. The left hemisphere is specialized for analytical functions, works in a linear and sequential way, and therefore usually processes activities such as language and mathematics. The right deals with information in a holistic way and synthesizes rather than analyzes. It forms overall impressions and deals with aesthetic responses. But few human activities are 'single minded' in the sense that they use one limited mental process to the exclusion of all others; the mind at work is much more complex than that. Particular instances which help to illustrate the general point include the following. Music is understood and interpreted aesthetically in the right hemisphere, and the creation of music uses this side of the brain also; but when musical skills are highly developed the skills of the left hemisphere are also used. Visual artists similarly develop analytical (left hemisphere) skills to support their holistic (right hemisphere-based) creative and appreciative work. Creative writing shows the same characteristics. There are also many instances of scientists who, while working logically and analytically, find new conceptual frameworks often in a moment of sudden insight and in doing so make use of the capabilities of the right hemisphere. The two hemispheres are interdependent but where they work together one or other is clearly in the lead. This is illustrated by a phenomenon well known to speech therapists who report how patients with a speech impediment may stammer when speaking but do not have problems when singing as the impediment is located in the left hemisphere and is overridden when the activity is led from the right. A number of commentators have observed that educational systems in the Western world tend to develop left hemisphere, serialist skills rather than right hemisphere, holistic ones. Often when there is a debate it tends to be on an either/or basis rather than one aimed at securing balanced approaches with recognition that some people's learning is led by step-by-step preferences, other's by holistic ones. The teaching of foreign languages illustrates this. The two extremes are the teaching of formal grammar, vocabulary and verb lists with much use of written language on the one hand, and the learning of sentence patterns used in real contexts on the other. Although many teachers now attempt to use a combination of both approaches, this is far from universal, the tendency to polarize remains. The use of teaching approaches that attempt to use both kinds of learning more evenly is growing (see, for example, Buzan) but widespread adoption seems a long way off. For this study the basic qualities of the two hemispheres of the brain are particularly helpful in understanding some of the ways in which people develop and use skills. It provides insights to which we shall return many times.

This fairly recent understanding of the workings of the brain is entirely consistent with the finding of some cognitive psychologists who have observed that people are of one or two thinking types. There are 'serialists' who learn, remember and recapitulate a body of information in terms of string-like structures, [the] items linked by simple data links [and] 'holists' who learn remember and recapitulate as wholes (Pask and Scott, 1975). It also supports the growing view that people do not possess one general intelligence and a number of specific and special abilities, but rather a number of separate intelligences. For example, Howard Gardner, a leading American researcher and teacher, identifies linguistic, musical, logical/mathematical, spatial, bodily/kinaesthetic and personal (awareness of self and inter-personal) intelligences and proposes a fairly exact physical location for some of them within the total physical structure of the brain (Gardner, 1985). Robert Ornstein, one of the pioneers of left-brain/right brain discoveries also now describes our total functioning of the mind as a 'Mental Operating System' in which there are a number of 'small minds' which may be 'wheeled' in or out of consciousness as required by changing circumstances (Ornstein, 1986). This is not the place to discuss the arguments for these theories but it is the place to notice the focus of research on the area where neurology, psychology and physiology meet and to note its potential for explaining why people develop different interests, and tackle life and problems in different ways. Here too we may find the essential links between our rational and instinctive behaviour[17] including things as various as our awareness of personal territory, our sense of possessing things, body language and courting behaviour.

Towards a Common Understanding

Current discussion by employers, academic policy makers and others is hampered by a lack of an agreed terminology and of a comprehensive view of the total range of activities capable of being regarded as generic. Even in formulations of the broad general type agreement is not complete. Communication, team work and problem solving all appear regularly but some statements include other areas (self-management, for example) as essential major areas. Further problems arise when these large areas are disaggregated, as the incomplete and diverse interpretations of the meaning of 'communication' show. But as soon as attention turns to more detailed classification new and different difficulties appear. One is the need to group skills and qualities into working clusters, recognizing that organizational purposes and values shape their selection. Another is the danger that the whole person will be lost in a welter of skills and traits. There is probably no totally satisfactory middle ground though an awareness of the level of aggregation at which one is working will help. A third problem area is that of level, in the sense of how elementary or advanced the activities are. All of these need further consideration if the needs of the major interest groups, employers and academics are to be understood. So also does the matter of what one group needs for its purposes but the other does not; academics need to be better informed about the needs of employers, but they also have needs which employers do not share and it is useful to make these explicit.

A description and discussion of some of the major skill areas will help to illustrate and clarify these issues further. The fifteen areas discussed below are at a secondary level of aggregation or generality. They are not proposed as a model; their only purposes are those stated.

Listening

Listening is one of the more difficult things to get right. John Wain catches the nub of common experience in his poem *Who speaks my language?*:

> Who that has ever tried to speak his mind,
> Assuming that his mind holds more than blended
> Refuse that other minds have dropped behind,
> Can feel assured his words were comprehended?
>
> Did those who listened get the message right?
> Could they repeat the tale when it was ended?
>
> Ah, no. It seems the simplest words take fright
> And shape themselves anew for every ear,
> Protected by a crazy copyright
> From ever making their intentions clear.
> (Wain, 1956)

Whatever the difficulties employers need accurate listeners who think actively about what is said, pick out important information and ask questions to ensure their understanding is complete. Then they think through the implications of what is said before they respond. Listening to lectures might appear to be good training in developing some of these; but probably they seldom are. The key is the amount of thought given to the content and many students listen only for the very limited purpose of transcribing what is said to be used as written material later. It might be better to say that they have heard the words but not listened to them. The lecturer in biblical studies who entered university teaching after some years in the ministry and opened his first lecture with a short extempore prayer illustrates the point. He looked up from his intercession to see the students taking his words down verbatim; the content and purpose of the words had not registered. The circumstances of the case may be unique but the practice is not.[18] Situations involving discussions such as participation in seminars, however, require active listening. They also require students to use their oral skills and this is considered further below under 'speaking'.

Speaking

Employers need speaking skills but these are much neglected in higher education. Once again English studies provide an illustration. One lecturer in a University Department of English pointed out that it was not impossible to gain a grade A in Advanced Level English, followed by a First Class Honours degree, without having said a single word about literature to anyone (Hammond, 1980).

But if some students can proceed through a university course in English literature without saying anything about literature and many complete such courses without having to say very much there have been attempts to develop skills and confidence in using the spoken word. The Department of English (later the Department of English and Related Literature) at the University of York provides a particularly strong example. In establishing its first courses and examining procedures following the foundation of the University in 1963 the Department recognized that the conventional three-hour examination paper required students to perform tasks which they would never be called upon to perform in later life and discriminated in favour of one kind of ability (the ability to argue in writing) and against another (the ability to argue in speech). These convictions together with an awareness of the requirements of the world of work resulted in a decision to develop and examine 'fluency and persuasiveness of speech' which were given the overall name of 'articulacy'. The main instrument for developing these skills was the seminar where typically a student would be expected to give a talk lasting about ten minutes upon a set literary theme. They were not allowed to read from a script and although permitted to use notes they were encouraged to use the techniques of the ancient teachers of rhetoric whose students imagined a theater and placed key words and phrases upon its pillars, posts and thatch. The rest of the seminar session was given over to discussion with other members of the group expected to contribute. Students attended two such seminars each week and received a mark both for the talks opening the session and also for con-tributions in the following discussion. There was room for appeal against specific performances or lack of contribution but at the end of the term there would be up to twenty individual marks from which a mark for the term could be derived (Jones, 1969).

The method remains in use. A student who graduated in 1990 summar-ized students' reactions:

Not all enjoy the oral work, especially those who are shy and prefer not to contribute in ordinary seminar situations. Often really talented students who go on to achieve first and upper seconds feel intimi-dated by more talkative people and therefore give impressions of boredom or aloofness through non-participation.

But many jump at the chance to be orally assessed and find the need to think and perform on-the-spot stimulating. The process of discussion also helps towards more thorough understanding of both text and criticism and gives people a chance to consolidate their ideas by talking them through, and to adjust their arguments to take ac-count of new information. Because discussion is, by its very nature, in front of other people there is an additional pressure for preparation and research to be thorough. Surprisingly though it gives the group a feeling of coherence since everyone is in the same boat and everyone helps one another out rather than competes. But although you learn to share, you also learn to have the strength of your convictions and arguments and to believe in yourself, though you respect other people's ideas and arguments too. Many of us found it more enjoyable all round.[19]

Two other features of the York initiative are instructive. One is that the Department of Music has adopted the oral presentation of prepared talks as a requirement of its course, and although the format is different, student reac-tions are similar. The other is that although some members of the original group of staff have moved to other institutions, they do not, so far as this author can ascertain, appear to have taken the method with them. Higher education institutions do not find it easy to adopt new practice developed elsewhere.

Since oral skills are so neglected in the process of higher education it is small wonder that Peter McManus comments on the timidity of British graduates when speaking to an audience.

Reading

Reading skills appear at first sight to provide more common ground between the academic world and that of employment. Both require the ability to read accurately (with an implied requirement of understanding the meaning of words in a precise way) and if possible quickly. But other issues arise at once. The sophistication of perception required in a study of literature illustrates the point. In an account of a particularly skilful teacher Lee Shulman (1987) reports:

Richly developed portrayals of expertise in teaching are rare. While many characterizations of effective teachers exist, most of these dwell on the teacher's management of the classroom. We find few descriptions or analyses of teachers that give careful attention not only to the management of students in classrooms, but also to the management of ideas within classroom discourse. Both kinds of emphasis will be needed if our portrayals of good practice are to serve as sufficient guides to the design of better education. Let us examine one brief account.

A twenty-five year veteran English teacher, Nancy, was the subject of continuing study by experienced teachers that we had been conducting. The class was nearing the end of the second week of a unit on Moby Dick. The observer had been well impressed with the depth of Nancy's understanding of that novel and her skill as a pedagogue, as she documented how Nancy helped a group of California high school juniors grasp the many facets of that masterpiece. Nancy was a highly active teacher, whose classroom style employed substantial interaction with her students. . . She was like a symphony conductor, posing questions, probing for alternative views - drawing out the shy while tempering the boisterous. . .

. . . Nancy characterized her treatment of literature in terms of a general theoretical model that she employed.

Basically, I break reading skills into four levels:

Level 1 is simply translation. . . It is understanding the literal meaning, denotative, and frequently for students that means getting a dictionary.

Level 2 is connotative meaning and again you are still looking at the words. . . What does that mean, what does that tell us about the character? . . . We looked at the Scarlet Letter. Hawthorne described a rose bush in the first chapter. Literal level is: What is a rose bush? More important, what does a rose bush suggest, what is it that comes to mind, what did you picture?

Level 3 is the level of interpretation. . . It is the implication of levels 1 and 2. If the author is using a symbol, what does that say about his view of life?

In Moby Dick, the example I used in class was the boots. The boots would be the literal level. What does it mean when he gets under the bed? And the students would say, he is trying to hide something. Level 3 would be what does Melville say about human nature? What is the implication of this? What does this tell us about this character?

Level 4 is what I call application and evaluation and I try, as I teach literature, to get the students to level 4, and that is where they take the literature and see how it has meaning for their own lives. Where would we see that event occur in our own society? How would people that we know be behaving if they are doing what these characters are doing? How is this piece of literature similar to our common experiences as human beings?. . . So my view of reading is basically to take them from the literal on the page to making it mean something in their lives. In teaching literature I am always working in and out of those levels.

Writing

Higher education gives much emphasis to the skills of writing but even here the emphasis is not uniform. Students on humanities courses get greater experience that those on science or engineering courses, for example. In the latter case levels of competence are sometimes poor though they are probably improving. Even on humanities courses the expansive essay style is more developed than terser more compact forms. From the employers' standpoint this is limiting. One consultant reports:

> . . .arts undergraduates often complain that their departments do not allow the numbering of points on paragraphs or the use of short and direct sentences and impose a high minimum number of words. . .
>
> A training in the writing of essays is not altogether a handicap, but it does maintain a false confidence, even superiority in both student and tutor. (Brancher, 1987)

The needs of employers in this case seem to be wider then the needs of academics but the matter raises the question of whether academic purposes would be better served by developing a wider variety of modes. Established academics certainly use summaries (in writing abstracts of articles for example) and present material in succinct lists in published works. It seems reasonable to teach students to do the same! Given this wider range of written forms most employers would probably be content with the ability to write as simply as the complexity of the material will allow, and to write unambiguously. Some might place a value on the ability to avoid jargon! Few would look for the other stylistic qualities, such as elegance and individuality which are sometimes quoted as essential components of style (Waugh, 1955). Indeed while some employers would appreciate individuality in expression,elegance is not obtainable. Within multicultural corporations English is the medium of expression of people from many very different backgrounds and written communication requires unambiguous clarity and no more; it is beyond reasonable expectations to look for elegance. But for higher education, certainly in the humanities lucidity is necessary but not enough. To be sure not all students write with ambiguous clarity even when they take their degrees. To the extent that they do not marks some failure in the education, for colleges and universities surely have a responsibility to ensure that students can write lucidly in the sense used in this paragraph. But in that higher education also has a cultural mission there is also a responsibility to develop elegance and individuality for what they contribute to the cultural good. However although appreciated by many teachers of the humanities, little seems to be done to develop them in a positive way. They may be admired and valued and even encouraged, but they are seldom taught.

Whether speaking or writing people who think in a linear way tend to construct verbal statements differently from holistic thinkers. The former find it is easier to make step by step statements than the latter who may write a paragraph (or speak its equivalent) including all the facts and arguments but poorly sequenced. Enabling such people to take their thoughts and resequence them is a clear task for skill development. The skill of listening to such statements is a necessary part of the perception of spoken language; and this may need patience especially on the part of those whose own processes are linear.

Looking

From the earliest times people have expressed their emotions and thoughts in a practical form and the world is full of things created to be looked at. Within Western culture high value is placed upon the visual arts in many forms. A few artists of good ability have been self-taught, but the vast majority learn the skills of their preferred media through formal teaching at an art school or college. There are many who work in a professional capacity making their living by creative work of one kind or another and many more who practise for pleasure. The appreciation of works of art can be a matter of impression or one of thoughtful understanding of structures, techniques and content. At its best it uses both.

Creating and looking are so interconnected that it is not easy to separate them out, but for the purposes of this study it is worth attempting.

Artists in training are taught not merely to draw, paint or take photographs, teachers of the visual arts teach their students to *look*. A teacher of art recently described the problem and the solution in these terms.

Elements of Seeing for the Artist

Seeing is a natural function, the eyes operate rather like a camera but they don't translate information into pictures as a camera does. The eyes work in conjunction with the brain producing information as a substitute for what they observe. The brain is adept at decoding the information it receives and informing us about the visual world. It can operate very efficiently from clues in the absence of complete evidence and it can both organize scanty information into objects and can also be deluded by information received thus coming to the wrong conclusions.

The brain is always trying to find objects in the information it receives from the eyes and it needs very little stimulus in order to produce them. Thus, we have the problem of seeing a small amount of information given to our brain, automatically supplying us with more visual suppositions than actually exist.

In order to use our eyes and brain as a more accurate recorder of information 'more successfully' and 'intelligently' we have to learn to be more visually enquiring, to reason visually, to analyze, to perceive the subject matter, to comprehend the situation as a whole, analyze the relationships between areas and objects through volume, movement, pattern, texture, colour, tonal values and light.

This can be done by being introduced to ways of seeing and looking with the aid of such things as verticals and horizontals — actual or imaginary and introducing these temporarily or permanently in basic visual, constructively observed drawings and paintings. This then enables the eye to relate these verticals in what is actually seen in relation to the subject matter. This helps to analyze the apparent distortion which occurs through the space between the foreground and background of the observed area. A basic awareness of the rules of perspective is also useful in this respect. In addition, in order to see more accurately, we have to learn to be visually selective by analyzing the main verticals, horizontals and the relationships within an area and then build up the information we require. It is only through practice and basic exercises that we build up a heightened awareness of what we see and are able to see with some accuracy and what in fact we wish to see.[20]

Most of the artist's processes are 'right-brained' but he or she also uses the logical processes of the left brain to support the activities of the right. There is perhaps here a more general lesson to be learned that all activities led by the right side can be enhanced by support from the right. Even more important activities on the left may be improved by using the special functions of the right.

The appreciation of painting, sculpture or other works of fine art as such are not a matter of great importance to the world of employment. But you do not have to move far from the world of the painter to enter that of the poster designer and book illustrator and only a short distance more to reach that of advertising. Close at hand too is industrial design where things are designed so as to be useful, functionally and ergonomically efficient and attractive to look at. In all of these the intention is to reach the mind of the looker through visual impact, part of it logical and capable of analysis, and part of it impressionistic and capable only of holistic understanding. The ability to observe is just as fundamental to the training and practice of product design, graphics and fashion.

Artists in training are taught to look in order to create. In so doing they also learn to appreciate. A few students in higher education, studying art history for example, learn to look so as to appreciate but without the intention to develop skills of creation. Outside of this higher education offers little by way of formal introduction to this part of our cultural heritage though some institutions do display paintings, pottery and other works of art. This can be useful even if the appreciation is entirely subjective, silent and unexamined. Perhaps even less is done to enable students to understand the visual content of the posters, photographs and book illustrations that they see in such profusion day by day. The same lack of attention obtains towards the visual and aesthetic qualities of product design.

Much more is expected in the related world of maps, diagrams, and charts. These forms of statement are fundamental in geography, economics, geology and many more disciplines. In all of them students are expected to look and interpret and then to use the process of observation solving the problems of their discipline. So the skills of looking, which are essential for the artist, are valid for other disciplines also.

They are also used increasingly in the world of management. For with the advent of computer-generated graphics the use of data presented in visual form has become easy and its use is now well established. Sir John Harvey-Jones (1988) is among those who prefer graphical presentation. He reports

> While I am a fast reader, I also like visual presentation of figures rather than tables, but I have worked with people who are the exact reverse. At different times in my life I have worked with two outstanding leaders who could only create mental pictures through the medium of numbers. They had an instinctive ability to correlate numbers into a sort of pattern and, whereas in my own mind I use numbers as a sort of coarse scale to check whether my pattern is true, in their case they could only conceptualise the other way round. (p. 202)

He goes on to describe the use of modern technology to display financial information which had previously been used only in tabular form. The new medium of presentation allowed him and his colleagues to 'indulge in a number of "what if" questions on the run' which would previously have been impossible and that moreover 'We found to our surprise that suddenly the whole of our business became alive to all of us' (*ibid*, p. 236).

Making Visual Images

The creation of works of art to be sold solely to give pleasure is usually a form of self employment; but it is employment nonetheless. However although an important part of Western culture it is marginal to the particular purposes of this study. All the other activities in which the skills of the artist are used however, are central to it. Just as there is a large element of logical thought in the artist's observation, so there is also in the artist's creative work. But there is a vitally important element of awareness of the whole as well, and the artist has to create works which will appeal to the emotional and aesthetic nature of the observer. It is much easier to describe the skills used in these creative processes that draw upon the logical faculties of the mind than to give an account of the development of skills that make statements which can only be understood by taking in impressions. But these are skills nonetheless and they are developed. In the world of employment as understood in this book employers use all the kinds of visual materials mentioned under the heading of 'looking'. But employers recruit specialist poster designers, illustrators and product designers and they contract their advertising out to specialist agencies. So the ability to produce these things is not specified in jobs advertised on an any-discipline basis. In all kinds of work too, the exposition of ideas uses increasingly visual images of all kinds to supplement the spoken and written word. Activities as various as planning meetings, staff development programmes and the presentation of company reports use diagrams, charts, maps and photographs. Indeed few things illustrate the importance to employers of the impact of well designed visual material as the annual report of public companies. Once again the work is done by specialist agencies. The use of diagrammatic and cartographic statements is also common in the exposition of some academic disciplines. At the level of sophisticated publication for example the opening paragraph of a recent paper reads 'This study utilizes a *precise diagrammatic exposition* (emphasis added) to analyze issues involving the stability of cities, land, rents and private and public local finance' (Hochman, 1990).

Maps, graphs, charts and diagrams are integral in the teaching of economics, geography and the biological sciences, to name only three disciplines.

Geographers are taught the fundamentals of cartography in a formal way as a basic part of their training. So are geologists, town planners and archaeologists. Historians and economists are expected to use maps but are not normally taught how to make them. There is, of course, a difference in the complexity and sophistication of the maps of a geographer and those of a historian but there is certainly an element of received practice in this. Historians might be better historians if they were taught to make maps to a quality expected of geographers. Economists might be better at making their statements if they were taught to the kinds of accuracy exemplified in the work of Professor Hochman. Additionally, there is probably scope to extend the number of disciplines in which graphical means of presentation are used. Two academics at the University of Georgia, for example, have argued strongly for the use of graphics in presenting the results of research in higher education. They draw attention to the 'heterogeneous characteristics of the types of research in higher education (for example, budget studies, student studies, faculty workload studies, and administrative work)' and argue for the encouragement of wide use of graphical means of communication in presenting data and conclusions (Williams and Strickland, 1976). But in making their case they quote an argument which can be applied more generally: 'If it were. . . realized how much depends on the method of presenting facts, as compared to the fact themselves, there would be a great increase in the use of the graphic methods of presentation' (Young, 1966 quoted in *ibid*). Visual statements then may be the logically constructed forms of the precise diagram or map or the impression-giving statements of the two dimensional artist. But the two are often combined. Advertisements are a particularly good example of this dualism, and here it may be quite difficult to distinguish the elements. Elsewhere we combine both ways of making and seeing things with a high visual content with yet other elements, for anything made by man has to be designed. Although there are a number of courses which prepare students for careers in the design-based industries, those disciplines where design is used, engineering or construction, for example, develop but little awareness of the visual elements of their products. This gap in the educational process has been commented upon many times.[21] For this study the important point is to notice that the skills of visual perception and the creation of things which we use, but also look at, are developed in a specialist way; but their use is diffuse in the extreme. Most disciplines undervalue such awareness.

Quantification Skills

The basic elements of quantitative skills are the ability to identify quantitative problems as such and to understand orders of magnitude; it includes the skills needed to work out solutions to quantitatively based problems and it contains also the ability to discern when quantitative techniques are not appropriate for solving problems and when they have only a partial applicability. Of all the skills considered in this book, quantitative skills are the most self-contained. In the world of employment the most important sub-group is statistics, where the ability to turn data into statistical form to compare similar operations either in different locations or in a time series, and to appreciate when statistical differences are significant are among the basic skills of management.

Training in the use of statistics was a compulsory element in the development of 'fast-track' civil servants in the 1970s. But unlike some skill areas (such as communication) where it is possible to argue that they are taught to or acquired by students along the way (like diagram making in economics) quantitative skills are either in the curriculum or they are not. In most humanities subjects they are not. In terms of preparing students for subsequent employment this is a serious lack. It may also have the effect of constraining the scope of the discipline. Geography, for example, was largely a descriptive discipline at one time. But it adopted quantitative techniques and it changed the nature of the discipline in the process. In the case of history, for example, increasing numbers of historical works use statistical data and this raises the question whether the discipline would be strengthened by making appropriate statistical methods a normal part of the training of historians (Floud, 1977; Wrigley, 1972). The possibility of improving academic performance by extending the range of intellectual skills at the immediate command of scholars is never far away in this discussion.

Like listening and speaking, reading and writing, looking at and creating diagrams and maps it would be possible to divide quantification and understanding on the one hand and producing statistics and other quantified materials on the other. But that would be merely pedantic. It proves in this case to be more convenient to treat them together.

Analytical Skills

These are partly the ability to identify the essential components of ideas, events, problems and processes, to see them both as components and also in relation to one another, where again there are two elements, namely the way components interact, and the way they constitute wholes. But analytical skills also include the examination of logical argument to test the steps and conclusions, the identification of the *non sequitur*, the identification and exclusion of the emotional, and the ability to distinguish between problems and context. Within employment, once a problem has been identified as existing, these skills are invaluable in 'unpicking' it and in laying bare its essentials. There are few academic disciplines that do not use analysis in one form or another. It lies at the heart of philosophy, and is fundamental to textual criticism and to the interpretation of historical sources. Allied to mathematics it is the essential intellectual process of the sciences and engineering. We have already seen how in one form it is used to strengthen the artists ability to 'look'. It is hard to find a discipline that does not use the skills of intellectual analysis. One of the many current uses of analytical thinking is 'critical thinking', an approach to thinking now enjoying a vogue in the United States. This has been broken into

— identifying and challenging assumptions;
— challenging the importance of context (and seeing when context is merely a weight around one's neck);
— imagining and exploring alternatives; and
— reflective scepticism.

There is a sizeable movement in American high schools to develop these skills and it is being taken up in some universities too (for a full account of critical thinking see, for example, Brookfield, 1987).

Synthesizing Skills

Synthesizing skills are used to construct general frameworks of ideas within which information and knowledge can be arranged and solutions to problems ordered. The three elements identified by

— the ability to deal with diverse kinds of material effectively;
— the ability to search for new connections and relationships between material;
— organising, integrating and understanding different facets.

Both analyzing and synthesizing skills contain common constituents, but analysis is concerned to see the elements within a whole, and to identify them accurately, while synthesis is concerned with building elements into new wholes. Whereas analysis is mainly a function of the left brain, synthesis depends more upon the power of the right. As a whole higher education is better at developing the skills of analysis though some disciplines (history, English, modern foreign languages, for example) do both. The skills of synthesis are fundamental in Roy Harrison's account of what the historian can contribute to management quoted above.

Imagination

Not all models include imagination as an important skill. But those employers who do list it value it highly, especially as an ability to generate new and original ideas. Within academic models imagination appears in two ways. One is in American models where experience of a major art form is seen as a necessary curricular experience. The other is within the more general skill area of synthesis where imagination is seen to form new relationships of abstract ideas. There may be a gap in our understanding here for while imagination is indeed apparent in all of these cases and provides a common thread among them, yet the fields in which it appears are different. Accepting for the moment the multiple view of human intelligence described by Howard Gardner then imagination may combine with intelligence so that it would be more appropriate to talk of multiple imagination just as it is more appropriate to talk of multiple intelligence. It is also useful to draw a distinction between synthesis and abstract imagination. Synthesis searches for new relationships and connections in a systematic way while imagination goes further to see further inherent possibilities. The distinction can be illustrated by reference to the work of forecasting centres. Much of their work is on the basis of extrapolation, identifying trends and evaluating the likelihood of their continuing, and then examining the way in which one trend might interact with another. But some forecasting centres also make use of the views of science fiction writers, who can go beyond the logic of extrapolation to see additional possibilities. Once again two forms of activity can be discerned, the one logical and linear the other less predictable and wider ranging. Once again the influence of the contrasting strengths of the two hemispheres of the brain is apparent. This accounts in part for the relatively infrequent consideration of imagination as applied to abstract ideas in the academic world, for academics use the facilities led from the left hemisphere more readily than those led from the right. One academic use is in the generation of hypotheses or the definition of areas for possible research where sometimes academics use the one intellectual approach and sometimes the other. But it remains, probably, an underutilized and underdeveloped skill area.

Clarifying Values

Some models include values clarification in analysis, and indeed, the process of values clarification does depend upon the ability to analyze. But values clarification deserves separate treatment partly because unless it is developed separately it does not develop fully; but also because people of some personality types rely so much more upon referring to values in making decisions. Within the education sphere the task is two-fold. Firstly there is the analytical task to enable people to see where opinions rest upon values, what those values are and to ensure they are consistent with other held values. Secondly there is the need to help people to develop their own value system and to use it in making decisions and forming opinions. Current perceptions in the United States increasingly recognize that analyses of problems, while apparently highly intellectual and dispassionate, are much more frequently bound up with values that have been absorbed from society in general than we have assumed in the past.

Intuition

None of the models quoted and discussed in this book include intuition as a skill. Yet in the United States especially, but elsewhere also, senior managers increasingly recognize the importance of intuition in making major decisions. The Geneva-based International Management Institute has recently launched a world-wide research project into the nature and potential of intuition in the business world (Agor, 1989, p. 218). The key word may be 'recognize' for intuition has been used in decision-making for many years though decisions made in this way have usually been supported by analytical data which confirms an already made conclusion. It is not only in the worlds of industry and business that intuition is used. The US Department of Defense is examining the possible use of intuition in their decision making (Rowan, 1989, p. 87). There are many other examples. One is that of chess grandmasters who play several games simultaneously and do so by 'intuition'; a few seconds glance suggests a good move 'although the player has no idea how the judgment was evoked' (Suman, 1989, p. 29). Closer to home educational managers use intuition too. The Director of a polytechnic said recently:

> Anything I might grandiosely call 'insight' comes at a time when I'm working on something else and in a context where I'm not expecting it. (Thompson, 1990)

As we have seen it is possible to respond to a work of art either by analysis or by appreciating it as a whole. This duality sets particular problems for the study of artistic forms in universities where the emphasis tends to be upon analysis while it is known that the work under scrutiny was produced by substantial use of intuitive processes. The usual expectation is that decision-making will be analytical and that artistic response will be holistic when in fact the alternative approach can be, and is, used in either case. We can also use both approaches in parallel (though not exactly simultaneously). Alfred Brendel, concert pianist and musical scholar speaks of musical analysis in these terms:

> For analysts the pipe dream of a system into which everything can be crammed and everything can be evaluated is a temptation that is rarely resisted. Masterpieces never give all their secrets away, not even those of craftsmanship. Invariably, only the few threads are disclosed. The word 'analysis' is, by common superstition, held to stand for a process that dissolves the whole into its component parts while it ought to serve as a guide from the particular towards the whole. (Brendel, 1988)

Holistic perception whether of a work of art or of a business situation parallels the process by which many scientific discoveries, works of art, and business decisions come about. Scientific discovery, musical and literary composition, and many other activities take place sometimes by the laborious application of hard won technique and sometimes by a flash of inspiration, the 'Eureka moment' or by a process in which the discoverer appears to be a recipient rather than a worker. Many scientists have reported that their discoveries 'came by a process of sudden awareness' (Goldberg, 1989a). Poincare, the mathematician, regarded both intuition and analysis as crucial in the advancement of mathematics and attested the importance of this combination in his own work (quoted in Vaughan, 1989, p. 53). Melvin Chalvin, the Nobel Laureate chemist, described the most exciting moment of his career as a researcher as occurring when he was sitting at the wheel of his car when quite suddenly and unexpectedly the cyclic character of the path of carbon became apparent to him, not in detail — that was worked out later — but with all the essential concepts clear and integrated (*ibid*, p. 55). Similarly James Watson, the biochemist, became 'suddenly aware' of the way in which the double helix of the DNA molecule could exist (quoted in Goldberg, 1989, p. 63).

Among poets A E Housman's experience is often quoted:

> As I went along, thinking nothing in particular, only looking at things around me. . .there would flow into my mind, with sudden and un-accountable emotion, sometimes a whole line of verse, sometimes a whole stanza at a time. (Housman, 1933, p. 49, also quoted in Graves, 1979, pp. 74 and 255)

In a slightly less well-known, but more specific case Siegfried Sassoon (1945) recorded:

> One evening in the middle of April I had an experience which seems worth describing for those who are interested in methods of poetic production. It was a sultry spring night. I was feeling dull-minded and depressed, for no assignable reason. After sitting lethargically in the ground-floor room for about three hours after dinner, I came to the conclusion that there was nothing for it but to take my useless brain to bed. On my way from the arm-chair to the door I stood by the writing table. A few words had floated into my head as if from nowhere. In those days I was always on the look-out for a lyric. . .so I picked up a pencil and wrote words down on a sheet of note paper. Without sitting down, I added a second line. It was as if I was re-membering rather than thinking. In this mindless, recollecting, manner I wrote my poem in a few minutes.
>
> When it was finished, I read it through, with no sense of elation, merely wondering how I had come to be writing a poem when feel-ing so stupid. I then went heavily upstairs and fell asleep without thinking about it again. . . The poem was *Everyone Sang* which has since become a stock anthology piece. (p. 140)[22]

Both Housman and Sassoon were also, of course, meticulous craftsmen who worked over some of their poems with intense care applying skills of con-struction learned by years of conscious effort.

Mozart, too, wrote of music coming to him fully formed and the cir-cumstances in which this occurred (coach journeys, solitary walks and beds) and the ensuing 'enlargement' of ideas which continued to develop as though he were an uninvolved witness. He also wrote that preparedness of mind was a precondition of composition in this way. (Goldberg, 1989b, p. 186).

The absence of intuition in the classifications and models of skills pro-duced by employers and by academics perhaps lies in the fact that the reported use of intuition in business is from the most senior of managers. There are several possible reasons for this. The most likely seems to be that because more reliance is placed upon analytical methods in most companies it is only the most senior and totally confident managers who will either use (or admit to using) such processes.

It is also more prominent in some managerial functions than others:

> Managers specializing in financial management, engineering, law and law enforcement have higher test scores of thinking vs intuitive ability

because these professions tend to place greater emphasis on facts and figures for decision-making, value hierarchical models of management and stress quantitative techniques of analysis. (Agor, 1989, p. 143)

Once again, however, choice of management task may relate to thinking style, and the implications for this are considered below in the section on teamwork skills.

Within higher education the same general emphasis upon one form of activity as opposed to another is apparent. Although many efforts are now being made to develop ways of assessing creative activities, higher education always finds it easier to evaluate or examine logical and linear activities than holistic ones. There is then a double constraint on acknowledging or developing the latter. The one point where existing models come close to accepting intuition is in the inclusion of imagination or creative skills. Intuition as discussed in this section seems to be much wider than any of these mentions would allow. It also appears to have characteristics which are separate, and in the interests of trying to open up the whole broad area, imagination is treated as a separate skill in this chapter. There may be other related activities of the human brain for subsequent inclusion. One American writer on intuition offers this list:

> Intuitive experiences include, but are by no means limited to, mystical insights into the nature of reality. Experiences which are commonly called intuitive include discovery and invention in science, inspiration in art, creative problem solving, perception of patterns and possibilities, extra-sensory perception, clairvoyance, feelings of attraction and aversion, picking up 'vibes', knowing or perceiving through the body rather than the rational mind, hunches and premonitions. (Vaughan, 1989, p. 40)

This adds precognition and extra-sensory perception to the fields already discussed in this section. These are also the subjects of much research and the American literature quotes many examples of precise precognition, such as knowing intuitively how much to offer in a sealed bid in an auction of a business. There seems to be a distinction to be drawn between judgments which, though made instantaneously and in a holistic way, are nonetheless made on the basis of information already known by the participant, and decisions made on the basis of the unknown or future events. And just as some American writers include them others will have none of it. So for example:

> (Intuition). . .is not some magical thing. . .it is the sub-conscious drawing from innumerable experiences that are stored. (Agor, 1989, p. 158)

If there is uncertainty on this particular matter among commentators and in the world of business, the world of education gives even less attention to it. There is probably, as yet, insufficient agreement over some fundamental characteristics of precognition and extra-sensory perception to attempt to include them in the discussion at this stage. But the world of education might do well to examine the potential of using the skills of intuition more fully.

Searching Skills

The worlds of employment and education alike depend upon information seeking, for we live in an information-based society in which the ability and skills to search for new and relevant information are essential. The skills of analysis and synthesis both work on material which is knowledge or information based. Analytical skills may identify gaps in information, and in the sequence of processes involved in solving problems (which includes identifying the problem and separating problem from context), there may be a requirement for fresh information. Searching for knowledge depends upon the skills of reading, listening and oral questioning. Indeed the Prudential Corporation include 'seeking information by oral means' as a communication skill. But it is probably more than this. One of the arguments for allowing examination candidates to see examination papers in advance or permitting them to take reference books with them is that it is more important to know where to look for information than to carry the information in one's head. So searching for information probably involves knowing where to look for reference books and how to use them. Immediately however this broadens the discussion to the breadth of the curriculum, for single discipline courses develop facility in a relatively restricted range of searching skills. Once acquired the ability to relate new knowledge to existing knowledge in a consistent way is needed. But even more important may be the ability to relate new to existing knowledge, and to see the implications of the new. Here the important abilities are not the purely technical ones but the ability to relate knowledge to conceptual frameworks that not only make sense of them, but also make connections between one set of concepts and another.

Interpersonal skills are needed to establish productive one-to-one relationships. The dynamics of such relationships are explained in part by interaction of the individual personality described by Myers-Briggs, but there are other forces at work too. Just one model of these forces is considered here. Its theoretical base was first described by Michael Argyle,[23] who sees relationships between individuals as the product of two fundamental aspects of behaviour. The first is the dimension of dominant or submissive behaviour and the other a tendency towards warmth or hostility. Robert Lefton, a consultant working in the field of improving interpersonal behaviour, defines these four characteristics as follows:

> *Dominance*: Dominance is the exercise of control or influence. It means asserting oneself, putting oneself or one's ideas forward, striving to make an impact on the way other people think or behave. A person who behaves dominantly takes charge and stays in charge, or guides and leads, or persuades and moves others to action.

> *Submission*: Submission is following the lead of others without first asserting one's own ideas. It's ready compliance, easy acquiescence, giving in with little or no attempt to influence the course to be followed.

> *Summary*: One good way to distinguish between dominance and submission is to say that dominant behaviour tries to make things

happen while submissive behaviour is more inclined to let things happen. Dominant behaviour is essentially active, dynamic, forceful, submissive behaviour is passive and deferential.

Hostility: Hostility is self-centredness coupled with a lack of regard for others. Hostile behaviour is insensitive and unresponsive to other people's needs, feelings and ideas. It's cynical about their motives and doubtful of their abilities. It is not synonymous with open anger.

Warmth: Warmth is regard for others coupled with trust, or at least open mindedness. Warm behaviour is sensitive and responsive to other people's feelings, needs, ideas. It's optimistic about people's motives and abilities. It is not synonymous with open affection.

Summary: A good way to distinguish between hostility and warmth is this: hostile behaviour is based on a negative or pessimistic view of others, which holds that a person shouldn't expect much of other people, and shouldn't offer much of himself in return; warm behaviour is based on a positive or optimistic view of others, which holds that one should approach them, at least initially, in an open receptive way. Hostile behaviour sees most other people as undependable at best, threatening or hurtful at worst. Warm behaviour takes a much more benign view. (Lefton, Buzzota and Sherberg, 1980, pp. 26–7)

Lefton and his colleagues go on to describe typical behaviour in each of the four combinations of these dimensions as it is observed between peers, towards subordinates and towards superiors.

Two examples are sufficient for the purpose of this chapter. Managerial behaviour towards subordinates in each of the four quadrants is typically like this:

Quadrant 1 (Dominant and Hostile)

Planning
Rarely involves subordinates. ('Why should I? Planning is my prerogative. I make the plans, and they carry them out. That's as it should be')

Organizing
Strong believer in tight organization. ('In my department I make sure everyone knows what to do and how to do it. I call the shots.')

Controlling
Very close supervision at all times. ('Any manager who isn't vigilant is asking for trouble. Subordinates need to know that they're being closely monitored and scrutinized.')

Leading
Pushes, demands, drives. ('Most people want a strong leader to tell them what to do. My subordinates know who's boss.')

Quadrant 2 (Submissive and Hostile)

Planning
Relies heavily on own boss. ('I prefer to pass along his plans. That way, my subordinate knows there's little room for deviation.') Or leans leavily on tradition when making own plans. ('If it's worked before, it should work again.')

Organizing
Follows policies and procedures stringently. ('When you go by the book, you can't get into trouble.')

Controlling
Sees self mainly as a caretaker. ('A manager is paid to keep things stable. I exert just enough control to make sure nobody disrupts established routines. There's no point in doing more than that.')

Leading
Downplays role as an influence. ('Don't kid yourself. No matter how hard you try to lead people, they're going to end up doing pretty much as they please.')

Quadrant 3 (Submissive and Warm)

Planning
More concerned with generalities than details. ('If you fence people in with too much planning you'll demoralize them. I prefer to be flexible and let my people do their jobs as they think best.')

Organizing
Loose. Relies on goodwill to get the job done. ('If people feel good about their jobs, they'll do their best without a lot of nit-picking regulations. My job is to make sure they feel good.')

Controlling
Expects high morale to produce hard work automatically. ('Control is secondary to morale. What subordinates need most is a good feeling about their jobs.')

Leading
Believes optimism and encouragement gets results. ('Being a manager is something like being a cheerleader. You can't let your people get discouraged.')

Quadrant 4 (Dominant and Warm)

Planning
Consults with subordinates whenever their thinking might prove helpful. ('I want the best plans possible. That sometimes requires ideas from other people. I don't have all the answers.')

Organizing
Believes in pragmatic organization, with policies and procedures to be adhered to as long as they work and changed if they don't. ('I'm a strong supporter of thoughtful, thorough, but not rigid, organization.')

Controlling
Tries to develop subordinates who whenever possible control themselves. ('Get people committed to their goals and they'll do a good job of supervising their own efforts.') Structures more rigid controls for those who can't control themselves.

Leading
Tries to guide subordinates to awareness and use of their potential. ('Leadership is helping subordinates do what they've got in them to do. A leader is a developer of people.') (*ibid*, p. 30)

Subordinate behaviour towards superiors in each of the four quadrants is usually like this:

Quadrant 1 (Dominant and Hostile)
Argues, displays negative emotions, or takes strong, dogmatic stands. Has I've-got-my-mind-made-up attitude. Overstates own achievements. Resists boss's attempts to explore the record. Reluctant to admit responsibility for mistakes or problems. Pushes own ideas in spite of contrary evidence. Doesn't explore superior's ideas. Rarely gives credit to others. Doesn't listen carefully; plows ahead with own views. Stubborn, resistant, argumentative.

Quadrant 2 (Submissive and Hostile)
Apathetic: unwilling to reveal own thoughts or get deeply involved. Seems afraid whatever he says will be used against him. Passively accepts boss's ideas. Responds in cautious, non-committal way. Stays neutral by saying little or stating views without conviction or refusing to ask questions. Rarely disagrees. Procrastinates; listens distrustfully. Remote, hard to read, uncommunicative.

Quadrant 3 (Submissive and Warm)
Over friendly and eager to please. Good-naturedly accepts boss's views without serious questions. Voices ideas in vague way; emphasizes positives, downplays negatives. Withholds underlying doubts. Rambles. Uninterested in details; settles for generalities. Enthusiastically agrees, but doesn't always show real understanding. Asks questions designed to produce happy answers. Doesn't seem to hear all that's said; screens out unpleasant facts. Genial, good-natured, accepting.

Quadrant 4 (Dominant and Warm)
Appropriately friendly. Candid and attentive. If she disagrees, she gives reasons; listens thoughtfully to boss's views. Seeks thorough discussion. Realistic and able accept criticism. Takes responsibility for errors. Doesn't alibi or rationalize. Takes credit for achievements without inflating them.

> Works hard with boss to develop insight into problems. Doesn't undermine boss, but insists on respect and a fair hearing. Asks sensible questions; expects straightforward answers. Businesslike, involved, growth-oriented. (*ibid*, p. 323)

As with the underlying tendencies defined by Myers-Briggs no individual operated on a fixed point. Someone who is usually warm and dominant may under stress become hostile and dominant. Again an individual may operate at a different position on the dominant/submissive dimension according to whether they are interacting with the boss or a subordinate. But this model established, there are three things that follow. Behaviour in the warm-dominant 'Quadrant Four' is more productive than any other. Secondly, the skills of behaving in this quadrant can be taught and learned. Finally, classroom interaction is based on these dynamics and, in particular, the relationships between teacher and student use these modes and students may learn from them. Once again Alverno College has been the pioneer. Recognizing that the way tutors respond to students is based upon the dynamics described by Lefton in the employment situation, the Faculty at Alverno have recognized that responsibility to develop interaction based upon the quadrant of dominance and warmth. Alverno Faculty define the four basic modes of transaction as

Assertive — rights, ideas and opinions of both parties valued. Assertive communicators invite other participants to resolve problems participatively and look to mutually satisfying resolutions of conflicts.

Aggressive — resolve problems by threat or hostility; tendency to rudeness and hostility, over-confident of their own opinions and abilities, tend to assume others are incompetent; uses commands.

Manipulative — places responsibility unfairly on the other person by exerting moral pressure or blackmail; does not respect the opinions or beliefs of others and manipulates other persons into behaviours they regard as inappropriate.

Passive — totally laissez-faire, assumes ideas and feelings are not valuable or important; allows others to ignore, exploit and make decisions for them.

Two of many examples quoted by Alverno staff are:

A student says to her tutor, 'I can't come to class, is it OK?'

Assertive 'I am not certain about how OK it is until you tell me the reason'.

Passive 'No problem'

Aggressive 'It's never OK to miss class'

Manipulative 'That's a pity because I had got some activities I thought would be specially helpful to you to the problems you have in class'

Or a student says

'I have a hard time in class because you talk too fast and use words I can't understand and ignore student comments'. Here responses might be:

Assertive 'I understand how frustrating it must be when you could provide me with some help by letting me know as soon as you find you need a different pace/I use a word you don't understand'.

Passive 'I usually talk too fast, I probably need to slow down'.

Aggressive 'Bring a tape recorder if you can't keep up'.

Manipulative 'You seem to be the only person in class having problems, have you thought about whether you should be here?' (Alverno College Faculty)

Team Skills

The relationship of people of different personality style also has a profound effect upon the way people relate to one another. Some of these are discussed in Isabel Briggs-Myers and Peter Myers, *Gifts Differing* (1980) whose understanding of personality type is outlined above.

Teamworking Skills

Team skills require interpersonal skills but go beyond them to the very core of personality. Sir John Harvey-Jones, former Chairman of ICI observes:

> . . .in the sort of committed style of management which I seek so many people are involved that. . .the composition and balance of the team is a most important factor. . .teams need a broad mixture of abilities and personal qualities. Teams of superstars each outstanding in their own area seldom win largely because their ability to analyze and criticize is high and their vanity and intelligence frequently make them bad listeners. . . Abandoning the purity of a position they know to be right is extraordinarily difficult and the belief in the importance of the shared aim is often not high enough to make such a 'sacrifice' worth while. (Harvey-Jones, 1988, pp. 97–8)

He goes on to list the essential personal qualities: 'involvement, mutuality of respect, the ability to recognise contributions no matter where they (come) from, the importance of multiple skills, and the need to stay together'. Elsewhere he elaborates these in regard to the team 'mix' he found essential in forming a company board grouping, identifying qualities in three areas. One is background where 'There must be on the board some people with a good financial background. . . Someone with experience of the different interactions between politics and economics in the various countries and areas of the world'.

Second is a mix of personalities which includes a balance of humour but also a balance between the 'instant-action' men with the 'philosophers', between the extroverts and the introverts, between those with strategic vision and those with tactical ability, and besides the essential requirements of honesty and integrity from every one of them, people who, at the least can respect each other, and hopefully can trust and like each other. The third area is a mix of different ages, ambitions and potential (*ibid*, pp. 249 ff).

This experience is reflected in current observation of team work undertaken by management consultants. To focus on the second of John Harvey-Jones' three areas, current thinking in management development often identifies eight styles of management. These are seen in close studies of managers at work in their jobs or in the way they work on management development exercises. The eight categories described by Margerison and Lewis have been summarized above on pages 71 and 72. Starting from a different theoretical base, the analysis of personality factors pioneered by Raymond Cattell (1965), R.M. Belbin (1981) also found eight identifiable styles and his own summary of these appears on page 97. The terminology differs but the overlap in substance is substantial. Neither categorization is rigid. Most managers have a predominant style and at least one, and often two, supplementary styles. Current practice seeks to use these strengths by building teams that between them provide all eight ways of getting things done.

Like many management statements these focus on the world of employment rather than life in general. They are outcome oriented. They are also more concerned with personal style than thinking style. It might be useful to management practice to extend its views of management style to include the complementary contribution that can be made by the four thinking styles of David Kolb and the differences of approach developed by different disciplines. The idea of teams built upon the strengths of different disciplines is more likely to be acceptable to academics than of teams built upon personality types. The development of a single view combining both thinking and personality style may provide common ground. Even so, the processes of higher education have a long way to go before they use learning experiences positively to develop team skills of either form. There are increasing efforts to use group methods of teaching in higher education but these seldom go beyond giving experience of the give and take of discussion. There is scope for major experimentation and research in this area. A difficulty may be the tendency for disciplines to attract people of similar thinking styles and personality type so that the construction of well balanced teams may not always be easy. But it is worth attempting and there are general experiences to be won from well structured group exercises such as too early commitment to an inadequate set of ideas. From this students can learn how easy it is to form group loyalty (to engage in group-thinking, to use the jargon expression) and how necessary it is for groups to be self-critical of their collective ideas.

Self-management

Self-management appears increasingly among employers' requirements, sometimes as an overall quality but more often defined in specifics. These

Table 6.2: Figure 2 of R.M. Belbin's summary of useful people to have in teams (p. 178)

Type	Symbol	Typical features	Positive qualities	Allowable weaknesses
Company worker	CW	Conservative, dutiful, predictable	Organizing ability, practical common-sense, hard-working, self-discipline	Lack of flexibility, unresponsiveness to unproven ideas
Chairman	CH	Calm, self-confident, controlled	A capacity for treating and welcoming all potential contributors on their merits and without prejudice. A strong sense of objectives	No more than ordinary in terms of intellect or creative ability
Shaper	SH	Highly strung, outgoing, dynamic	Drive and readiness to challenge inertia, ineffectiveness, complacency or self-deception	Proneness to provocation, irritation and impatience
Plant	PL	Individualistic, serious-minded unorthodox	Genius, imagination, intellect, knowledge	Up in the clouds, inclined to disregard practical details or protocol
Resource investigator	RI	Extroverted, enthusiastic, curious, communicative	A capacity for contacting people and exploring anything new. An ability to respond to challenge	Liable to lose interest once the initial fascination has passed
Monitor evaluator	ME	Sober, unemotional, prudent	Judgment, discretion, hard-headedness	Lacks inspiration or the ability to motivate others
Team worker	TW	Socially oriented, rather mild, sensitive	An ability to respond to people and to situations, and to promote team spirit	Indecisiveness at moments of crisis
Completer-finisher	CF	Painstaking, orderly, conscientious, anxious	A capacity for follow-through. Perfectionism	A tendency to worry about small things. A reluctance to 'let go'

include the ability to manage time, to plan one's own work (including taking responsibility for one's ongoing learning) and to work to deadlines. More subtle skills include the awareness of one's own potential and the ability to evaluate one's own performance objectively and accurately. Here development can only go hand in hand with general maturity, but they are more than the product of maturity alone. Another skill which has something of the same quality about it is the ability to engage in a discussion without being the centre of it (the ability to 'decentre' as the jargon has it). Coming to terms with objectivity is difficult for some. 'That was a boring lecture' says one student, so categorizing the event by their subjective reaction to it. 'I was bored by that lecture' says another, so allowing the possibility of other evaluations. Another commonplace example is provided by the student who is unable to modify his/her opinion in the light of discussion: 'I accept what you say but still think that. . .' This is an area where education has a particular responsibility since it emphasizes individual over group achievement, upholds the right of the individual to hold his/her point of view, and tends in consequence to support self-regard. There is also judgment, a difficult quality to define though lack of it is more readily recognized.

Other Taught Areas

Other areas of competence sometimes appear in lists of competence. Two which appear frequently are the ability to use computers and knowledge of foreign languages. Both are increasingly sought by employers, and can be combined with almost any of the other fourteen skill areas. Any search for a completely comprehensive and totally acceptable formulation is likely to be unsuccessful. The line between what is learned explicitly as knowledge and what is learned by process is seldom clear.

Many of the skill areas are contained within larger disciplines. But it does not in any way reduce the status of great disciplines for some of the skills they have made available to be regarded as 'transferable', and to have them described in limited terms. Philosophy, for example, might be thought of as the 'home' of analytical skills. And quantification skills can be subsumed within mathematics, at once one of the great intellectual achievements of mankind and source of the intellectual tools upon which so many of the discoveries and physical achievements of the modern world, from theoretical physics to the built environment, depend.

Many of the sub-skills can be placed under more than one heading and some belong together in ways which have not so far been mentioned. Even in the most disinterested model-building it is difficult to be free from the influence of purpose. So the subtler skills of understanding the written word so effectively developed by Lee Shulman's example in the teacher Nancy, and the appreciation of painting could be as well considered, and for some purposes far better, under a heading of 'Aesthetic Perception'. For the same reasons while 'teamwork' has real meaning, the popular global groupings of 'communication' and 'problem solving' have little. For each draws in skills for particular circumstances. Communication draws upon listening, speaking and interpersonal skills sometimes accompanied by the ability to make presentations in graphical forms. Or it uses the written word helped by other means of representation. Most modern journalism uses several kinds of presentation simultaneously. The *Economist* and *New Scientist*, to quote but two examples use the written word, maps, diagrams, cartoons and photographs. It is an effective combination. Problem solving may require analysis, values clarification, searching or additional information and synthesis. But above all skills are manifest in whole people and no matter how carefully their individual gifts are analyzed or their skills defined, each remains unique. Some essential qualities defy definition. Belbin is clear: 'Character counts whenever an important job lacks takers. In one case what is needed is moral courage, in another exacting self-discipline or in yet another a readiness to endure tedium' (*ibid*, p. 130).

Some Related Issues

A basic assumption underlies the thinking in this book — that skills transfer from one situation to another. It is not unreasonable, for the distinctiveness of *homo sapiens* lies in the ability to think and to remember what has been learned in one situation so as to apply it to another. But not all attempts to transfer succeed and the limitations upon successful transfer have been the subject of laboratory investigation for many decades.

There are two broad aspects of transfer; one that attempts are made to transfer skills but they prove to be the wrong ones, the other that skills tend to be used only in the context in which they were learned. As to the first aspect, in the case of the graduate taking up a job, skills which have been developed in the process of higher education may prove to be of little use in employment while skills which have been neglected suddenly become of great importance. It is not necessarily that graduates do not use the skills they possess, but that the skills they transfer are inappropriate. 'He thinks about alternative ways of doing the job rather than getting on with it', complained one bank manager to the other. 'Last week I gave him a problem to sort out and he wrote an essay about it, describing the history (which I already knew) and exploring half a dozen irrelevant ramifications. I wanted the job done, not explained.' The unfortunate graduate employee had transferred the skills he had learned but they were largely inappropriate in the job he had been given to do.

For all the work that has been done to bring the worlds of the academy and employment closer together significant differences remain. Some writers see the large discontinuities between operating in an academic and an employment environment as critical areas. P.C. Candy and R.G. Crebert (1990), for example, point to differences of overriding purpose similar to those reported in this chapter: 'Goals L (in higher education) are directed at acquiring knowledge, skills and process while in (the workplace) they are directed at producing goods or services for profit'. They quote Szanton (1981) in listing the particular ways in which this shows: differences of 'attitudes towards driving interest; use of time; modes of thought, expression and work; and the end result of their efforts'. So the manager may be pragmatic in arriving at decisions but hate an absolute concern for deadlines, while the academic with a greater concern for the demonstrably right as opposed to an adequately usable answer, may be a stickler for method and prefer to go on seeking evidence rather than meet a deadline. The manager who needs solutions to problems is unlikely to adopt the latter approach. Candy and Crebert (1990) summarize the differences in the neat phrase 'elegant answers versus practical solutions'. They point also to major differences in the way learning takes place. Within higher education most learning is formal and uses lectures, tutorials, the reading of set texts, the writing of essays as its means. Much learning at work is informal, achieved on-the-job by chatting to colleagues over coffee, picking up job-related information in meetings, from memoranda or correspondence. It is then small wonder that the skills developed in higher education may fail to be effective in the world of employment.

Candy and Crebert (1990) see the solution along lines similar to those proposed in this chapter.

> Within tertiary institutions what is needed is a far greater emphasis upon strategies designed to foster self-directed learning. . . Students should be encouraged to participate actively in all forms of learning whether in lecture seminar or tutorial form and more programmes based on problem-solving should be introduced into the curriculum.

Cognitive psychologists who have worked on the problems of transfer of learning have found it a particularly difficult area for experiment since rigour requires the elimination of variables which distort or invalidate findings while the process of transfer from academe to employment is so multi-faceted as to defy this kind of treatment.[24] Apart from the difficulties of observing the process of transfer which can be inferred from the differences identified by Candy and Crebert there are distortions of motivation. Those who have worked with trainees on Youth Training Programmes for example have found 'a new task or working environment may be much more interesting or motivating (than school)' (Mathews, 1986). Psychologists working on these problems have been especially interested in learning and problem solving (using problem solving in the narrow sense necessary for scientific enquiry). Of the problems worked on by academic psychologists for more than three decades two are of particular relevance here. One is the relationship between general thinking skills and the knowledge base on which it is used. 'There *are* general cognitive skills; but they always function in contextualized ways' (Parkins and Salamon, 1989, p. 19)[25] and this context is provided through a knowledge base. As a result a high level of abstract thinking ability can be relatively ineffective when the knowledge base is thin and lesser intellectual power can be very effective when there is a sound knowledge base to work on. The other main area of importance is the extent to which the human mind is structured to attempt transfer at all. Perkins and Salamon comment

> A casual look at the research on transfer might suggest that our cognitive apparatus simply does not incline very much to transfer. But this would be a misapprehension. On the contrary, when faced with novel situations people routinely try to apply knowledge, skills and

specific strategies from other, more familiar domains. In fact people commonly ignore the novelty in a situation assimilating it in to well rehearsed schemata and mindlessly bringing to bear inappropriate knowledge and skill yielding negative transfer. (*ibid*, p. 22)

Perkins and Salamon conclude that although there is much evidence of situations where transfer does not take place it does nonetheless occur provided certain conditions obtain:

It became evident that transfer is possible but that it is very much a matter of how the skill is acquired and how the individual now facing a new situation goes about trying to handle it. Given appropriate conditions such as cueing, practising, generating abstract rules, socially developing explanations and principles, conjuring up analogies and the like. . .transfer from one subject domain to another can be obtained. (*ibid*)

Although this approaches the problem of transfer from one discipline to another and does not deal with transfer from academic to employment situations, the conclusions are at least similar to those reached by Candy and Crebert; education can do a lot to develop thinking skills in ways which do transfer. Some problems of context — purpose, deadlines, and pragmatism — remain. But it is possible that even these are not totally intractable. For although academics and employers place markedly different emphases upon these things, neither excludes the other completely. Moreover if our understanding of learning style is accurate they derive not only from the needs of the situation but from preferred ways of working. Indeed such differences of personality may partly explain why transfer sometimes takes place and sometimes does not.

The development of the intellect as a fundamental purpose, the use of abstract reasoning to produce elegant answers do distinguish academic from other activities. But underlying this chapter are two convictions; one, that higher education would for its own purposes be enhanced by using a wider range of processes and the other, that this done the academic purpose does not overlap completely with that of other employment. But as higher education moves to change its processes perhaps employers have a responsibility to meet academics part way down the road; there will always be some onus on the employer to release the potential of skills learned in an academic environment. And the employers who write in this book do just that.

A central, perhaps the central, issue raised in this book is the extent to which courses in higher education should be attuned to the needs of employment, and to what extent should they be answerable only to academic values. A basic argument often offered against change is that higher education in the liberal tradition cannot be both vocational and liberal; it must be either one or the other. This tradition and this specific aspect of it have generated a considerable literature both in Britain and in the United States. The underlying positions in the two countries are substantially different. For the British standpoint a definition written by L.C. Knights in 1938 is a good starting point.

The essential function of a university is to produce men who are 'equipped to be intelligent and responsible about the problems of contemporary civilization'. It must then set itself to cultivate these qualities:

(a) A sensitive and flexible intelligence that can be brought to bear effectively upon the problems which concern the individual or the individual as a member of society.
(b) A potentially mature sense of values: an ability to respond to what the past has to offer (in literature and art, in philosophy and religion, in general ways of living) that may be of value in the present.
(c) A sense of the relativity of one's immediate standards — a sympathetic understanding of human modes essentially different from those that are familiar (something that is not incompatible with firm judgment).

Unless a university performs this fourfold function — unless it turns out a fair proportion of men who are educated in this sense — it is not a university at all. (Knights, 1938, pp. 363–4)

Many things have changed in that half century since that was written. Traditional universities are not now the only providers of higher education though it is important to ask whether they have features which make them distinct from other providers. Our own times would also find the implied exclusion of the education of women from the responsibilities of universities unacceptable to an offensive degree. But for this study a detectable change in the relationship between university education and employment is more important. Knights did not refer to employment and although it might be subsumed within the 'problems which concern the individual' that would be to strain the sense of his carefully worded definition beyond fairness. Moreover Knights included no vocational discipline among his examples of 'the instruments of knowledge' through whose mastery a person becomes educated. Again while asserting that research and the training of teachers 'can hardly serve their higher purpose unless carried on in close relation to a university', he saw no such relationship as necessary for the work of technical colleges. So there was for him a clear divide between liberal education which is non-vocational and taught in universities on the one hand, and technical education (used as a synonym for vocational education as it was until well after the Second World War) on the other. Robbins signalled an end to the divide by including the development of 'skills suitable to play a part in the general division of labour' among his four aims of higher education and placed it first lest it be overlooked. As this has become more widely accepted the focus of the discussion has changed and now centres upon two issues, the extent to which preparation for employment should be explicit and how to define and preserve the essential and distinguishing qualities of the university. Lady Warnock's *Universities: Knowing our Minds* (1989) deals with both. It was written in the immediate context of the implementation of the Education Reform Act of 1988 and in the wider setting of the discussion of what makes graduates employable and the distinctiveness of university education. Lady Warnock concludes 'that, before it is too late, we must try to reach some kind of agreement on what the universities are actually supposed to do' (*ibid*, p. 10) and responds in the terms indicated earlier in this chapter. She continues:

> Moreover in a democratic society, increasingly and properly demanding the right to understand, one must add the ability to explain issues, both narrow problems and wider implications, to people not themselves experts in a field, but with a legitimate interest in it. (*ibid*, p. 35)

Other characteristics appear elsewhere in the same publication:

> . . .universities. . .should release people. . .from the tyranny of present-mindedness. (*ibid*, p. 36)

> Graduates are. . .trained to be. . .critical of their own and other peoples ideas (*ibid*)

Lady Warnock states the distinguishing features of a university education in different and in less precise terms from Knights, yet the two sets of views are entirely consistent with one another. But whereas vocationalism was not an issue for Knights it has to be tackled in 1989. In doing so Lady Warnock first places universities and other 'providers of post-school education' in separate categories. The avoidance of an expression such as 'other higher education' helps to heighten the sense of distance. While deploring the 'confusion over relations between. . .university and other providers' she does not look at what the distinctive role of the others is or might be. Here Lady Warnock has a different and more difficult task than Knights, for the role and characteristics of the polytechnics and colleges of higher education need to be taken into account. Knights did not need to say what a technical college actually did; it was so different from a university that no delineation was needed. Lady Warnock draws a three-fold distinction

> between wholly vocational subjects (such as hairdressing and carpentry) and subjects which are either not vocational at all (such as mathematics or medieval history) or are vocational, but with a strong academic content (such as medicine or law). Only the latter two should be studied for a degree the others for diplomas. (*ibid*, p. 12)

Because the examples are so clear-cut they avoid the issues of where the boundary is drawn between them. 'Carpentry' may not seem right for the inclusion in degree studies, but at its more advanced levels the techniques of construction using wood has a content in common with engineering. The boundaries are not easy to draw. But Lady Warnock does point out the usefulness of the skills of analysis for managers (*ibid*, p. 36) and although the weakness of this position has already been noted above it does indicate two important changes from the views of Knights. One is that in 1989 the connection between what happens in the process of university education and its subsequent application afterwards is worth mentioning. The second is that the connection is made in the area of transferable skills. Specific vocationalism is unacceptable'; but the acquisition of an intellectual skill useful in employment is, by implication, valid. At a more general level the proposition is made that 'We should rethink the concept of the useful' (*ibid*, p. 32). Although there is no ground given on the possibility of adapting curricula to be more explicitly aware of vocational needs the concept of 'the useful' is now open for examination.

American writers have less difficulty in seeing higher education as preparing people for employment, but the main differences between the American and British traditions are in their view of specialism and breadth. Knights was clear that the educated person would be a specialist, though not necessarily in only one discipline, and he expected a university education to develop a sense of value; (albeit not to a mature state) by processes which he did not define but which involved responsiveness to literature, art, philosophy and religion. Lady Warnock is not specific on the issue of specialization but does not challenge current practice. The expectation that the educated person will be a specialist though not necessarily in only one discipline in the tradition in Britain (and particularly in England and Wales) differs substantially from American expectations.

A good example of the current American thinking is provided by Derek Bok, President of Harvard University who defines the goals of liberal education to be:

> Undergraduates should acquire an ample store of knowledge, both in depth, by concentrating in a particular field, and in breadth, by devoting attention to several different disciplines. They should gain an ability to communicate with precision and style, a basic competence in quantitative skills, a familiarity with at least one foreign language, and a capacity to think clearly and critically. Students should also become acquainted with the important methods of inquiry and thought by which we acquire knowledge and understanding of nature, society, and ourselves. They should develop an awareness of other cultures with their differing values, traditions, and institutions. By having the chance to explore many opportunities, they should acquire lasting intellectual and cultural interests, gain in self-knowledge, and ultimately be able to make sound choices about their future lives and careers. Through working and living with a wide variety of follow students, they should achieve greater social maturity and acquire a tolerance of human diversity. Last but not least, they should enjoy their college years or at least look back on them later as a time when their interests and enthusiasms were engaged in a particularly memorable way. (Bok, 1936, pp. 54–5)

The importance of breadth could hardly be put more strongly. Harvard has for many years been at the forefront of the concern to hold on to this aspect of higher education in the United States so that an unequivocal statement in its support is to be expected from its President. But similar views are expressed more generally. The recent statement of the Association of American

Colleges, *Integrity in the College Curriculum* (1985) shows that commitment to the general principle remains strong. Pursuit of a core of common knowledge has also been increasingly difficult with the constant expansion of the total range of human knowledge, nonetheless it remains an underlying aim. From it has followed a recurring interest in the nature of knowledge and in defining its many forms. Philip Phenix's *Realms of Meaning* (1964) is a fine example of this continuing quest for definition and classification.

In Britain it is otherwise. In England and Wales choices which narrow have become normal in schools from the age of 14, and studies within the sixth form are essentially specialist. The National Curriculum Council is addressing both issues and it is clear will require a better balance to the age of 16 than has obtained universally in recent years. Change beyond 16 may be much more difficult to achieve. Two attempts by the Schools Council to achieve more breadth (in 1968/69 and 1978) failed, as did also the recommendations of Professor Higginson's Committee in 1988.[26] On entering higher education specialization becomes even more marked and few institutions in England and Wales regard breadth as important.[27] The significant exceptions have been the University of Keele with its four-year degree course, and the University of Sussex with a structure of degree studies that requires some study across normal disciplinary confines. Both of these institutions have had to retreat a little from their original positions as time has passed. In more universities specialism remains the norm. Scottish practice, as in so much else, is different especially for the age group beyond 16. But in recent years most Scottish universities have moved closer to degree studies based on the special honours pattern of England and Wales and in doing so have lost much of the breadth which one time marked them out as significantly different. Polytechnics in England and Wales have however offered much broader honours degrees, often in combined studies.

At a general level there have been two significant attempts to move the structure of degree studies in the direction of greater breadth. In 1958 Lord Hailsham, when Lord President of the Council, tried to persuade the Cabinet, 'to push the universities into adopting less specialized degree courses, and so reduce the pressure on sixth forms to specialize. The Chancellor of the Exchequer, Derick Heathcote-Amory, who then had responsibility for university grants, refused a general inquiry into the universities on the grounds that it would infringe their autonomy.'[28] About a decade late Professor A E Pippard, a member of the Swann Committee, argued for university science to be taught in two phases of two years each. The first two years would be an education in general science with an introduction to a specialism, the second two years would develop the specialism (Pippard, 1968). Professor Pippard was unable to convince his colleagues and his proposals appeared only in an annexe to the main report. In practice the trend in universities in England and Wales has been in the opposite direction. For in the last thirty years the universities founded in England in the nineteenth century and up to 1950 (but excluding Keele) have reduced both the base of intermediate studies and ceased to offer three subject general degrees. The breadth and specialism issue has so far been discussed in purely educational terms and particularly as differing aspects of the British and American traditions. Employers also have a perspective. In Britain this has been put by Sir John Harvey-Jones, the former Chairman of

ICI, who believes 'The great need is for more breadth. We need practical, well educated, broadly-based young people. The next group of young people to join industry will need breadth of view and depth of understanding' (Harvey-Jones, 1985).

Although breadth in America has remained an important aim, the balance for some commentators is still not sufficiently weighted towards it. One recent overview of major trends in the world and their implications concluded:

> The notion of life-long learning is already replacing the short-term approach to education and employment whereby you went to school, graduated, and then that was that. . . The long-range perspective may signal the need to return to the ideal of a generalist education. If you specialize too much you may find your specialty becoming obsolete in the long run. As a generalist, committed to lifelong education, you can change with the times. (Naisbitt, 1984)

There is one other aspect of the breadth/specialist balance. A society which attempts to respect the individual and regards autonomy as important must respect the right of the individuals to choose. The tendency to prefer one broad set of intellectual activities to another as understood by Kolb (and outlined above) develops a predisposition towards some form of specialism in most of us. Part of current culture is resistant to forcing people to study particular things because they are 'good' for the student. Yet if the fully autonomous human being is to be effective in a complex world some breadth is inescapable. For Lady Warnock a fundamental distinguishing feature of the universities is their ability to develop a particular 'cast of mind.' This would probably be widely accepted though many would claim that it is not a preserve of the universities alone and that other institutions develop the same quality. A recurrent theme in the statements of employers is their need for particular attitudes. So the wider issues include not only the breadth of the curriculum, the processes of teaching it and the transferable intellectual skills they develop, but also the attitudes developed by the experience of higher education. Most critical of all is whether there is an intractable incompatibility between the attitudes and habits of mind developed through higher education in the liberal tradition, and those required by employers. It is not easy to separate attitudes from the exercise of skills, the pursuit of a discipline or a profession, or other activity such as pursuit of a hobby. For just as competence is possessed but can only be assessed when it is demonstrated in practice, so also attitudes remain hidden until they appear in behaviour. Some of the major attitudes of mind developed in higher education are

- intellectual objectivity;
- respect of evidence and the ability to evaluate it critically;
- intellectual curiosity and the ability to pursue a line of enquiry or argument 'whithersoever it goeth';
- respect for the opinion of others, subject to their being based upon the same principles;
- coherence and consistency of opinions; and
- intellectual humility and an awareness of one's own limitations

None of these seem to be inconsistent with the need for tenacity and drive sought by employers. But there is a potential mismatch between intellectual curiosity and the pursuit of lines of enquiry and arguments to their conclusion and the need to meet deadlines and to be confined by objectives. The need to meet deadlines by completing study assignments provides some training in meeting deadlines and the related skills of self-management, but the nature of higher education is less constrained by predetermined objectives. Yet on some occasions the more open, less constrained qualities may be just the ones needed in employment. Nor does there seem to be any overriding reason why these two particular approaches should not rest in the same person; the requirement is to know when to switch from one mode to the other. But just as the ability to think analytically was a necessary but not a sufficient intellectual product of higher education, so the attitudes developed in higher education are useful but not of themselves enough. Just as attitudes are bound up with skills so also they have a relationship with values. An American statement helps to put the issues in a stark form:

> Impact studies should consider the role of college in developing such qualities as courage, the capacity for effective leadership and fellowship. Machiavellian skills, competitive skills, cut-throat types of behaviour and the capacity to exploit intellectual style and jargon, . . .to deceive and be deceived, and to relate to people of different backgrounds. (Ellison and Simpson, 1973, pp. 57–8)

Although this statement could hardly be more extreme, it is useful since it highlights the fact that it is not the attitudes to intellectual processes, but the purpose to which they are put and the values that govern what we decide is acceptable and unacceptable behaviour that matters. Intellectual honesty in the pursuit of study is a useful attribute to acquire. But there are two other factors. One is that students also learn from the way their institutions are run, and the second that one of the failures frequently attributed to institutions of higher education on both sides of the Atlantic is that they have abdicated direct responsibility for developing values in their students. They may provide them with the intellectual skills to discriminate among values or to analyze values, but teach them a value system by which to live they do not. As with so many of the areas touched upon in this chapter, there is a vast literature on this matter too.

If the area where incompatibility lies is in the field of values then there is reason to hope that academics can continue to look towards the more explicit development of skills in the process of teaching. As this occurs so there are benefits for the academic world too, for the development of some skills required in employment will enhance the educational process itself; it will sometimes enhance existing academic objectives, and sometimes it will require their modification. For these skills are developed more by the process of teaching and learning than imparted as knowledge. At the moment most courses are knowledge dominated.

Process is part of the curriculum and is recognized as such in some institutions; but we have still far to go before the balance is satisfactory for academic as well as employment purposes. All this said there should and there will remain objectives, content and processes which serve academic purposes, but which do not serve employment purposes and which are, at most, neutral towards it. Most of the discussion here is about humanities graduates. It is a legitimate focus, but the issues are pertinent to scientists, engineers and social scientists, too. As long ago as 1965 Anthony Sampson commented:

> A young graduate taken on for his broad horizons (a favourite man-agement cliche), will find himself in a thicket of specialist problems with no glimpse of an horizon in sight and specialization is worse for the young technologist moving from the university lab to a works lab with little scope for handling people. 'The arts graduate need not worry about competition from the scientist', said one Personnel Officer expert, 'because they're like pigmies. They treat people as if they were chemicals, they want to wait until all the variables have been eliminated'. Thousands of scientists escape from laboratories to be-come managers helped by frequent weakening of scientific curiosity at the age of about thirty or so.

Another issue, related to that of breadth, is that of two preferences, shown by higher education. One is a preference for the logical and linear disciplines and ways of teaching them over rational, and equally valid, holistic studies and methods. Second, and closely related, is the preference given to people of certain personality styles. Success in higher education is more easily achieved by introverts than extroverts, even though intelligence is spread evenly among people of both types. These are not easy predispositions to overcome for we tend to recruit students who are like ourselves. And once recruited we teach students according to our own style. A teacher of foreign languages will teach in a linear way requiring lots of vocabulary to be learned from lists of the next most useful words if he or she is a serial, left-hemisphere led thinker while a right-hemisphere holistic thinker might build vocabulary in a less structured way using whole sentences and emphasizing the context of their use. Serialist-thinking students will respond more readily to the former, holistic-thinking students to the latter. But within higher education the balance is already in favour of the serialist teacher and learner. There are parallel challenges to employers. A further issue is the emphasis given in education, and especially higher education, upon individual achievement. In employment the need is for people who can work with others towards shared goals. Again there are parallel challenges to employers. Senior and middle management is certainly dominated by people who combine the Myers Briggs preference of sensing, thinking and judging. Teams may be built up with regard to the need to have a balance of styles within them, but are sometimes selected according to sub-conscious preferences for people of our own style. Responses from the institu-tions of higher education are urgently needed on all of these issues. Change is real in some institutions and is effected by many individuals. But the gen-eral position is not fast moving. Michael Young, the sociologist points out,

> Whenever there is a challenge to the customary, people's first reaction is to find out the *status quo ante* and to re-affirm it, if with·some tiny modification. The most telling argument in almost any debate about

what should happen is that it is in accord with the practice of the Constitution or any constitution, of the Gospel or of a gospel. The presumption is in favour of the past. (Young, 1988, p. 199)

Although Michael Young is making a general point about human behaviour, his conclusions fit the world of higher education with deadly accuracy. Self-perpetuation of the system, the self-interest of its workers, and conformity to tradition all raise further questions about the ability of institutions of higher education to challenge the assumptions on which they operate. For most of this century the essential traditions of higher education in Britain were tied to specific types of institution. The universities were characteristically research-led, their first degree courses were almost exclusively full-time and they attempted to provide residence in purpose built halls for students, partly in the belief that it was a valuable part of the educational experience. Until 1964, too, the universities were set apart from other higher education by their monopoly of degree awarding powers.[29] Given legal force through university charters this monopoly was sustained by a conviction among many policy makers that only the universities could guarantee the essential qualities of degree study.

Higher education within the technical colleges had traditions quite distinct from these. They were led by the needs of employment, looked for ways of applying knowledge and had a special responsibility towards part-time students.[30] Although many thinkers (especially within the universities) had been unable to recognize them as belonging to the world of higher education at all, their importance is seldom questioned today. One of the last significant expressions of the distinction as applied in policy appeared in the establishment of the colleges of advanced technology. The CATs were the flagship of technological higher education in the decade 1955–64 yet they were unable to teach for degrees. The technological and applied nature of their work made the University of London external awards unsuitable for their purposes and their degree level work led to the award of Diploma in Technology.

The teacher training colleges, barely recognized as belonging to higher education at all before 1964, represented another tradition, marked by a concern for the actual processes of learning and for the welfare of individual students.[31] Among other aspects of the higher education tradition two were particularly important. One was the strong sense of status attaching to the different kinds of institution. The other was the slow rate of change within them which meant that new needs were often met by adding to the stock of institutions rather than by reforming existing ones. Implementation of the Robbins Report after 1963 lessened some of the more damaging differences. However while institutionalization of the distinction between universities and colleges of technology along the binary line made the funding of new growth for employment-led polytechnics easier, (they were funded less generously than universities) it did little to lift their lower status. This structural anomaly will be resolved as the reforms proposed in the 1991 White Paper, *Higher Education : A New Framework* are implemented. All institutions providing mainly higher education will operate within a university system with its state funding coming from one body. It will not of itself resolve the status problem but should help to reduce it. One new issue will then arise. The multi-faceted nature of our society requires a variety of types of higher education. No doubt the emerging pattern will see universities of different dominant cultures, some led by research, others by employment needs. All will have to attempt to be more responsive to a wider range of needs than in the past, and some will no doubt try to achieve balance without dominance. Attempts to resolve these issues will be helped by a greater emphasis on the processes, as opposed to the content, of courses. And it is the argument of this chapter that the development of a range of intellectual and personal skills fully understood and intelligently modelled will be fundamental in defining useful process.

Notes

1 A Joint Statement by the University Grants Committee and the National Advisory Body for Local Authority Higher Education, published simultaneously (1984) in *A Strategy for Higher Education in the Late 1980s and Beyond* (NAB) and *A Strategy for Higher Education into the 1990s* (UGC).

2 The University of Sheffield Personal Skills Unit 'Employer Survey'. One of the researchers in this Unit also comments that a survey of advertisements for posts in marketing two years previously found only 38 per cent of such mentions. The sample was smaller and the field restricted but since advertisements in marketing tend to include a higher than average specification of personal skills the growth in such mentions seems to be increasing rapidly.

3 Letter to the author from Procter and Gamble previously quoted in Bradshaw (1985).

4 Harrison expresses here a personal, rather than a British Coal, view.

5 The second of Wellens' themes quoted here has recently been developed by Mangan, J.A. in a series of studies which include (1986a) *Athleticism in the Victorian and Edwardian Public School*, Lewes, Falmer Press and (1986b) *The Games Ethic and Imperialism*, Harmondsworth, Viking Press.

6 Dixon (1976 and 1987) examines numerous case studies and explores the many facets of the psychology of military leadership and management. Although not his main concern, his deeply researched and highly readable works show how a high level of commitment without professional competence and powers of judgment are more likely to lead to disaster than success. Industrial failures may not receive the same public exposure but there is no reason to believe that the same principles do not apply.

7 Letter to the author from Professor Maurice Kogan.

8 Doncaster Metropolitan Institute of Higher Education, application for approval for a Diploma in Higher Education, March 1989.

9 The Training Agency (1988) *Enterprise in Higher Education: Guidelines for Applicants*, London, The Training Agency; Wolverhampton Polytechnic (1988) *Enterprise in the Black Country*, Proposed to the MSC for an Early Start under the EHE Initiative; Polytechnic of Wales (1987) *Enterprise in the Polytechnic of Wales*, a Proposal for the Development of an Enterprise Culture.

10 Additionally the dividing line between 'further' and 'higher' education is drawn in differently in other countries. Some of the curriculum for national diplomas in the United Kingdom, for example, would be pursued as degree studies in the United States. See, for example, Department of Education and Science (1989).

11 All of the definitions and descriptions in this section on Alverno are taken from Alverno Faculty (1989).

12 Our Lady of the Lake University, San Antonio, Texas Program Profile for the National Commission on Excellence in Education. (1982)

13 Researchers report that in workshop situations one in twenty people display an equal facility in all modes.

14 For a survey of the relationships between personality type and employment see Macdaid, McCaulley and Kainz (1986). For an exposition of the significance of interaction between people of different type in school education see Keirsey and Bates (1984) especially pp. 97 ff.

15 The definitions are those of Margerison, McCann and Davies (1986). The summary of their definition is quoted from Bradshaw (1989). This article explores some of the issues of developing team work and the under implications for education more fully than is possible here.

16 For a survey of the research into, and current understanding of, the differential functioning of the hemispheres of the brain see Springer (1989).

17 There are many books about body language. The best known popular accounts of those aspects of human behaviour which derive from our evolution prior to the emergence of *homo sapiens* are those of Desmond Morris. See, for example, Morris (1967, 1969, 1977 and 1985).

18 Privately contributed.

19 Letter to author.

20 Private communication to author from Mr Stephen Reddy, Doncaster Metropolitan Institute of Higher Education.

21 Design Council (1976) *Engineering Design Education*, report of a Committee chaired by Dr Alex Moulton, London, The Design Council; Design Council (1977) *Industrial Design Education in the United Kingdom*, report of a Committee chaired by Mr David Carter, London, The Design Council; Design Council (1980) *Design Education at Secondary Level*, report of a Working Party chaired by Professor David Keith-Lucas, London, The Design Council.

22 In his later years he referred several times to other occasions when he wrote in this way. See Corrigan (1973).

23 There is a vast literature on the nature of interaction between individuals and between individuals in groups. The best introductory studies are probably those of Michael Argyle. For example, Argyle, M. (1969) *Social Interaction*, London, Methuen; and Argyle, M. (1983) *The Psychology of Interpersonal Behaviour*, Harmondsworth, Penguin.

24 Psychologists are themselves constrained by the confines of their discipline and its procedures (and sometimes by the context of whatever school of psychology they belong to); they are themselves 'context bound'.

25 See also Perkins, D. and Salamon, G. (1989), 'Transfer and teaching' in Perkins, D.N., Lockhead, J. and Bishop, J. (1987) (Eds) *Thinking: The Second International Conference*, Hillsdale, NJ, Lawrence Erlbaum Associates, pp. 285–303.

26 Standing Conference on University Entrance and the Schools Council Joint Working Party on Curriculum and Examinations (1969) *Proposals for the Curriculum and Examinations in the Sixth Form* (The Q and F proposals), London, Schools Council; Schools Council (1978) *Report of the Joint Examinations Sub-committee*, Working Paper No 60 (The N and F proposals), London, Schools Council; The Higginson Committee of Enquiry (1988) Advancing A Levels, London, HMSO.

27 The story of the change from a generalist to a specialist model for higher education in England is told in Heyck (1984).

28 *Times Educational Supplement*, 6 January 1989, commenting on the 1958 Cabinet Papers then just released under the thirty-year rule.

29 The monopoly cannot be described as absolute since the Archbishop of Canterbury also held degree-awarding powers.

30 Many of the differences are described in Marris (1964). Apart from the high quality of its analysis the book is particularly valuable historically as its research was done as one of the studies undertaken for the Robbins Committee and so caught the system as it was before the changes of the 1960s began.
31 For a fuller description of the college of education tradition within higher education see Bradshaw (forthcoming).

Bibliography

AGOR, W.H. (1989) 'Test your intuitive powers' in AGOR, W.H. (Ed.) *Intuition in Organizations: Leading and Managing Productively*, Newbury Park, CA, Sage Publications.
ALVERNO FACULTY (1989) *Liberal Learning at Alverno College*, Milwaukee, WI, Alverno Publications.
ALVERNO FACULTY (forthcoming) 'Interpersonal problem-solving: The teachable movement', *User Friendly Guidelines for Teaching Social Interaction*, Milwaukee, WI, Alverno College.
ASSOCIATION OF AMERICAN COLLEGES (1985) *Integrity in the College Curriculum*, Washington DC, Association of American Colleges.
ASTIN, A. (1981) 'Measuring the quality of undergraduate education', proceedings of the Conference on Quality in Baccalaureate Education, Austin, University of Texas, quoted in NORTHEAST MISSOURI STATE UNIVERSITY (1984) *In Pursuit of Degrees with Integrity*, Washington, DC, American Association of State Colleges and Universities, p. 9.
BARNETT, C. (1986) *The Audit of War*, London, Macmillan.
BELBIN, R.M. (1981) *Management Teams, Why They Succeed or Fail*, London, Heinemann.
BOK, D. (1936) *Higher Learning*, Cambridge, MA, Harvard University Press.
BOYS, C.J., BRENNAN, J., HENKEL, M., KIRKLAND, J., KOGAN, M. and YOULL, P. (1988) *Higher Education and the Preparation for Work*, London, Jessica Kingsley.
BRADSHAW, D. (1985) 'Transferable intellectual and personal skills', *Oxford Review of Education*, II, 2,
BRADSHAW, D. (1989) 'Higher education personal qualities and employment: Teamwork', *Oxford Review of Education*, 15, 1.
BRADSHAW, D. (forthcoming) 'Other colleges' in MCNAY, I. (Ed.) *Visions*, Milton Keynes, Open University Press.
BRANCHER, D. (1987) 'Words used skilfully are vital instruments in today's industry', *The Times*, 26 November.
BRENDEL, A. (1988) 'The Last Three Piano Sonatas of Schubert' (The Edward Boyle Memorial Lecture).
BROOKFIELD, S. (1987) *Developing Critical Thinkers*, Milton Keynes, Open University Press.
BTEC (1986a) *Common Skills and Core Themes*, London, BTEC.
BTEC (1986b) *Common Skills and Core Themes General Guidelines*, London, BTEC.
BUZAN, A. (1983) *Use Both Sides of Your Brain*, New York, E.P. Dutton.
CANDY, P.C. and CREBERT, R. (1990) 'Teaching now for learning later: The transfer of learning skills from the academy to the workplace'. A paper presented to the eighth Australian Conference on Language and Learning Skills, Queensland University of Technology, Brisbane, 11–13 July.
CATTELL, R.B. (1965) *A Scientific Analysis of Personality*, London, Penguin.
CHEMICAL AND POLYMERS GROUP OF ICI (1988) *Getting Results*, London, ICI.
CORRIGAN, D.F. (1973) *Siegfried Sassoon: Poet's Pilgrimage*, London, Victor Gollancz.
COUNCIL FOR INDUSTRY AND HIGHER EDUCATION (1987) *Towards a Partnership: Higher Education — Government — Industry*, London, CIHE.
COUNCIL FOR NATIONAL ACADEMIC AWARDS (1988) *CNAA Handbook*, London, CNAA.

DEPARTMENT OF EDUCATION AND SCIENCE (1963) *Higher Education* (Report of the Committee appointed by the Prime Minister under the chairmanship of Lord Robbins), London, HMSO.

DEPARTMENT OF EDUCATION AND SCIENCE (1987) *Higher Education: Meeting the Challenge*, Cm 114, London, HMSO.

DEPARTMENT OF EDUCATION AND SCIENCE (1989) *Aspects of Higher Education in the United States of America*, London, HMSO.

DEPARTMENT OF EDUCATION AND SCIENCE (1991) *Higher Education: A New Framework*, Cm 1541, London, HMSO.

DIXON, N.F. (1976) *On the Psychology of Military Incompetence*, London, Jonathan Cape.

DIXON, N.F. (1987) *Our Own Worst Enemy*, London, Jonathan Cape.

ELLISON, A. and SIMPSON, B. (1973) 'Does college make a person healthy and wise?', quoted from WILSON, J. (1981) *Student Learning in Higher Education*, London, Croom Helm.

FORREST, A. and STEEL, J.N. (1982) *Defining and Measuring General Education Knowledge and Skills*, Iowa City, The American College Testing Program.

FLOUD, R. (1977) 'Quantitative history: Evolution of methods and techniques', *Journal of the Society of Archivists*, 5, 7, April.

GARDNER, H. (1985) *Frames of Mind*, London, Paladin Books.

GOLDBERG, P. (1989a) 'The many faces of intuition' in AGOR, W.H. (Ed.) *Intuition in Organizations: Leading and Managing Productively*, Newbury Park, CA, Sage Publications.

GOLDBERG, O. (1989b) 'The intuitive experience' in AGOR, W.H. (Ed.) *Intuition in Organizations: Leading and Managing Productively*, Newbury Park, CA, Sage Publications.

GRAVES, R.O. (1979) *A E Housman: The Scholar Poet*, London, Routledge & Kegan Paul.

GREEN, S. (1989) 'Biological science graduates — employment prospects and flexibility', *Biologist*, 36, 4.

HALL, E.T. (1959) *The Silent Language*, New York, Doubleday & Co.

HAMMOND, B.S. (1980) 'University English and the spoken word', *Spoken English*, Southport, The English Speaking Board.

HARRISON, R. (1986) 'History and employability: History is business', *Welsh Historian*, autumn.

HARVEY-JONES, J. (1985) 'Industry and education: The partnership to success', a speech at the University of Bradford.

HARVEY-JONES, J. (1988) *Making it Happen: Reflections on Leadership*, London, Fontana/Collins.

HAYES, C. (1989) 'Qualifications for an uncertain future', paper presented to the Annual General Meeting of the Association of Colleges for Further and Higher Education, February.

HENNESEY, P. (1989) *Whitehall*, London, Secker & Warburg.

HEYCK, T.W. (1984) *The Transformation of Intellectual Life in Victorian England*, London, Croom Helm.

HIRSH, W. and BEVAN, S. (1988) *What Makes a Manager? In Search of a Language for Management Skills* Brighton, Sussex University, Institute of Manpower Studies.

HITCHCOCK, G. (1987) 'Transferable skills: A DipHE contribution to the debate', *Journal of Further and Higher Education*, 11, 3, autumn.

HOCHMAN, D. (1990) 'Cities, scale economics, local goods and local governments, *Urban Studies*, 27, 1.

HOUSMAN, A.E. (1933) *The Name and Nature of Poetry* (The Lesley Stephen Lecture, 9 May), Cambridge, Cambridge University Press.

JESSUP, G. (1990) *Common Learning Outcomes: Core Skills in A/AS Levels and NVQs*, London, NCVQ.

JONES, R.T. (1969) 'Multiform assessment: A York experiment', *Cambridge Review*, 15 November.

JUNG, C.G. (1923) *Psychological Types or the Psychology of Individuation*, London, Kegan Paul.

KEIRSEY, D. and BATES, M. (1984) *Please Understand Me: Character and Temperament Types*, Del Mar, CA, Gnosology Books.

KNIGHTS, L.C. (1938) 'The modern universities', *Scrutiny*, VI, 4.

KOLB, D.A. (1983) *On Management and the Learning Process*, Cambridge, MA, Massachusetts Institute of Technology.

LEFTON, R., BUZZOTA, U.R. and SHERBERG, M. (1980) *Improving Productivity Through People Skills: Dimensional Management Strategies*, Cambridge, MA, Ballinger Publishing.

MACDAID, G., McCAULLEY, M.H. and KAINZ, R.I. (1986) *The Myers-Briggs Type Indicator Atlas of Type Tables*, Gainesville, FL, Centre for the Application of Psychological Type.

MAHER, P.T. (1983) 'An analysis of common assessment center dimensions', *Journal of Assessment Center Technology*, 9, 3.

MARGERISON, C. and LEWIS, R. (1981) *Mapping Managerial Styles*, Bradford, MBC Publications.

MARGERISON, C., McCANN, D. and DAVIES, R. (1986) 'The Margerison-McCann team management resource', *International Journal of Manpower*, 2.

MARRIS, P. (1964) *The Experience of Higher Education*, London, Routledge & Kegan Paul.

MATHEWS, D. (1986) 'The accrediting of ability to transfer skills and knowledge to new situations', *FESC Information Bank No 2201*, Blagdon, Further Education Staff College.

MINTZBERG, H. (1976) 'Planning on the left side and managing on the right', *Harvard Business Review*, July/August.

MORRIS, D. (1967) *The Naked Ape*, London, Cape.

MORRIS, D. (1969) *The Human Zoo*, London, Cape.

MORRIS, D. (1977) *Man Watching*, London, Cape.

MORRIS, D. (1985) *Body Watching*, London, Cape.

MYERS, I.B. with MYERS, P.B. (1989) *Gifts Differing*, Palo Alto, CA, Consulting Psychologists Press.

NAISBITT, J. (1984) *Megatrends*, London, Macdonald.

NORTHEAST MISSOURI STATE UNIVERSITY (1984) *In Pursuit of Degrees with Integrity*, Washington, DC, American Association of State Colleges and Universities.

ORNSTEIN, R. (1986) *Multimind*, London, Macmillan.

OUR LADY OF THE LAKE UNIVERSITY SAN ANTONIO (1982) 'Program Profile for the National Commission on Excellence in Education', San Antonio, Texas.

PASK, G. and SCOTT, B.C.E. (1975) 'Learning strategies and individual competence' in WHITEHEAD, J.M. (Ed.) *Personality and Learning*, London, Hodder & Stoughton.

PERKINS, D.N. and SALOMON, G. (1989) 'Are cognitive skills context found?', *Educational Researcher*, January/February.

PHENIX, P. (1964) *Realms of Meaning: A Philosophy of the Curriculum of General Education*, New York, McGraw Hill.

PIPPARD, A.E. (1968) 'Outline of a proposal for reorganizing university education', annexe E of the Report of the Working Group on Manpower for Scientific Growth, *The Flow into Employment of Scientists, Engineers and Technologists*, Cmnd 3760, London, HMSO.

REPORT OF THE HARVARD COMMITTEE (1946) *General Education in a Free Society*, Oxford, Oxford University Press.

RODERICK, G.W. and STEPHENS, M.D. (1978) *Education and Industry in the Nineteenth Century: The English Disease?*, London, Longmans.

ROWAN, R. (1989) 'Intuition: What it is' in AGOR, W.H. (Ed.) *Intuition in Organizations: Leading and Managing Productively*, Newbury Park, CA, Sage Publications.

SAMPSON, A. (1965) *Anatomy of Britain Today*, London, Hodder and Stoughton.

SAVILLE AND HOLDSWORTH LTD. (1988) *Occupational Personality Questionnaires*, brochures issued by Saville and Holdsworth Ltd., Esher.

SASSOON, S. (1945) *Siegfried's Journey*, London, Faber & Faber.

SHULMAN, L. (1987) 'Knowledge and teaching: Foundations of the new reform', *Harvard Educational Review*, 57, 1.

SIMON, H.A. 'Making management decisions: The role of intuition and emotion' in AGOR, W.H. (Ed.) *Intuition in Organizations: Leading and Managing Productively*, Newbury Park, CA, Sage Publications.

SPRINGER, S.P. and DEUTSCH, G. (1989) *Left Brain, Right Brain*, New York, Freeman & Co.

SZANTON, P. (1981) *Not Well Advised*, New York, Russel Sage Foundation.

THOMPSON, K.B. (1990) address of welcome to a conference on 'Assessing Transferable Skills in Business, Social Science and Humanities', Staffordshire Polytechnic, June.

UNIVERSITY OF SHEFFIELD PERSONAL SKILLS UNIT (1990a) *A Conceptual Model of Transferable Skills*, Sheffield, University of Sheffield.

UNIVERSITY OF SHEFFIELD PERSONAL SKILLS UNIT (1990b) *Employer Survey, Sheffield*, University of Sheffield.

VAUGHAN, F.E. (1989) 'Varieties of intuitive experience' in AGOR, W.H. (Ed.) *Intuition in Organizations: Leading and Managing Productively*, Newbury Park, CA, Sage Publications.

WAIN, J. (1956) 'Who speaks my language?' in *A Word Carved on a Sill*, London, Routledge & Kegan Paul.

WARNOCK, M. (1989) *Universities: Knowing Our Minds*, London, Chatto & Windus.

WAUGH, E. (1955) 'Literary style in England and America' in *Books on Trial*, reprinted in GALLAGHER, D. (Ed.) (1983) *The Essays, Articles and Reviews of Evelyn Waugh*, London, Methuen.

WAYNE STATE COLLEGE (1985) 'Statement for APEP', previously quoted in BRADSHAW, D. (1985) 'Transferable intellectual and personal skills', *Oxford Review of Education*, II, 3.

WELLENS, J. (1959) 'The anti-intellectual tradition in the West', *British Journal of Educational Studies*, VIII, 1.

WHISSON, M.G. (1986) 'Why study anthropology', *Anthropology Today*, 2, 1, February.

WIENER, M.J. (1981) *English Culture and the Decline of the Industrial Spirit*, Harmondsworth, Penguin.

WILLIAMS, J.E. and STRICKLAND, W.G. (1976) 'The importance of the graphic approach to research in higher education', a paper presented at the Southern Conference on Institutional Research, Georgia State University.

WRIGLEY, E.A. (Ed.) (1972) *Nineteenth Century Society: Essays in the Use of Quantitative Methods for the Study of Social Data*, Cambridge, Cambridge University Press.

YOUNG, M. (1988) *The Metronomic Society: Natural Rhythms and Human Timetables*, Cambridge, MA, Harvard University Press.

YOUNG, P.V. (1966) *Scientific Social Surveys and Research*, New York, Prentice Hall.

Chapter 7

Employment, Skills and Career Orientations: English and History Undergraduates Compared with Other Undergraduates

Chris J. Boys

The relationship between higher education and employment is complex. The type of employment obtained by a graduate is affected by the state of the economy, individual employer preferences, his/her aspirations, personal and social attributes, as well as by educational factors. These will include the type of subject studied, the type of course attended, the type of institution attended, the degree classification achieved, and 'A' level grades. The most important educational variable, in terms of employability and employment, appears to be the subject studied.

Annual surveys of graduates some six months after graduation reveal a fairly consistent subject pattern. Table 7.1 shows, for example, the average unemployment and temporary employment rates between 1975 and 1986 for the six subjects which I am comparing in this chapter — English, history, economics, business studies, physics and electrical engineering. Humanities graduates tend to suffer higher rates of unemployment than their peers. This may be dismissed as a transitional problem, if a problem at all. However, I have argued elsewhere that unemployment and temporary employment six months after graduation correlates with other indicators of 'success' in the labour market over the longer term: obtaining jobs aspired to, career opportunities, salaries, and the status of jobs obtained (Boys and Kirkland, 1988). There is something of a paradox between the poorer showing of humanities graduates in employment compared with their peers and claims that courses in the humanities develop broad skills relevant to a wide range of occupations. Is the claim about skills correct? The question is important because of the implications for what is taught and how it is taught at a time when governments in many countries want closer links between education and employment. In attempting to answer the question I shall draw on findings from a sample survey of final year undergraduates carried out as part of a project sponsored by the Council for National Academic Awards (CNAA) and the Leverhulme Trust Fund at Brunel University between 1984 and 1987 (Boys, *et al*, 1988).

Table 7.1: *Percentage of polytechnic and university graduates employed or in temporary employment six months after graduation between 1975–86.*

Subject	Percentage unemployed
English	21.0
History	19.3
Economics	16.9
Business studies	12.1
Physics	11.5
Electrical engineering	6.1

Source: CNAA Students Database

Skills

Table 7.2 shows the results of a question put to students in their final year about the extent to which they felt that they had improved various skills or qualities as a result of being in higher education. The list predated the various initiatives aimed at improving skills in higher education including enterprise skills (the Training Agency), capabilities (Royal Society of Arts), and 'transferable intellectual skills' (CNAA). This does not matter for my purposes and, in any case, there is an overlap between the skills referred to here and those referred to in these initiatives. The aim is to establish if there are subject patterns in the types of skills undergraduates feel that they have developed in higher education and to relate these patterns to employer preferences for graduates from different subjects and particular skills in their recruits. Before looking at the patterns revealed in table 7.2, I shall summarize some of the findings about employer preferences.

Employer Preferences

A survey of employers conducted by Gordon in 1981 found that they tended to value different qualities in graduates from different subjects. (Gordon, 1988). It should be noted that there was no consensus among employers about any of the skills required. 'High ability' generally was the reason most often cited for recruiting graduates and the 'ability to learn quickly' was also cited by a large number of employers. The emphasis on high ability is not surprising given the importance attached to good 'A' levels by employers in an earlier employer study conducted in 1981 at Brunel University (Roizen and Jepson, 1983). Relevant knowledge was cited by Gordon as the main reason why employers recruited science graduates whether pure or applied but this did not figure among reasons for recruiting arts graduates. The most often cited reason for employing arts or social science graduates was their ability to communicate. Numeracy was among the reasons for recruiting scientists and lack of numeracy was cited by a number of employers as a disadvantage in employing arts graduates.

A more recent and large scale study has thrown further light on employer preferences although not with the amount of detail on skills as in the earlier

Table 7.2

Skills

To what extent have you improved in any of the following as a result of your experiences in higher education either inside or outside your degree course?

Score −1 for deterioration; 0 for stability; +1 for marginal improvement; +2 for quite an improvement; +3 for great improvement.

(i) Thinking

	History	English	Economics	Business studies	Physics	Electrical engineering
Critical thinking	2.20	2.25	1.82	1.79	1.47	1.47
Objective thinking	1.77	1.63	1.63	1.62	1.31	1.23
Original thinking	1.72	1.79	1.62	1.39	1.20	1.23
Mean	1.90	1.72	1.67	1.60	1.33	1.31

(ii) Understanding concepts

	English	History	Economics	Business studies	Electrical engineering	Physics
	1.89	1.84	1.64	1.51	1.45	1.39

(iii) Breadth of understanding

	English	History	Economics	Business studies	Electrical engineering	Physics
Understanding Social Issues	1.76	1.82	1.82	1.44	0.94	0.93
Understanding Ethical Issues	1.53	1.40	1.17	0.90	0.90	0.79
Understanding other Subjects	1.20	1.23	1.11	1.05	1.12	0.98
Mean	1.50	1.48	1.37	1.13	0.92	0.90

(iv) Absorbing information/quickness of learning

	History	Economics	English	Business studies	Physics	Electrical engineering
Absorbing Information	1.47	1.37	1.46	1.38	1.26	1.29
Learning Quickly	1.19	1.26	1.16	1.11	1.14	1.02
Mean	1.33	1.32	1.31	1.25	1.20	1.16

(v) Working independently

History	English	Economics	Business studies	Electrical engineering	Physics
1.88	1.79	1.65	1.61	1.48	1.36

(vi) Communication

	English	History	Business studies	Economics	Physics	Electrical engineering
Written Communication	1.93	1.93	1.52	1.10	1.01	0.90
Oral Communication	1.75	1.73	2.01	1.63	1.36	1.32
Mean	1.84	1.83	1.76	1.76	1.36	1.18

(vii) Numeracy

Physics	Electrical engineering	Business studies	Economics	History	English
1.18	1.11	0.96	0.90	-0.12	-0.13

(viii) Interpersonal

	Business studies	Economics	Physics	English	Electrical engineering	History
Ability to work with people	1.79	1.26	1.32	1.32	1.25	1.16
Leadership	1.57	1.10	1.04	1.01	1.04	1.03
Mean	1.68	1.18	1.18	1.16	1.14	1.09

(ix) Personal

	Business studies	Economics	History	English	Physics	Electrical engineering
Self Confidence	1.77	1.62	1.70	1.63	1.52	1.51
Drive and Ambition	1.45	1.15	1.05	0.93	0.87	0.87
Reliability	1.04	0.91	0.73	0.65	0.77	0.71
Mean	1.42	1.23	1.16	1.07	1.05	1.03

Gordon survey. Surveys conducted for an interdepartmental government review show that roughly half of employers are looking for general abilities while the other half are looking for specialists, although this varies considerably between types of employment (CIHE, 1990). When private employers were asked: 'If you could choose the subjects your graduate recruits studied, would you have any preferences?', 60 per cent said that they would and gave at least one subject area for their choice. Preferences were more likely to be expressed in the manufacturing and construction industries and for technology and engineering subjects. Over 50 per cent of employers in the service industry expressed no preference. When pressed further on these hypothetical subject preferences, 20 per cent of respondents emphasised that the personal qualities of the individual were more important to them than their stated subject preferences. This resonates with the Brunel survey of employers, in which personal or non-academic qualities were also important to employers (Roizen and Jepson, 1983).

Subject Patterns

One of the main features of table 7.2 is that the subjects tend to pair into English and history (humanities), business studies and economics (in which there is an overlap in subject matter), and physics and electrical engineering. To some extent we might expect each pair to draw on similar populations of students.

A second major feature of table 7.2 is that history and English score relatively better on many of the groups of skills identified, certainly on those listed in (i) to (vi) which include those skills and qualities more readily associated with academic study (critical thinking and understanding concepts related to the subject for example).

The differences are not always so large as to set English and history students that much apart from their peers. For example, there is not much difference in the ability to learn quickly which Gordon found to be a skill employers looked for generally and which, along with other academic skills, may be associated with 'high ability' which also featured in the findings about employer preferences.

A third feature of table 7.2 is that the main differences between subjects tended to match the value placed on skills by employers found in the Gordon survey. For example, communication skills score highly in history, English, business studies and economics. In the two humanities subjects, a substantial minority of respondents felt that their numerical skills had atrophied. In this, English and history graduates stand out from the other subjects in the survey.

A fourth feature of table 7.2 is the relatively high scores in business studies on what might be called personal or interpersonal skills (those featured in (viii) and (ix). This is significant because these, together with communication skills, are now considered to be 'core' skills by the National Curriculum Council (NCC) and the National Council for Vocational Qualifications (NCVQ). These skills are likely to be among the personal qualities looked for by employers. The relatively high scores in business studies reflect changes to the curriculum in recent years with the introduction of business skills.

The findings do not show English and history undergraduates to be at a disadvantage in the skills that they develop in higher education except in numerical skills. The fact that a substantial minority of history and English undergraduates felt that their numerical skill had declined during their time in higher education implies that they may be deterred from applying for jobs requiring these skills. They may also be turned down by employers should they apply. The Brunel survey of employers found that a substantial number of them would like to see a more numerate graduate population. (Roizen and Jepson, 1983) Referring to essential numeracy, a Council for Industry and Higher Education publication on the humanities stated:

Companies which recruit large numbers of graduates have recently noted that arts graduates otherwise ideally qualified have to be turned down for management jobs because they are unable to handle quantitative data. Managers must have the confidence to reason with and extract information from numbers, and must be able to do so accurately.

We think that humanities courses that excuse their students from respectable numeracy and everyday understanding of science (sic) will come to be seen as putting their students at an inexcusable disadvantage. We are encouraged to see the growth of humanities courses which reinforce numerical skills and which familiarize their students with technology, including the use of computers. (CIHE, 1990)

As with other subjects, there is also room to develop interpersonal or personal skills which are less developed than most other skills in higher education.

The relatively higher scores in business studies on these scores (see (viii) and (ix)) indicate that changes to the curriculum and to teaching can develop types of skills as perceived by students.

A recent CNAA review of humanities courses (CNAA, 1990) revealed that staff teaching courses in this area were generally cautious about some of the methods currently in vogue to make teaching applicable to the world outside academe and, in particular, to make it applicable to students' future working lives.

The caution expressed by staff in the humanities may have something to do with their belief that transferable skills are an implicit part of what is required to study the humanities. Not withstanding this belief and their wariness towards some of the new skills based approaches to teaching, staff are conscious that they have some part to play in catering for students' working lives. Examples of changes cited in the humanities review include teaching through information technology which is increasingly deployed as either an additional or an integral method of learning, teaching for transferable skills or competence, and negotiated learning through independent study.

The question I posed earlier in this chapter was: is the claim that courses in humanities develop broad skills relevant to a wide range of occupations correct? We have seen the answer is yes but numeracy may be a problem and personal skills could be more developed. I want to add a further question which may better explain why humanities students appear to be worse off in the labour market: are the types of careers sought by humanities undergraduates and their attitudes towards employment different from career aspirations and attitudes of undergraduates in subjects which appear to be more successful in the labour market?

Findings from the student survey to which I have been referring showed that a relatively high proportion of English and history undergraduates entered their courses needing time to decide on an occupation, few chose options in order to enhance their career prospects, and during their final year just over a third had still not decided what type of job they wanted to do. This contrasted with electrical engineers and business studies undergraduates who were much clearer about the types of jobs they wanted to do. In addition, English and history and, indeed, physics graduates, were less concerned about extrinsic rewards (including high salaries, opportunity for rapid promotion, good fringe benefits, a chance to exercise leadership, and to take responsibility) than economists, electrical engineers, or business studies undergraduates. In contrast the humanities undergraduates were more likely to want altruistic rewards (the opportunity to help others, the potential for improving society).

In short, humanities graduates are less conscious about finding employment, tend to have different career related values, and to want different jobs from those who appear to be more successful in the labour market. (Boys and Kirkland, 1988) This leads me to my conclusion: while humanities undergraduates may develop a wide range of skills which employers may want, they are not as conscious of their value as other undergraduates. They need, I suggest, to be made more aware of their value on the labour market. Arguably this may be best achieved through assessing and recording skills throughout an academic course. This could also be linked to work experience. When asked if they would have liked to have experienced a period in employment as part of their degree course, just less than a third of English undergraduate and a quarter of history undergraduates replied in the affirmative.

Taken together, these findings are encouraging for programmes such as the enterprise initiative which aims to develop transferable skills that will be useful to undergraduates in work and in their lives after graduation. Such programmes also require students to undertake periods in the working world. It will be interesting to see whether, in the long run, these programmes make any difference to the employment of humanities graduates.

References

Boys, C.J., Brennan, J., Henkel, M., Kirkland, J., Kogan, M. and Youll, P. (1988) *Higher Education and the Preparation for Work*, London, Jessica Kingsley Publishers.

Boys, C.J. and Kirkland, J. (1988) *Degrees of Success: Career Aspirations and Destinations of College, University and Polytechnic Students*, London, Jessica Kingsley Publications.

Council for Industry and Higher Education (1990) *Towards a Partnership: the Humanities for the Working World*, London, CIHE.

Council for National Academic Awards (1990) *The Nature and Structure of Humanities Provision in the Polytechnics and Colleges*, London, CNAA.

Gordon, A. (1988) 'Attitudes of employers to the recruitment of graduates', *Educational Studies*, 9, 3.

Roizen, J. and Jepson, M. (1983) *Expectations of Higher Education: An Employers Perspective*, Guildford Society for Research into Higher Education.

Chapter 8

Humanities Graduates in the Labour Market

Eva Stina Lyon

Introduction

The relationships between degree courses and the labour market have been shown to be varied and complex. Few disciplines taught as degree studies in higher education possess a single vocational objective, yet almost all graduates have secure employment in their preferred occupation a few years into the labour market. A high proportion of graduate jobs in the labour market do not require vocational or specialist degrees for entry, and the skills looked for by employers seeking graduates have been shown often to be of a more general kind. Despite this rather optimistic overall picture of the employability of graduates whatever their degree subject, there are, however, variations in the nature of the process of transition from study to work for graduates from different disciplines. With the government increasingly set on a course of making both the content and structure of higher education more accountable to the economy, such variations have become an issue of concern as has the contention that not all graduates are equally well equipped for the demands of an increasingly high technology and enterprise economy. Though it would be true to say that few courses, if any, disclaim all responsibility for what happens to students after finals, there are major differences in the extent to which different types of courses and different disciplines prepare their students for particular occupations and tasks in the labour market. Humanities courses have increasingly come under criticism for not being sufficiently responsive to employers and the labour market, and for not doing enough to help prepare their graduates for the demands of the world of work.

This chapter aims to look a little more closely at the complex interaction between the aspirations and characteristics of humanities students and their destinations in the labour market. It aims to give a brief overview of employment experiences and related attitudes of humanities graduates to the employment relevance of their studies, which I believe adds up to a picture of some importance for course planners in the field, as well as for employers of humanities graduates. This evidence points both to the need for some changes in approach to the humanities curriculum to accommodate student needs in the labour market, and to the desirability for a greater awareness by both employers and politicians of the aspirations and orientations of humanities graduates. I will use evidence from publications and research data which has emanated from a series of CNAA-funded research projects on the relationship between higher education courses and the labour market and on the process of entry to it by graduates from different courses and disciplines. One of these projects I will refer to in some detail, the HELM Graduate Panel Survey. This project, recently completed, looked at the employment experiences and destinations of course-based samples drawn from two cohorts of CNAA graduates, that of 1982 and 1985. For the 1985 cohort, comparative information was also ascertained from university graduates in a few disciplines selected as approximately equivalent to subject areas offered in polytechnics. The samples were in both instances chosen to reflect main teaching areas of CNAA-validated institutions. This included the subject area of 'humanities', i.e. a sample of courses so referred to in CNAA handbooks and documentation. As humanities courses in polytechnics usually comprise combinations of English and history, these two subjects were chosen to represent university humanities courses. The chapter is not intended as a summary of the research and all its findings, which has been, and will be, done elsewhere. For the purposes of this chapter it will use select evidence from these surveys to illustrate major issues pertinent to the general discussion about humanities graduates in employment. (Already published summary reports from the CNAA Graduate Panel Surveys are Brennan and McGeevor, 1988, Lyon, McGeevor, Murray, 1988. The final report of phase two of this project was published through the auspices of the CNAA in 1991.)

Employment Orientations and the Choice of a Humanities Course

After a decade of research on graduate entry to the labour market it now seems confirmed beyond doubt that the nature of courses and subject areas in higher education in important ways structure the subsequent process of entry to employment. Vocationally specific courses and subjects serve sectors of the labour market different from degrees of a non-vocational kind such as those in humanities, and each such market is governed by different rules of entry (Brennan and Silver, 1988). This means that for the students, the choice of course to study acts as an important mediator between occupational aspirations, orientations and interests on the one hand and, on the other, the nature and demands of specific labour markets at any one time. The desire for higher education is not a uniform wish for a unitary product. By choosing a particular type of course and subject area, students aim for different types of jobs and different sorts of career rewards. Indeed, for some students the experience of higher education is seen as much as a way of furthering personal development and postponing career decisions, as a passport to immediate employment. Students applying for vocationally non-specific courses are naturally less likely to see their choice of subject as career and job related than students on courses designed with a particular occupational outcome in mind. Though economic incentives may guide the pursuit of higher education in that most graduates are rewarded at the end with higher incomes than non-graduates, students also choose to study for reasons other than those of obtaining specific labour market skills. Such reasons bear a strong relationship to their general social and educational background and location.

There is agreement in many studies on student orientations that students choosing vocationally non-specific subject areas such as humanities, social sciences and arts do so with more 'intrinsic' rewards in mind, than those entering more vocational or vocationally oriented subjects such as engineering, law and varieties of commercially-related disciplines, for whom more extrinsic rewards of career relevance, status and income have been shown to matter more (Dippelhofer-Stiem *et al*, 1984; Sanyal, 1987; Redpath and Harvey, 1987; Boys *et al*, 1988). Evidence from the HELM panel surveys shows the comparative lack of employment orientation by humanities students. The courses in both the 1982 and 1985 cohort samples with the smallest percentage stating that they had chosen their degree subject in order to improve career prospects, or to help them get a particular job, are those of polytechnic and university humanities courses and courses in fine arts. For humanities graduates in the 1985 cohort, this was only the motivation of approximately a third of the students.

The graduate panel data from the 1982 cohort enabled further exploration of the notion of student 'orientation' in order to isolate clusters of factors that enter into labour market aspirations. These clusters can be related to subject of study and to other student characteristics of relevance to labour market entry. Graduates were asked a range of questions directed at their occupational orientations and self-perceptions. They were asked to indicate the importance of a series of items of their choice of a long-term job, and to mark the importance of various spheres of life to them, as well as to give an indication of how they thought of themselves. Factor analysis of these sets of questions allows the isolation of different orientation types, three of which I will look at here: 'careerist', 'inner-directed', and 'altruistic' work orientations. The factor here labelled 'careerist' was shown to correlate strongly with items such as 'a strong possibility of rapid promotion', 'high prestige and social status', 'high salary', 'job security', 'opportunity for professional development' and 'the chance to exercise leadership'. The highest scorers on this factor were shown to be courses of a vocational nature, and the least 'careerist' are graduates in fine art, environmental science, English literature and humanities. The 'inner-directed' work orientation factor strongly correlates with the following: 'the opportunity to be creative', 'the opportunity to use one's special skills and abilities', 'relative freedom from supervision from others' and 'work that is continually challenging'. It is perhaps not surprising that the art and design courses occupy the first position here, with humanities courses close by. Finally, the 'altruistic' orientation is defined by a high correlation with items such as 'opportunity to help others', 'potential for improving society' and 'opportunity to work with people'. The subject areas included in the survey where the greatest proportion of 'altruistically' motivated students were to be found are those of nursing, pharmacy, psychology and humanities. Such findings are in agreement with earlier evidence from other cohorts which show that significant minorities of humanities graduates do not consider their course choices in the light of career benefits, but pay more attention to interest in the subject, altruistic aims and a desire to be generally better educated (Boys *et al*, 1988).

A pattern is emerging of a relationship between aspirations and subject studied, which may be part of the explanation of differential patterns of entry to the labour market.

Labour market orientations such as those discussed above are not, however, evenly spread across the student population, but relate to other student characteristics such as gender, age, social class and interrelated with these that of previous educational achievement. Students with a 'careerist' orientation tend to be on courses where average entry qualifications are higher and more selective, which indicates that labour market orientations relate to educational choices earlier down the ladder of credential accumulation. It is also the case that more women students, particularly mature students and students from lower social class backgrounds express more of an 'inner directed' and 'altruistic', than a 'careerist' orientation. The 'altruistic' career orientation of women students in education has been much discussed, and is related both to earlier socialization into female roles as well as to the realistic anticipation that work in 'service' and 'caring' professions, rather than in high status career contexts of finance and industry, are more conducive to fit in with family concerns (Acker and Warren-Piper, 1984; Thomas, 1990; Metcalfe, 1990). For mature students, and students from a background without a tradition in higher education, aspirations may be more general, and express a search for cultural, educational and personally developmental goals on the way towards finding a route out of low grade routine work. Certainly, a degree can allow for more time in which to decide on career paths, which has been shown to be a desired aim of more than half of one cohort of humanities students (Boys *et al*, 1988).

It would be wrong to argue from this that humanities graduates do not feel their degree course should be of value in the labour market. When asked what they feel higher education in general ought to be about, the humanities graduates show the same values as graduates in most other subjects. There is a considerable amount of agreement amongst the graduates on the ranking of the top functions of higher education with 'personal growth' and 'research and the production of knowledge' coming highest on the list. But close after in the list of values comes 'training for industry and commerce', which also humanities graduates put in third place, before more altruistic and cultural motives. They rank this aim as highly as do business, science and engineering graduates. Like students in other areas, those with humanities degrees want higher education to bear some relationship to work, but for many of them this is not the main reason for which they choose this particular subject of study. As shown in the study by Boys *et al* (1988), a substantial minority of humanities graduates are unlikely to know what kind of job they want towards the end of the third year of their studies. I will return to this somewhat contradictory view of the higher education experience later, when discussing the doubts some humanities graduates express when asked about the value of their degree course once at work. Humanities graduates do not have the kinds of aspirations which would make one believe either that they are very 'geared up' in their search for employment, or that they are likely to present themselves across all areas of the graduate labour market. This does not mean that they do not want jobs, only that finding a high-status, well-paid job with good career prospects has so far not in itself been a major priority in their choice to pursue higher education.

Humanities Graduates: Who Are They?

The 'social catchment' of humanities courses differ in important respects from that of other subject types in higher education and thus there are important consequences for how one interprets both student motivations and the labour market outcomes for graduates. The most important background characteristic known to determine career orientations, choice of course and labour market progression is that of gender. The persistent gender 'divide' between the technological and human sciences in higher education is well documented, as are its consequences for the experiences of women in the labour market (Acker and Warren-Piper eds, 1984; Lyon and Murray, 1992; Thomas, 1990). A high proportion of humanities graduates are women, and with both higher education and the labour market sharply segmented along gender lines, this will affect their future career profiles in ways not always adequately discussed. There is an ongoing interaction between gender, career orientations and secondary and tertiary educational credentials which starts in school and carries on well into what is also for graduates a gender-segmented labour market. For reasons to do with both their earlier educational choices and expectations, as well as future career expectations, women enter different areas, and levels, of the graduate labour market than men, which is likely to depress the overall picture of the employment destinations, status and income of humanities graduates.

Humanities courses also attract mature students. Polytechnic courses in social sciences and humanities have by far the largest proportion of mature students, (i.e. students over 21 at entry). In the 1982 sample it was shown to be 39 per cent, in the 1985 cohort 31 per cent. The survey showed a major difference here between polytechnic and university courses, with the latter having an average of mature entrants of only 6 per cent. In his analysis of the early destinations of mature graduates, Tarsh (1989) notes that in comparison with school leavers, older students, already in the labour market, are less likely to take degrees with a direct link to employment, and more likely to go to polytechnics than universities. However it should be noted that this may not hold true of all mature students in higher education. Ethnic minority students, larger proportions of whom go to polytechnics than to universities, were shown to be largely absent from humanities courses. They are present in greater numbers on more vocationally oriented degrees such engineering and technology, administration, business and social studies. This absence of minority students on humanities courses, despite the fact that they more often enter as mature students, may relate to the stronger vocational orientation shown. This may be fostered by greater awareness of labour market demands and by realistic fears about potential discrimination in the labour market. Due to the shortage of minority students on humanities courses, it is difficult to say anything further here about the issues they face as humanities graduates in the labour market (Brennan and McGeevor, 1990; Lyon, 1991).

The attraction of polytechnic humanities courses to mature students needs further exploration than that undertaken here. There is undoubtedly in the choice of a humanities course as in the choice of social sciences, a search for a broader cultural educational experience, and the development of personal interests and skills. In view of the lower unemployment rates amongst graduates than amongst non-graduates, there is probably also an element of faith in the value of a degree as such. There may, as Tarsh argues, also be more mundane reasons for such a choice in that humanities and social sciences courses, especially in polytechnics, usually require less specific subject knowledge, especially in more 'numerate' subjects, before entry than for example courses in economics, business studies, science and engineering. Sometimes this is a result of a conscious policy of widening access to higher education, but it may also be a result of institutional competition for student numbers. It is, therefore, important to look at the profile of background qualifications that humanities students carry with them into higher education, as such profiles strongly relate to both gender, age and class, and constitute an important factor influencing student choice of course, as well as employer attitudes to potential graduate recruits (Roizen and Jepson, 1985).

Courses vary considerably in their openness and accessibility to potential candidates. The better the 'A' level results, the better the chance of entering a university rather than a polytechnic, and of getting a place on one's chosen course of study. Students taking a science 'A' level are likely to have a higher average 'A' level score than those taking a social science or an art subject 'A' level. The Graduate Panel Surveys point to the different entry pattern of particular courses and show a tendency for courses in some subject areas especially in polytechnics to offer wider opportunities for entry to applicants without 'A' level qualifications, or with lower 'A' level scores. (Scores are calculated on a combination of level of results and numbers of qualifications, with one 'A' level grade A making up a score of 5, grade B scores and so on.) The variations in average 'A' level scores of entrants range from under 25 per cent with a score of 6 or above in polytechnic biology courses, social sciences and, interestingly, science, to above 60 per cent for polytechnic estate management and law. All university courses surveyed had more than 70 per cent of their students with an 'A' level score of 6 or above.

As mature entrants to higher education are less likely to possess 'A' levels, or to enter with high 'A' level scores (which may constitute one reason why they did not go for higher education directly upon leaving school) such students are also both attracted to and more easily accepted on humanities and social sciences courses. Lack of science and numeracy qualifications are likely both to depress 'A' level scores, and to narrow the number of different courses in higher education for which some school leavers and non-standard entrants can be considered. We here see a major difference between university and polytechnic humanities students. The quality of educational experience, as measured by breadth of certification, that polytechnic humanities graduates bring with them to higher education is shown to be considerably less than that of university humanities students and students in other subjects (table 8.1). In view of employer attitudes to secondary qualifications, these differences in educational background are likely to constitute an important factor in explaining differential progress in the labour market. It is also an issue which relates to the question of numeracy as a competence in demand in the labour market. I will return to this when discussing the notion of transferable skills in the humanities curriculum.

Educational qualifications in school and beyond relate not only to gender and age, but also to class. With a high proportion of mature students, and lower barriers to entry than on many other courses, it is not surprising that

Table 8.1: *Percentage 'A' level points and 'O' level passes 1985 cohort*

	9+ 'A' level	6+ 'A' level	Maths O-pass	English O-Pass
Humanities/CNAA	7	34	57	94
Humanities/University	82	87	94	99

polytechnic humanities courses, along with those in social sciences and engineering, have the lowest proportion of students with fathers of senior professional or managerial status. This is also an area where there is a major difference between polytechnic and university students in the sample. Whereas 28 per cent of polytechnic humanities students in the 1985 sample have fathers in manual work, this is only true of 15 per cent of those from university. By comparison it is interesting to note that this is only so for 20 per cent and 7 per cent respectively of polytechnic and university accountancy graduates. Again, the nature of a graduate cohort is stratified not only by gender, but also by a range of other background characteristics known to affect both educational achievement and labour market aspirations and outcomes. The attraction of humanities courses to students 'new' to higher education is undoubted. The hope that all mature students will want access to higher education in order to 'retrain' and 're-equip' themselves for the world of work in a directly vocational sense, as expressed by the Council for Industry and Higher Education (1987), looks in the light of the above to be somewhat unrealistic. Given the indications we have about the nature of the career orientations expressed by non-traditional entrants, the demand for non-vocational humanities courses will continue despite the many concerns expressed about the nature of employment opportunities for some of their students.

The Process of Finding Graduate Work

Destinations in Transition

Given the diffuse nature of the relationship between humanities courses and particular occupations, and the nature of the 'social' catchment' of such courses, it is not surprising that on leaving college, humanities graduates do not immediately enter full-time employment with the same speed as students from courses with more direct labour market links. I will in this section first look at the nature of their destinations after leaving college, both after six months and later into employment, and then turn to some evaluations offered by the graduates themselves of employment related benefits brought by their chosen course of study.

One indicator of early graduate entry to the labour market is that provided by the Early Destinations Statistics, which show what graduates are doing six months after graduation. Less than half of the humanities graduates are in permanent employment, approximately a third are in research or further education of some kind, and a sizeable minority are still unemployed (see

Table 8.2: *Arts humanities graduates 1982 cohort: Employment status 1983–1985 (%) (in brackets % for all courses)*

	1983	1984	1985
Full-time employment	36 (54)	65 (75)	71 (80)
Full-time study	25 (18)	5 (7)	6 (5)
Unemployed	32 (23)	15 (8)	8 (4)

CNAA, 1989, figures 1 and 2). These statistics show a slight improvement between 1982 and 1985 in the proportion of graduates in permanent employment. The proportion of students in further education and training has dropped, as has the number of unemployed students six months after graduation. For the 1982 graduates the labour market was at a low ebb, and with an improvement in the general demand for graduates over the following years, better employment profiles were to be expected. However, we have to treat the explanations of this change with some caution. The improved rate of entry to work may not necessarily be as a result of a more receptive labour market, but could be attributable to the students' anxieties resulting in the decision to take the first job offered, rather than holding out for a more attractive one or postponing the search by going for further training.

The evidence provided by the Early Destinations Statistics, however, needs to be seen in the light of what happens to graduates over a slightly longer time than during the first six months. The HELM Graduate Panel Surveys show that for all graduates, but especially for graduates with degrees without well-defined occupational objectives, the first few years after graduation are a period of transition and change, characterized by varieties of short-term employment, vocational study, interspersed by periods of voluntary or involuntary unemployment, which together make up the process of trying to find more desirable work. Humanities graduates take longer and experience more job changes than many other students before they find a job in which they wish to stay.

Starting off with higher unemployment rates than many other courses, the amount of change taking place for the humanities graduates of the 1982 sample, but also for the cohort of graduates as a whole, over the first three years into the labour market was notable (table 8.2). A similar pattern of change from the employment situation six months after graduation can be seen when we look at the 1985 cohort two years into employment (table 8.3). It is still the case, however, that two years into employment humanities graduates are both studying and unemployed in greater numbers than graduates from other courses in the sample. Information from the 1982 cohort shows that graduates from both social sciences and humanities courses are still two years after graduation searching for graduate work in comparison with those from more clearly vocationally oriented courses, for example, engineering and business studies. At that point almost half of all the humanities graduates in the 1985 sample state that they want a different job than the one they now are in (table 8.4). Over the period 1982 to 1986 humanities graduates from universities did better on the whole when it came to finding employment soon after graduation

Table 8.3: Humanities graduates 1985 cohort: Employment status 1987 (%)
(in brackets % for all courses)

	Men	Women
Full-time employment	55.2 (81)	57.2 (88.9)
Full-time study	14.8 (10.5)	11.1 (8.9)
Unemployed	16.3 (4.2)	9.0 (3.8)

Table 8.4: Changes in employment status/search for work: 1982 cohort (%)

	Changed employment status		Actively seeking different work	
	1983/84	1984/85	1983	1985
Engineering	20	6	19	15
Business studies	17	7	12	12
Social science	51	26	32	19
Art/humanities	61	27	36	21

than those from polytechnics and colleges (CNAA, 1989). Evidence from Early Destinations Statistics suggests that differences between universities and other institutions in the rate of unemployment are more pronounced in the less vocational subjects (Boys and Kirkland, 1988). The difference in the overall profile of background characteristics should be remembered here, with university students having in general wider range of 'A' level qualifications and a greater likelihood of some qualification giving evidence of basic numeracy skills. This should make university students available for a greater *range* of jobs than those from polytechnic humanities courses. As we shall see, this situation is reflected in the differences in the type of work they entered.

A Continuing Education

One important element in the transitionary period immediately after graduation is postgraduate vocational training. Such training is usually of two years duration, and the proportion of humanities graduates in some form of further education or training drops considerably for both cohorts two years after graduation. Evidence from the 1982 sample shows that postgraduate study is normally vocational in character, and that it appears to be successful in preparing graduates for the work they do and assists them in getting it. After three years a quarter of all humanities graduates (from the 1982 cohort) had acquired a Postgraduate Certificate in Education and a further quarter had gained other types of vocational qualifications (Brennan and McGeevor, 1988). Many fields of graduate employment are characterized by 'closure', i.e. entry to the occupation is regulated by a structure of professional vocational qualifications. In subject areas where the first degree does not subsume within it elements of a specific professional training, further study must fill that need. Interestingly, only a third of the 1982 humanities graduates saw their post-graduate study as bearing a direct relationship with their previous degree course. Though not necessarily 'retraining', some postgraduate education could perhaps be described as 'conversion', as it is often not continued training in the same field though a degree in itself is a necessary prerequisite for entry to the training. Unlike, for example, nurses and lawyers, for whom there is a well-defined relationship between undergraduate study postgraduate education and professional employment, humanities graduates (from vocational postgraduate courses) take on an added labour market significance. There is a growth of such courses serving both graduates fresh from college, and later returners looking for updating and new specialisms. For students entering higher education by alternative non-standard routes, and with a less wide educational background from earlier schooling, a general non-vocational degree in many ways serves as a stepping-stone towards a higher level post-graduate qualification and hence ultimately for professional employment. Given the general absence of a well-defined vocational orientation amongst humanities students, and the diffuse relationship between degree study and work, it may be that course developers in humanities need to see vocationally oriented postgraduate *courses* as the first step for which to prepare their students.

Varieties of Employment and Employers

Like other graduates, those from humanities degrees enter a wide range of types of work with different kinds of employers. Both the Early Destination Statistics and the HELM Graduate Panel Survey show that a large proportion of CNAA humanities graduates enter some form of public service, with an originally smaller but recently rising proportion working in commerce. For the humanities students in both the HELM cohorts, a quarter entered teaching. With some recategorization of occupations done for the 1985 sample, 41 per cent reported themselves as in varieties of work described as clerical and administrative 'management support'. The rest of the humanities graduates are spread over a very wide field, including occupations such as selling, hotel and catering, etc. With teaching as a large category, it is not surprising that for both cohorts a constant 65 per cent was shown to work for employers in the public sector, traditionally a strong employer of female labour, with a quarter entering the commercial sector, which leaves few graduates employed in the manufacturing sector of the economy. The courses in the HELM samples with over 60 per cent employed in the public sector are, apart from humanities, those of fine art, biology, social science and education.

Comparisons based on the Early Destinations Statistics between university graduates and those from polytechnics have shown that a much higher proportion of those graduating from university enter jobs in some form of commerce (CNAA, 1989). Looking in greater detail at the 1985 cohort, we find an interesting difference in the most important categories of work done by polytechnic and university humanities graduates (table 8.5). Accountancy is an important profession for the university humanities graduates, but not in equal measure for those from polytechnics. University humanities students

Table 8.5:   Most important type of work entered % (1985)

Humanities-CNAA		Humanities-University	
General Administration	17	Teaching	18
Teaching	13	General Administration	13
Clerical	11	Accountancy	10

Table 8.6:   Aspects of job quality and career development 1985 cohort — two years into employment (%)

	Trad grad job	Degree essential	Graduate ability required	Long-term job	Feel over-qualified
Humanities Graduates–CNAA	20	18	28	29	56
Humanities (history/ English)–university	27	30	33	39	34

also enter banking and finance. The greater prevalence amongst university students of background qualifications showing evidence of numeracy skills is probably important in allowing more varied job opportunities, as are overall employer assumptions about the general skills and qualities of a university graduate. It also likely to be the case, however, that the greater proportion of mature students in polytechnics, not on the whole characterized by their 'career motivation', make choices away from jobs in the commercial field. As has been argued above, graduates *place* themselves in particular job markets, they do not all seek jobs across the board. Nor do polytechnic graduates in general have equal 'access' to employers in the private sector. There have been shown to be institutional variations with a higher percentage of university than polytechnic graduates gaining access to employer 'milk-rounds' or other types of institutional visits to recruit students whilst in their last year of study. This is reflected in the greater likelihood of university graduates in general working for large organizations (Boys and Kirkland, 1988).

There are also real differences between humanities graduates from universities and those from polytechnics when it comes to the perceived level and quality of the jobs in which they are employed. As can be seen from Table 8.6, which is based on the responses of the 1995 cohort of the graduate panel survey, a higher proportion of university humanities graduates are in traditional graduate occupations and in jobs where a degree is essential for entry, or graduate ability is required. More university graduates see themselves as being in their long term job, and considerably fewer feel overqualified for the job they do than is the case with the polytechnic graduates. It should be noted that for all the graduates coming from humanities courses, a comparatively low percentage of students see themselves as working in traditional areas of graduate employment, or doing work for which a degree is essential for entry. With the supply of graduates increasing, particularly in humanities and social sciences, it is perhaps to be expected that there may be difficulties for them in finding employment making use of their graduate skills. It may be that jobs in such areas as clerical and administrative management support are increasingly becoming graduate professions (Wilson *et al*, 1990). These types of jobs have traditionally been held by non-graduate women, which reflects the importance of looking at gender differences in labour market entry by men and women graduates. It will be interesting to see whether in the long-term the increase of participation of women in higher education will have as one of its effects that of making traditional female clerical and administrative posts graduate jobs, rather than helping women to break new grounds in traditional graduate professions.

A Gendered Transition to Work

As with the labour market as a whole, a notable gender segmentation is present also in the graduate labour market, with women graduates entering lower level work in areas traditionally characterized as female employment and earning less money for the jobs they do. Such segmentation is also present within the humanities category of graduates. Along with social science students, humanities graduates earn on average less than others, which is clearly related to both to the type of work they do and to the fact that a large proportion of them enter work in the public sector. But this situation is also related to the gender distribution in the subject. Whereas for the 1985 cohort, the average income of male humanities graduates two years into employment was £8438 it was only £6570 for women. Though there are few differences in the proportion of men and women humanities graduates in full-time or part-time work, 55 per cent of the women but only 31 per cent of the men in the 1985 cohort sample want a different job. Interestingly, there is, as table 8.4 showed, a higher proportion of male humanities graduates who are unemployed, than female ones. Male graduates are looking for higher level work than the women. When comparisons are made between men and women as regards their sense of being overqualified for the job they do, 74 per cent of women say they feel overqualified as opposed to 51 per cent of the men. The willingness of women graduates to take on lower grade work has to be seen in the context of the relation between gender and the exercise of family responsibilities. One of the most important differences between the employment status of men and women graduates lies in the high proportion of women not actively seeking work, almost 10 per cent in the 1985 cohort. Family responsibilities lie heavier on the shoulders of women graduates. Analysis of both the 1982 and the 1985 sample shows the differential impact of the relationship between family and gender roles for male and female graduates in that two years after graduation 79 per cent of the male graduates with dependent children are in full-time employment whereas this is only true for 41 per cent of the women. Only 4.3 per cent of men with dependent children give family responsibility as a reason for not seeking work, but 25 per cent of women with children do. The proportion of single men and women in full-time employment two years after graduation is approximately the same at 80 and 81 per cent. For a subject area with a high proportion of women students, many of whom are mature, labour market destinations are as much determined by family responsibilities as by the availability of jobs or the nature of the course itself.

A Useful Degree?

The various explanations offered above of the relatively slower labour market entry of humanities graduates cannot necessarily be construed as justification for curricular inaction when it comes to preparing the students for entry to the labour market. Whatever their background characteristics and vocational orientations, humanities graduates feel that they have had a difficult time entering the labour market, and that their chosen course of study did not help them very much in the process. Of both the 1982 and the 1985 cohort sample, approximately half of the humanities graduates said they had experienced difficulties in finding a job. Though generally pleased with their course, as evidenced by the fact that over 80 per cent of humanities graduates said they were satisfied or very satisfied with it, the graduates do not on the whole feel the content of their degree course has been of value in employment. Of the 1982 and 1985 cohort samples an average of 35 per cent felt their course had been of value in the labour market, and less than half, 44 per cent think it will be so in the future. This is a sentiment humanities graduates share with students from specific vocational courses where there is slack demand in the labour market. It is, however, the lowest evaluation of employment relevance of any of the courses looked at in the HELM panel surveys. Many humanities students, almost 40 per cent in the 1985 sample, would in *retrospect* have chosen another subject to study. A negative retrospective evaluation is of course an 'after thought', and does not mean that even if graduates had known in advance of the lack of employment value of their course, they would have chosen otherwise. The questions asked did not allow for consideration of what other kinds of courses they might have been qualified to apply for, given the lower and less numerate profile of their background qualifications. But the evidence of perceived problems in employment relevance should lead to some questions being asked about the nature of the notion of 'relevance' in the curriculum and the perceptions of this expressed by the graduates themselves.

Work Related Benefits and the Humanities Curriculum

Higher Education and Transferable Skills

With a sizeable proportion of graduate vacancies available to students from any subject background, and employers increasingly putting an emphasis on the demand for general 'transferable' rather than specific vocational skills, debates on the employability of humanities graduates have recently gone to the heart of the humanities curriculum and what it has to offer. Can humanities graduates, especially those graduating from polytechnics, compete in the demand for 'generalists', and why do employers express such concern about the quality of general skills that non-specialist graduates bring with them into the labour market?

The alleged mismatch between employer needs, education and the nature of employment-related general skills has been examined in some depth by Bradshaw (1985). Using evidence from company recruitment policies, advertisements and graduate training programmes, Bradshaw shows the employer demand for general skills which go over and beyond those at present indicated by a degree qualification itself. The list of core qualities required is long, ranging from the ability to write, to social skills with strangers. Most of these so called 'transferable skills' or 'competencies', can be seen, albeit somewhat ambiguously, to fall under the general headings of critical analytical and problem solving skills (both quantitative and qualitative), communicative and interactive skills, and finally judgmental skills of value identification and clarification. There has been some critical discussion about the conceptual and pedagogical usefulness of inventories of skills or competencies (Lyon, 1988, Ashford and Saxton, 1990). But two important points can be seen as emerging from Bradshaw's review of employer needs: first that disparate companies present the same priorities, and secondly, that major issues common to degree teaching have been obscured in recent debates about degree subject and employment prospects. As Bradshaw states, the response in Britain to employer needs has been more in the development of subject specialists than in the fostering of generic skills capable of transformation into a variety of vocations in programmes of general skills-oriented education. He contrasts this situation with that of the US higher education system where some form of core of general education has commonly been part of the undergraduate curriculum for all students.

Looking more specifically at the needs and shortcomings of unemployed graduates, Morgan and Scott (1987) also focus on the specific qualities and skills sought by graduate recruiters. The skills they isolate are those of technical capacity (for example, numeracy and computer application), brain power, communication, leadership, teamworking, problem analysis and solution, achievement and adaptability. Morgan and Scott refer to such abilities as 'enabling skills' because it is assumed that they enable the holder to develop, apply and put into practical effect his/her ideas. Employers look beyond subject knowledge towards the more dynamic aspects of skills capable of providing initiative, action and leadership. The acquisition of such skills, they argue, is particularly important for graduates in subjects which are less vocationally specific, and with less clear labour market outcomes, both in the human and the natural sciences. On the basis of their study they conclude that students unable to sell specialist vocational skills in demand in the labour market are especially in need of a better range of *general* skills indicating flexibility and capacity to learn and change in work situations demanding Jacks-(or-Jills) of-all-trades. They also emphasize that some form of numerical competence and knowledge of mathematics is often a preferred attribute in the list of abilities looked for. The technical capacity to handle numerical data is a skill which as we shall see later creates one of the more difficult problems in attempts to tighten the links between employer demands on graduate skills and the humanities curriculum.

Traditionally academics have often seen the issue of generic graduate skills in terms of the demands of the discipline: knowing the basic tenets of the subject, having the ability critically to analyze and synthesize, applying general principles to particular instances. Each discipline has its own conception of who is a 'good student' over and above being knowledgeable in the subject, but how in practice such general skills are successfully taught is unclear, as is the process whereby both the teaching methods and the outcomes are to be evaluated. One academic approach to generic skills teaching has been through the concepts of study skills and teaching methods. The central tenet of this approach is that generic skills development need not be seen as a thing apart from subject teaching, but can be fostered through the process of teaching and learning in project work, group exercises, role playing and a variety of realistic field work exercises. Such a view of research and study skills as transferable skills I have elsewhere referred to as 'the happy coincidence' theory of generic skills training, and it is in evidence in a couple of articles on the humanities curriculum which are of relevance to some of the graduate evaluations I will later discuss (Lyon, 1988).

In his article on humanities and the world of work, Southgate (1988) points to the personal skills and qualities fostered by humanities disciplines and courses. He identifies three areas of skills that can all be subsumed under the term 'communication skills': writing, speaking and interpersonal skills. Through the teaching methods used in essays and seminars students develop their abilities to construct and present coherent and persuasive arguments in speech and writing. The interpersonal skills enabling one to communicate successfully with the widest possible range of people are well fostered in humanities students in their knowledge of literature and history, and through the emphatic imaginative effort required in reading and listening.

Southgate is right in pointing out that such personal skills have traditionally been well fostered by a liberal arts and humanities education and are of great relevance to the world of work as well as to culture and society at large. But in his exclusion of computing and numeracy skills as not relevant except in the study of numerical data in history, he leaves a problem. Brecher and Hickey (1988) in their paper on the humanities, skills and employability present the curriculum and structure of the BA (Hons) Humanities degree at Brighton Polytechnic in the light of employer demands for 'flexibility, intellectual resourcefulness, problem, solving capacity, and so on'. These are skills, they argue, which have been at the heart of humanities teaching since the time of Socrates. What has been an implicit part of subject teaching should be made explicit and assessed. They emphasize the need to disentangle 'the narrow vocational relevance' of general transferable skills from their role in fostering personal growth and development more widely. The pedagogical tool for fostering personal growth and development is an *active* participation and involvement in the learning process, group work and oral presentations. The objectives are defined mainly within the discipline itself with the 'research function' being identified and transferable: identification of information, analysis, synthesis and presentation of the findings of inquiry. Questions are never raised, however, of how transferable into the labour market these skills really are for a student with no general background knowledge in science, mathematics or computing. In their study of curricular responsiveness to labour market demands, Boys *et al* (1988) found a strong faith in the humanities as a subject worthy of study for its own sake and one of the subjects least responsive to external manipulation.

So, what for employers constitutes the bread and butter of 'employability' appears for academics a useful byproduct of the development of scholarship. The byproduct is 'marketed' as servicing the future employment prospects of students. How do graduates themselves feel about what they get from their humanities course? Do such courses in their estimation offer required employment-related benefits, or would they like to have been offered something over and above the core of the discipline of their choice?

Some Student Evaluations

The evidence presented by the two cohorts studied in the HELM graduate surveys shows that there is some support for the contention that students see their degree courses as offering *both* general intellectual and personal skills and abilities of relevance to their work, but not on all courses in equal measure. There is also doubt expressed by some students on some courses about the absence of emphasis on some very basic transferable skills. The evidence also appears to throw some further doubts on what I have referred to as the 'happy coincidence' approach to skills teaching. Such an approach may work well for some of the general intellectual and individual skills discussed above, but there are some kinds of skills, both social, personal and intellectual which unless *positively* defined as relating to the work roles envisaged for particular graduates do not appear to be learned as a byproduct of good teaching and learning practice in individual disciplines. If accepted as an essential part of 'competence' training in higher education, general skills need to be much more positively thought about in the development of undergraduate programmes.

What kinds of general intellectual and social abilities do the graduates feel are enhanced during their higher education experience? Which abilities would they in retrospect like to have had more support for? Both the 1982 and the 1985 samples were asked whether their experience of higher education had helped them in a range of what can be described as work related abilities. Again, a considerable amount of consensus was shown, with general intellectual skills such as the 'ability to think critically', 'act independently', 'organize one's own work' and the 'ability to apply new knowledge', perceived by all graduates to have been considerably improved by the higher education experience. These are all abilities which most students would pick up 'on the way', simply by spending time in a traditional academic environment of learning and assessment. But at the other end of the list of perceived benefits the critics of skills teaching in higher education may have found some ammunition. The more practical skills of 'written and spoken communication' were less shared across the board of courses with differences shown between subjects. For example, computing graduates feel they have only been helped by a small amount as regards the ability to write, and as might be expected, humanities graduates are happier about their improvement in writing abilities. Engineering students have not gained much as regards spoken communication, where language students report themselves as having gained more in that respect. Humanities students perceive gains somewhere in between a 'fair' and a 'small' amount.

When it comes to interpersonal and social skills, those of 'cooperation', 'leadership' and 'responsibility' are all abilities required in most graduate careers.

Yet graduates across most courses in the HELM surveys, and humanities graduates in particular, felt they have benefited rather less with respect to these skills. It is interesting to note that these interactive abilities are seen as subject to the greatest improvement by students in professional courses such as nursing, law, performing arts education and sports. These are all subject areas where group interaction and the occasional exercise of authority and leadership are part and parcel of the 'curriculum itself in a variety of practical and clinical settings. This is clearly not so for humanities students, where such skills if they are to be developed need to be much more consciously thought about as curricular objectives. The fact that a large number of humanities graduates are women and/or mature students should perhaps add an extra impetus to imaginative thinking about how during the course of teaching the subject, student confidence in exercising such skill could be enhanced. One way of helping students develop employment-related interpersonal skills has traditionally been that of providing them with real work experience in the field. When asked about the value of work experience as part of the course, graduates in both cohorts who had such an experience for more than two weeks felt positive about it. It is interesting to note in this context that for those in the 1985 cohort of humanities graduates who had no work experience as part of their course, 56 per cent said they wished they had been offered the opportunity. The 'latent demand' from students in non-vocational subject areas for some form of work experience can be discerned. Vocational elements in courses may be used to provide compensation for low entry qualifications (Boys *et al*, 1988; Boys and Kirkland, 1988).

Finally, we come to the issue of numeracy and computing skills. As stated in recent papers published by the Council for Industry and Higher Education, there is a growing awareness in education that the curricular breadth associated with a well-rounded person in contemporary society must include aspects of numeracy, science and technology as part of the foundation for a liberal and general education (CIHE, 1987 and 1990). The 'ability to handle numerical data' is clearly a notion which means different things for different types of graduates. But whatever meaning is attributed to it, it cannot be described as a general skill which students acquire through participation in some form of higher education experience as such. For both cohorts surveyed numeracy is the one ability that least fits the pattern of a 'general ability' improved across the board (Brennan and McGeevor, 1988; Lyon, McGeevor and Murray, 1988).

It could, of course, be argued that students do not seek to study humanities in order to do computing and numeracy and hence are not disadvantaged in not getting it. Do humanities students in retrospect as graduate employees feel they were given sufficient opportunity to develop numeracy or computing skills? Both the 1982 and the 1985 samples were asked this question and on average 40 per cent of the humanities graduates felt that they had not been given sufficient opportunities to develop numeracy skills and the same was true for computing skills. This constitutes a large number of students feeling there was something in which they could have had more instruction. This supports earlier findings made by Boys *et al* which showed that humanities graduates felt that their numeracy skills had in fact declined during their course of study in higher education.

There is perhaps a lesson here about the continuing place of humanities in 'the two cultures'. If we bear in mind that humanities graduates are likely to come from non-numerate backgrounds, but subsequently enter employment as teachers or in various positions involving administration and management support, then the lack of perceived help in the development, or 'maintenance' of numeracy takes on some significance. If it is correct, as Morgan and Scott (1987) argue that students from non-vocational courses are more easily employable if they have some form of numeracy skills, and that this is a factor in the better employment prospects for university students, then clearly here is an argument for looking at ways in which polytechnic humanities students in particular can be offered help. Recent curricular reforms for secondary schools are designed to increase school leaver knowledge in the areas of numeracy, science and technology and the effect of these reforms will soon be felt in higher education. But these reforms will not, however, in any way have an impact on the large numbers of mature students encouraged to seek higher education. The experience of those humanities courses that have attempted seriously to take on the issue of numeracy and computing and offer students some form of 'service teaching' in the ability to handle numerical information, might usefully be assessed and compared. How to offer such instruction, whilst at the same time continuing to attract non-numerate students wishing to avoid work with numbers, is clearly a curricular challenge.

Conclusion: Humanities Graduates into the 1990s

There are many indications that humanities courses are here to stay. The pressure from policy makers for an expansion of student numbers in higher education is strong, and with declining cohorts of school leavers this expansion must come in part from students traditionally attracted to humanities courses. The important compositional changes expected in the output of graduates in the 90s are those of rising proportions of mature graduates, women, graduates from non-traditional educational backgrounds, and minority graduates. The proportion of graduates from polytechnics and colleges will grow relative to that from universities and overall there is likely to be a decline in the proportion of graduates from engineering and technology (Pearson and Pike, 1989). In view of structures of funding in higher education increasingly being based on more market oriented principles with the ability to attract students as a measure of worth, institutions will have to continue to provide broad arts based courses catering for the personal interests of students with more varied and non-traditional entry qualifications and with less clear cut occupational aspirations and motivations. In its report *Towards a Partnership: Higher Education — Government — Industry*, the Council for Industry and Higher Education gives its support for the continuation of a strong commitment to arts and humanities in higher education and notes that as employers 'many of our best and most creative recruits in many departments and at many levels have their educational backgrounds in the arts' (CIHE, 1987). This will continue to be the case for any humanities graduates, especially when everything points towards a growing demand for managerial and professional skills in the labour market but if by 'best and most creative' is meant someone young, with well defined career orientations, broad background qualifications and well exercised leadership skills, then many humanities graduates will continue to face the kind of difficulties in the labour market that have been discussed above.

The above situation puts an onus on both higher education and employers. For course leaders it will increasingly become important to look towards student evaluations of what is being offered. With courses in humanities increasingly acting as a 'bridge' for many students between on the one hand their needs and aspirations for an interesting course, a general education, a more worthwhile quality of life and work, and on the other an increasingly skills oriented labour market, then this role has to be acknowledged and a truly 'general' education provided. Forms of constructive compromise have to be found focusing on curricular breadth and changing teaching methods based on the expressed needs and retrospective evaluations of the students themselves. The concept of a 'liberal' education may have to change to include knowledges and skills traditionally not seen to be within its domain in higher education, to compensate those students that arrive in higher education through alternative routes, yet have to compete on equal terms in the labour market. Given the important role played by postgraduate training, preparation for such training must be an important part of this. There is a great deal of curricular challenge in attempting to reconcile students' demand for an education in the humanities with their demand for interesting graduate work in a changing labour market. As Slee (1990) has recently argued in a paper seeking to define the parameters for a consensus between manpower needs and higher education, a 'broader framework for learning' with a well defined concept of an undergraduate curricular generic 'core' needs to be identified.

There is also an important onus on employers to change and adapt to the changing nature of higher education. First, the recurrent emphasis on a changing skills base in graduate work as a result both of changes in the economy and of technological and organizational change within individual employing organizations, cannot in full be met by changing student demands for more 'relevant' courses and subjects. Individual needs for personal development may not be as easily reconciled with the needs of employers to adjust to technological, economic and social change as assumed by the Council for Industry and Higher Education, and higher education has to serve both sets of needs. Employers themselves will have to become more involved in providing and funding 'compensatory' need-related training for its staff, once employed. Secondly, the employers' concept of 'the best and the brightest' will have to change and new recruitment sources and strategies will have to be found amongst graduates not traditionally seen as 'high flyers'. Many companies are already beginning to respond more to the needs of women employees and a similar change of attitude towards the recruitment of mature students without standard secondary school qualifications will have to come. As noted by Pearson and Pike (1989) in their report on the graduate labour market in the 1990s, unless recruiters adapt to the changing supply of graduates and graduates attune themselves more to the rules and expectations of the labour market, there is likely to continue to be a growing segmentation in the graduate labour market with a shortage of skilled labour co-existing with graduate unemployment. Herein lies the challenge for both educators and employers of humanities graduates.

Eva Stina Lyon

References

ACKER, S. and WARREN PIPER, D. (Eds) (1984) *Is Higher Education Fair to Women?* Surrey SRHE/NFER-Nelson.

ASHWORTH, P.D. and SAXTON, J. (1990) 'On, competence', *Journal of Further and Higher Education*, 14, 2.

BALL, C. (1989) *Aim Higher: Widening Access to Higher Education* (Interim Report for the Education/Industry Forum's Higher Education Steering Group) London RSA/ Industry Matters.

BOYS, C., BRENNAN, J., HENKEL, M., KIRKLAND, J., KOGAN, M. and YOULL, P. (1988) *Higher Education and the Preparation for Work*, London, Jessica Kingsley.

BOYS, C. and KIRKLAND, J. (1988) *Degrees of Success*, London, Jessica Kingsley.

BRADSHAW, D. (1985) 'Transferable intellectual and personal skills', *Oxford Review of Education*, 11, 2.

BRECHER, B. and HICKEY, T. (1988) 'Humanities, skills and employability: The humanities degree at Brighton Polytechnic', paper presented to the CNAA/British Steel Conference, Redcar.

BRENNAN, J. and MCGEEVOR, P. (1988) *Graduates at Work*, London, Jessica Kingsley.

BRENNAN, J. and MCGEEVOR, P. (1990) *Ethnic Minorities and the Graduate Labour Market*, London, CRE/CNAA.

BRENNAN, J. and SILVER, H. (1988) *A Liberal Vocationalism*, London, Jessica Kingsley.

COUNCIL FOR INDUSTRY AND HIGHER EDUCATION (1987) *Towards a Partnership: Higher Education, Government, Industry*, London, CIHE.

COUNCIL FOR INDUSTRY AND HIGHER EDUCATION (1990) *Towards a Partnership: Humanities for the Working World*, London, CIHE.

CNAA (1989) *Humanities Graduates: Degree Results and First Employment Destinations*, Information Services 'Outcomes' Paper 3.

DES (1987) *Higher Education: Meeting the Challenge*, Cm 114, London, HMSO.

DES (1990) *Highly Qualified People: Supply and Demand* (Report of an Interdepartmental Review), London, HMSO.

DIPPELHOFER-STIEM, B. *et al* (1984) 'Students in Europe: Motives for studying expectations of higher education and the relevance of career prospects, *European Journal of Education*, 19, 3, 1.

GORDON, A. (1983) 'Attitudes of employers to the recruitment of graduates', *Education Studies*, 9.

LYON, E.S. (1988) *Academic Abilities and Transferable Skills: A Discussion* HELM Working Paper 7, London, South Bank Polytechnic.

LYON, E.S. (1991) 'Black minorities in higher education' in CALDER, J. (Ed.) *Disaffection and Adult Learners*, Lewes, Falmer Press.

LYON, E.S., MCGEEVOR, P. and MURRAY, K. (1988) *After Higher Education: The Experience of a Sample of 1985 Graduates and Diplomates Two Years After Graduation*, HELM Publication, London, South Bank Polytechnic.

LYON, E.S. and MURRAY, K. (1992) 'Graduate labour markets and the new vocationalism in higher education' in PAYNE, G. and CROSS, M. (Eds) *Sociology in Action*, London, Macmillan (forthcoming).

METCALFE, H. (1990) *Retaining Women Employees: Measures to Counteract Labour Shortages*, IMS Report No. 190, Brighton, Institute of Manpower Studies.

MORGAN, W.J. and SCOTT, N.T. (1987) *Unemployed Graduates: A Wasted National Resource*, Nottingham, University of Nottingham, Centre of Labour and Management Studies.

PEARSON, R. (1985) 'The Demands of the labour market' in JAQUES, D. and RICHARDSON, J. (Eds) *The Future of Higher Education*, Guildford SRHE/NFER-Nelson.

PEARSON, R. and PIKE, G. (1989) *The Graduate Labour Market in the 1990s*, IMS Report No. 167, Brighton, Institute of Manpower Studies.

REDPATH, B. and HARVEY, B. (1987) *Young People's Intention to Enter Higher Education*, London, OPCS, HMSO.

ROIZEN, J. and JEPSON, M. (1985) *Degrees for Jobs: Employer Expectations of Higher Education*, Guildford SRHE/NFER-Nelson.

SANYAL, B.C. (1987) *Higher Education and Employment*, Lewes, Falmer Press.

SILVER, H. and BRENNAN, J. (1988) *A Liberal Vocationalism*, London, Methuen.

SLEE, P. (1990) 'A consensus framework for higher education' in WRIGHT, P.W.G. (Ed.) *Industry and Higher Education*, Milton Keynes, Open University Press/SRHE.

SOUTHGATE, B.C. (1988) 'Non-vocational? Humanities and the world of work: comment', *Journal of Further and Higher Education*, 12, 2.

TARSH, J. (1989) 'New graduate destinations by age of graduation', *Employment Gazette*, November.

THOMAS, K. (1990) *Gender and Subject in Higher Education*, Milton Keynes, Open University Press/SRHE.

WILSON, R.A., BOSWORTH, D.L. and TAYLOR, P.T. (1990) *Protecting the Labour Market for the Highly Qualified*, Coventry, Institute of Employment Research, University of Warwick.

WRIGHT, P.W.G. (Ed.) (1990) *Industry and Higher Education: Collaboration to Improve Students' Learning and Training*, Milton Keynes, Open University Press/SRHE.

Part C

Aspirations and Expectations of Students and Graduates

Chapter 9

Student Perceptions of Their Personal Development Through Higher Education and Their Preparedness for Employment

Sue Drew and Roger Payne

Introduction

What are students' views of their personal development through their higher education experience? Do they feel their personal skills and qualities change and grow whilst on their courses and if so how? This chapter is based on work being carried out at Sheffield City Polytechnic which focuses upon student perceptions. George Kelly, the originator of personal construct theory, said 'If you don't know what is wrong with the patient, ask him, he may tell you' (Bannister and Fransella, 1980, p. 78). We have adopted a similar principle, asking the students what is right (or sometimes not so right) about them and how they got to that point.

We are aware of the limitations of such an approach. Perceptions about a single teaching session may vary not only between staff and students but between individual participants, and may only be seen as useful in retrospect, possibly even years later. However the experience and perceptions of individual students are clearly important and there are common themes. We are attempting to seek students' views more overtly in this particular area, and to achieve a greater depth than is afforded by the more usual questionnaires or discussions at staff-student consultative committees.

In the present climate, where increasing pressure on resources is combined with growing demands from government and employers upon the HE system, students' views may not be heard very loudly. Our material will hopefully help to redress the balance.

Personal Skills and Qualities

Perhaps we need to begin by defining what we have chosen to call 'Personal Skills and Qualities' (PSQ). The term embraces the personal transferable skills

147

referred to elsewhere in this book, such as those relating to communication or interpersonal abilities, and also includes qualities such as initiative, confidence or perseverance without which an individual may be unable to maximize skills. An individual's motivation, attitudes and values are also important, since they may determine whether or not she/he chooses to exercise a particular aspect of PSQ. In short, the term refers to the personal attributes which enable individuals to cope as students and which tend to be sought by employers.

We have been engaged since 1987 on a project aiming to encourage good practice in the development of students' PSQ through their courses. We brought to this project our past experience as careers advisers, a role involving not only a direct interface with employers but also a student-centred approach, with the focus upon the clients and their needs.

This chapter refers to two types of research activity:

(i) structured group sessions with students, developed initially for the Unit for the Development of Adult and Continuing Education (UDACE) project on learning outcomes;

(ii) in-depth studies of samples of students on four courses.

How We Obtain Student Perceptions

Structured Group Sessions

Our structured group technique is based on ideas from Wirral Metropolitan College on developing inventories (1990) and an account by David Boud (1986) of nominal group technique. Students individually complete an inventory of student statements derived from our in-depth studies, and then work in small groups identifying learning outcomes all can agree with, which may or may not be from the inventory and which are outcomes they either hope to achieve or feel they have achieved, depending on their stage in the course. After clarifying and comparing the lists from the small groupings, the students individually note the learning outcomes of most significance to them personally. We also collect information on the learning outcomes penultimate or final year students wish they had covered better. The focus throughout is on positive information, and we attempt to avoid sinking into 'grumbling'. As outsiders we are able to listen to and note students' views without feeling the need to defend or justify, and students appear to welcome this. At the time of writing we have run timetabled sessions with students from five arts courses.

In-depth Studies

In 1987 we agreed with the course teams of four courses (one arts, one professional with an arts bias for some students, and two non-arts) that we would carry out termly interviews of small samples of students for the duration of their courses. The briefs varied slightly, since this monitoring process had to be acceptable to course teams, but the information gathered from all four

courses was concerned with student perceptions of their personal development and the influences upon them.

Two of the studies are now complete and two unfinished, hence the
interim nature of these findings. A total of thirty-five students have participated, each being interviewed from forty-five minutes to one hour at approximately termly intervals. The sample included students from a wide range
of backgrounds: young/older; black/white; male/female; gay/heterosexual;
local/non-local; etc.

Both researchers use client-centred interview techniques, identifying in
advance the issues to be covered, for example: reasons for being on the course;
support mechanisms; current and recent concerns; change and influences; non-
course activities; career plans. This chapter takes as its starting point the views
expressed by the arts students in the study, but incorporates where appropriate supporting material from the remaining courses.

Some Preliminary Findings

Are Career Prospects Important to Arts Students?

Do students actually want their courses to lead to improve employment prospects? Preliminary findings from a postal survey of current students carried
out by colleagues from Sheffield City Polytechnic's Survey and Information
Analysis unit ('The Student Experience') indicates that this is the case.

The survey information is still being analyzed and there is as yet no
breakdown by course. However, a breakdown by site is available. The students at a site containing all arts courses (site A) rated career prospects as a
reason for choosing their course as follows:

Table 9.1: Career prospect as a reason for choice of course

	No influence %	Some influence %	Very influential %	Not influential %	Sample (n)
Site A	27	36	17	20	71
Other sites	11	35	47	8	837

In total 53 per cent of students at site A claimed career prospects to be an
influence, a majority but much less than the 82 per cent of remaining students.
However, it is difficult in postal surveys to cover all eventualities, and we
suspect that had a different question been asked 'How influential were the
following in deciding to do a *degree course?*' many more students at site A would
have claimed career choice as an influence. Arts students may expect HE in
general to improve their career prospects but possibly not their particular
subject of study.

Our research would certainly support this view. Student in the structured
group sessions although given the option of ranking learning outcomes did

not do so, suggesting that their motivations are complex and the outcomes interrelated. Students at every stage, first year, penultimate and final year, virtually without exception, listed improved career options as both one of their sub-group agreed outcomes, and as one of their personally most important outcomes.

First year —   'Better job prospects — job satisfaction/enjoyment'
                'Job opportunities'

Penultimate year — 'Good career prospect, career options I didn't have before'
                'A clearer knowledge of career options'

Final year —   'More realistic approach to the job market'
                'Career awareness, job opportunities'

The majority of students in the in-depth study expected and hoped the course would influence future careers.

As first years 'The degree will open up options for me'
'I don't have any clear ideas for the end of course but
I hope I'll acquire one as I go through'

Several of those monitored were mature students who felt they had reached a dead-end before the course, had experienced insecure work situations or reached a point where they could not progress further. These students hoped the 'bit of paper' of a degree would bring security or more options. How far career prospects figure in students' statements vary with the stage of the course (the Polytechnic postal survey did not differentiate between years), in the middle period of a course students tending to be more concerned about immediate issues. What happens after the course seems to be a theme throughout the course for most students which comes to the fore at particular decision points, for example in deciding on options or as the end of the course approaches. Our research indicates that the majority of students regardless of age expect the course to affect their lives after graduation for the better in terms of employment (though their definitions of 'for the better' may vary).

What PSQ Do Students Develop?

From both structured group sessions and from our in-depth studies we have accumulated a mass of information on student views of their PSQ. Some of this information is idiosyncratic, relating to individuals or to specific course, some is more generalizable. The following is intended to give an indication of the PSQ fostered in students rather than being a comprehensive listing. We have sorted the PSQ identified by the structured group sessions into themes, but must emphasize that this 'systematization' is ours and not the students. As far as the in-depth studies are concerned we give an indication of the major issues for the students and areas where they perceive change or development.

    The following student statements from the *structured group sessions* are intended to give a flavour of student views and have not been selected to illustrate development between the years. First and penultimate years are referring to outcomes hoped for, final years to those achieved.

General awareness
'Broaden my mind, have a broader outlook on life' (penultimate year) 'A balanced, fair, informed view of society' (final year)

Critical skills
'Not taking criticism personally' (first year) 'Analysis/ criticism of text, a critical mind' (penultimate year) 'More self critical' (final year)

Research
'Research effectively' (penultimate year) 'Able to find background information relevant to projects' (final year)

Aesthetic/creative
'To be as creative as I possibly can' (first year) 'Be original, find innovative approaches to the subject' (penultimate year)

Self management
'To balance work and play' (first year) 'More independent — can look after myself better, more self-reliant' (final year)

Direction
'To know what you are doing in life' (first year) 'Become focused on what I want to do with my life' (penultimate year)

Learning skills
'To be able to continue to learn and change' (first year) 'Develop learning skills' (penultimate years) 'Adapting to new areas, expanding knowledge, having an open mind' (final year)

Interpersonal skills
'Be socially aware/sensitive to those around me' (first year)
'Organizing others, team work, delegating' (penultimate year)
'More considerate to others but not to be taken advantage of or taken for granted' (final year)

Communication
'To write well, critically and coherently' (penultimate year)
'I can listen and understand more what people have to say' (final year)

Attitudes
'Confident of own opinions' (penultimate year) 'A much more speak up for myself sort of person' (final year)

Problem solving decision making
'Be able to make rational decisions — work and socially' (first year) 'More able to approach problems in a realistic way' (final year)

In addition to PSQ outcomes students also identified practical or technical skills.

'Knowledge of current technology' (first year)
'Word-processing' (penultimate year)
'Wider understanding of skills and techniques' (final year)

As indicated earlier, career related outcomes were also frequently mentioned.

The *in-depth studies* provide more opportunity to explore student perceptions, the structured group sessions producing much more of a 'snapshot' view. At the beginning of their courses the majority of students in the samples tend to have difficulty in talking about PSQ and refer more often to those they feel are lacking. By the second year they are much more able to describe PSQ and by the third often able to identify major areas of change. This apparent shift may be influenced to some extent by a developing relationship between interviewer and interviewee and the students becoming clearer what the interviewer is looking for. The monitoring process itself may improve self-awareness as well as the course and higher education experience enabling personal reflection. Perhaps all of these factors contribute. Although the students have found the monitoring process valuable in providing time to talk over personal issues, *they* do not feel their higher education experience has been significantly altered by it.

By the second year issues emerge which seem critical to certain students, and which recur in their monitoring interviews. Whilst they are of particular significance to these specific individuals, they do indicate the range of concerns in the area of personal development.

— developing skills of criticism and analysis;
— being good at operating in a group but wishing to be also able to operate alone;
— maintaining a balance between activities;
— commitment, either being extremely committed or finding commitment difficult;
— social skills, for one realizing they are a major asset and for another a major difficulty;
— pushing oneself;
— philosophical or political stances;
— limitations on finance affecting both social life and concentration on the course;
— space (usually in an emotional context).

Those students participating in the monitoring process who have already graduated, had views on major area of change in PSQ which included:

'Persistence, that's my key thing. I'm much more persistent'

'I've got more of an ability than I thought at organizing other people and delegating'

'I'm getting feedback that when I put myself forward it works and I don't get rejected'

'I've got the enthusiasm to make things happen for myself'

'I've become more self-protective, not so vulnerable'

'I'm not as self-important as I was, seeing the importance of myself but in relation to something bigger'

'Just learning who I am and where I'm going'

What Seems to Help in PSQ Development?

Our structured group sessions do not attempt to identify views on influences and change, but only on the outcomes of learning experiences. The in-depth studies, however, provide a considerable opportunity to explore change and what helps. We feel that it is possible to identify a number of major themes in this area, but, a word of caution, none of these themes stand alone. Any one experience for a student may incorporate several if not all of these themes and they should be seen as elements in a complex situation. Also we must emphasize that the thematic scheme is ours, not the students', and aims only to provide a convenient way of looking at the issues. Students seem to be affected both by external factors and by factors within themselves.

External Factors

  (i)   Encountering difficulties, problems and challenges
  (ii) Structure, for example, knowing the rules.
 (iii) Extra curricular activities, employment, use of vacations, contacts with the outside world
 (iv) Feedback
  (v) Support and stimulus from others
 (vi) Pressure
(vii) Freedom

Internal Factors

 (viii) Seeing the relevance of course activities
  (ix) Self-awareness, seeing the need for change, and having a clear personal direction
  (x) Accepting responsibility for themselves
 (xi) Making effective relationships

External Factors

(i) *Encountering difficulties, problems and challenges*

Students face difficulties and problems both on the course and outside, which can range from a landlord wiring his freezer to your electricity supply, to needing a part-time job because of parental non-contributions, to domestic difficulties and divorce. Course-related difficulties may include inadequate resources, or unfamiliar ways of working.

The following table (table 9.2) indicates the range of the non-course difficulties with which our sample have been or are grappling:

Table 9.2: Range of non-Course difficulties

Number of students	Difficulties/problems
15	Relationship making or breaking
14	Illness (relatively short)
13	Difficulties with others sharing accommodation
9	Overdrafts and debts
9	Accommodation problems
6	Burglaries, theft, mugging
4	Parents separating/divorcing
3	Parent/close relative died recently
3	Ongoing serious health problems
3	Car crash
2	Medical operation
2	Involved in a court case
2	Being arrested

Out of difficulties and problems often seems to come considerable personal development.

'. . .away from home for the first time, big effect on me, making me more independent, no Mum and Dad to help.'

'I've been forced to do something about being quiet because I was so lonely.'

'Being away from home has made me more independent' (mature student). 'It's red tape. You spend weeks trying to see people to get help. People say it's not me it's that person. You end up by going round and round so you just do it yourself.'

Problems can also overwhelm '. . .the struggle with paying the rent. . .you can't concentrate on your work'.

Challenges are the positive side of the same coin. Whereas paying for a landlord's freezer might be perceived as a problem by most of us, what is a challenge for one person may not be for another. The course may present challenges to students which must be undertaken to proceed. Whilst students are often extremely anxious about such situations, surviving them brings not only relief but new confidence.

'Worst event this term was giving a presentation, didn't put too much effort into it and I totally failed. I was really low, thinking 'Oh God I won't be able to give the talks and speeches' but I asked if I could do it again and did it properly with notes, diagrams, got my OHP's sorted out and I got 62 per cent and thought 'I can do it if I try'.

'Giving the seminar was the first thing I felt I'd achieved. It really bucked me up.'

'It's a brilliant experience (the dissertation) just trying to write 5000 words' (from a student with poor academic success at school).

Occasionally if the challenge is severe the student may opt out, but be disappointed.

> 'A large part of it is my responsibility. There were group activities but I didn't go.'

(ii)   *Structure*

The structure of the course seems to be a major factor not only in determining the type of activities undertaken but the pressures experienced and issues which emerge for the students. Students tend to experience the philosophy and aims of a course through its structure. Where it is very open with the majority of activities self-directed, issues which arise include students setting challenges for themselves, self-imposed pressures, making decisions about how to use time, the balance between structured and unstructured elements. Students frequently refer to, for example, self-motivation, and accepting responsibility.

> 'I'm more emotionally independent of support. I've got to cope with what comes along.'

> 'You have to find everything yourself.'

> 'I was deciding when something was right or wrong, that was something I had to learn.'

For students on more structured courses, issues might include those relating to externally imposed pressures and dealing with required elements of the course. Students refer to, for example, learning to cope with pressure, and problem solving.

> 'Since March it's been work, work and more work. I've stopped playing volleyball and everything and had to concentrate on assignments and exams. I'm just glad it's all over.'

Students on the more self-directed course refer more often to structure than do those on other courses, and they experience structure as providing support. You need to justify activities to tutors, you belong to an educational institution, have the status of 'student', and have some, albeit low, level of financial security (this tends to be for mature and independent students). Lack of structure can cause frustration and anxiety, perhaps if course organization is seen to be lacking, or assessment criteria unclear.

The structure of the course underlies many of the other themes in this section. For example, on more unstructured courses the need for feedback may be particularly significant ('You need points where you can be assessed and reassess yourself'), and students on the more self-directed course seem to use peers for support more than do those on more structured courses.

(iii)   *Extra-curricular activities, employment and placements*

Self-chosen extra-curricular activities are generally personally relevant activities for the students. They take responsibility for them and they may form part of personal development plans. Such activities therefore relate closely to other themes in this section (themes (vii), (viii) and (ix)). They include leisure, holidays, employment or political involvement.

'I'm more influenced by friends I grew up with.'

'I take a lot of baggage both ways — I take a lot of things from my personal life to the course and from the course to my personal life.'

'I learned a lot more about people from my part-time job.'

'I didn't understand the full possibilities of teaching before I did Bunacamp. It changed my views on teaching quite a lot.'

'Political involvement has helped my public speaking.'

The students undertake course-related activities off Polytechnic premises, for example, projects, involvement with the community or short placements.

'The placement has definitely changed my outlook and probably what my future will be.'

'. . .it gives me a lot of confidence when people you work with have faith in you. There's no bigger boost than being told there's a job waiting at the end of the course. It's better than getting As at assignments because that only shows you're good at assignments.'

'If you just work in college for three years, what happens when you finish?'

(iv) *Feedback*

Feedback is particularly important in the early years of courses, becoming less so when the students begin to feel confident about their own judgment, or possibly important for different reasons, for example to provide alternative perspectives rather than to say the student is 'right' or 'wrong'.

'The more confident I become, the less other people's views matter.'

Students seek reassurance or advice from a variety of sources, especially at times of uncertainty.

'Self-criticism is no good without criticism from others.'

They use friends, students on later years of the course, even a landlady.

'It's easier to get criticism from second or third year students because they don't have to be with you all the time.'

Clearly the opinions of lecturers are seen as important, initially they are the 'experts' and in an authority role, and ultimately they will grade work.

'. . .to get confidence. . .I need a lecturer to say 'don't worry, you've understood what I've told you, you've asked good questions'.

The way in which feedback is given is important. The students want specific comments. 'You're doing fine' may not be perceived as helpful or as being likely to be converted into a good grade. Feedback can reduce confidence, especially where comments are written and presented impersonally.

'It's not enough to read a tutor's comments. You need discussion.'

Feedback is a significant thread throughout these themes. Interpersonal relationships, for example, may be unlikely to improve if individuals remain unaware of their effect on each other.

(v)   *Support and stimulus from others*

The structure of the course may cause students to seek support from different sources, but what is common is that all students need support and stimulus from others. Generally close friends (sometimes on the same course), people they live with, family, other students and staff seem to be most important, roughly in that order. However where activities are largely self-directed and interests shared, other students are most significant as supports. They are more readily accessible, have similar problems and you can appear vulnerable to them.

'I wouldn't mind the other students knowing things about me but not the lecturers.'

'It's discovering that everybody has the same kind of problems that's made me happier.'

Tutor support is particularly valuable in times of personal crisis.

'The tutor was really helpful when I told him the problem.'

Being a woman, from an ethnic minority group, or gay, can make a student very aware of staff attitudes to them.

'I don't like the tutor commenting on my appearance, it's too personal.'

Some women actively seek out women tutors, though in certain areas there are few women staff. Generally the staff are the backbone of a course.

'The staff are the structure and supports. You find things out yourself. It's only then you can hang things off them.'

Whilst staff generally are supportive in times of great need, ongoing nagging problems may go unaided but have a considerable influence on the student's development, for example an individual's difficulty in relating to fellow students to tensions within a group.

'There was never any middle ground in our group.'

'The others aren't like me, they're loud and middle class.'

Outside influences can provide considerable stimulus and support: social groups, unlike those at college, provide new perspectives (but also sometimes bring about identity crises), family members, people sharing the same interests, work-colleagues, all play their parts. As the final year progresses students refer increasingly to outside support — old friends, new contacts — and in this sense the transition from college begins well before the course ends.

One observation (from the researchers rather than the students) is that whilst all seem to need support, some are better at getting it, and the very behaviours which may militate against obtaining support may mask needs for it, for example withdrawing from others or aggression.

(vi) *Pressure*

The structure of the course seems to determine to a large extent the nature of the pressure on students. Assessment is a major factor in creating this pressure, and can dominate students' lives for courses where there is a continuous and heavy requirement to produce work for assessment, (some even see it as a plot!).

> '. . .I think it's on purpose, how come all the assignments have to be handed in within a certain few weeks. I think they could assess us in another way or give us some more assignments through the year. In some subjects they do. All students complain but staff don't want to do anything about it because it's part of the assessment to put us under pressure.'

Where work is negotiated, uncertainty about criteria and what is required can cause pressure. The run up to the final degree assessment is experienced as enormously pressurising for the majority.

> 'The tension is flying in the air.'

Incidentally, students seem to want assessment to:

- — provide reassurance
- — require them to think about and justify their actions;
- — provide feedback, ideas and suggestions;
- — provide stages to be reached;
- — provide final validation;
- — provide structure and clarify what is expected.

Additional pressures come from a variety of sources, for example, as a result of problems and difficulties or because of a particular course activity perceived as a challenge. At the beginning of courses students are confronted by not only a new course but new leisure activities and living arrangements.

> 'Anything that comes up, I don't want to miss out on anything and so double book and every single minute is taken up.'

They then begin to discriminate

'I've withdrawn from quite a few things to clear my head, there was too much to think about.'

'It's not coming into college that counts, it's what you are doing.'

Where there is considerable scope for self-direction pressure is often self-imposed, and often relates to time.

'Almost every day I've said, this is a great situation, make the most of it.'

Self-imposed pressures may also result from inadequate advance planning, and reflecting on this can help an individual amend future behaviour.

(vii) *Freedom*

One of the courses in the in-depth study provides considerable freedom and scope for self-direction. The following statements are from those who experienced this freedom.

'The freedom of the course is developing new skills and qualities. Knowing that I'm not wasting that freedom but taking myself as far as possible. I can't overstate how important that is.'

'It's a brilliant environment for self development.'

'It's trying to turn freedom into something useful.'

Freedom also brings with it risks and being allowed to get things wrong.

'I don't think college should dominate people. They shouldn't be trying to protect you. Getting you to think instead of trying to envelop you.'

'I feel a lot happier about the mistakes. You spend weeks on something that doesn't come to anything, but you learn a lot through it.'

For students on more structured courses freedom, as far as course activities are concerned, seems to be confined to choice of options or projects, or their way of carrying out those activities. As students grow in independence and confidence they are more able to make use of the freedom available, form their own views and if necessary challenge lecturers. Initially this can take the form of grumbles; later students have clear ideas of what they would find helpful.

There is a tension between freedom and course requirements. Those who experience a high level of self-direction have their work ultimately graded by others. Those who are more led throughout their courses by assignment requirements make their own freedom by choosing or adapting parts of the course to make them more personally relevant.

The internal themes which follow presuppose some measure of freedom for students to incorporate their own needs and interests in courses. Those who are allowed considerable freedom acknowledge the difficulties in maintaining a balance between this and their need for structure, challenges and the other external themes. Perhaps this is the theme which connects external and internal factors.

Internal Factors

(viii) *Seeing the relevance of course activities*

Students seem to spot 'games' quickly and activities which appear unreal or irrelevant may be grumbled about rather than taken advantage of. Although some activities are seen as irrelevant by virtually everybody, others are relevant for some only. The student who wishes to develop critical skills may view seminars as vital, others may not. Where an activity is personally relevant to a student, self-development is often acknowledged, but where not there is a tendency to criticize the process rather than accept responsibility for being part of it.

> 'Everybody didn't want to be held back by every one else's ideas when we did the group projects.'

In all the courses students are required to give oral presentations, often assessed, and although this often creates anxiety, all accept it as relevant.

> '. . .didn't enjoy it all but gained an awful lot of confidence in my speaking from the work we did on verbal presentations, interviews, presenting reports and conducting committee meetings.'

(ix) *Self-awareness, seeing the need for change and having a clear personal direction*

Many of the students are unused to talking about personal strengths and weaknesses.

> '. . .get on OK with people, not a sort of loud mouth. Never thought about it.' (first year)

Others have clear ideas right from the start about themselves and areas they feel they need to develop.

> '. . .strengths: working class,. . .active social life, good experience of life. . .want to work in an inner city area, can communicate and relate to people, in touch with fashion, caring and unselfish attitudes to life, a thinking person. Weaknesses: extremely arrogant, can't see two sides of an argument, need to calm down and develop confidence to stand up and give presentations.'

Generally most students expect and want to change.

> '. . .the course will develop me as a person, give me enthusiasm, an awareness of what's going on, ideas of what to do next, make me more able to talk about things. At 19 I've done nothing, been nowhere. I hope to get somewhere, be somebody.'

'I want to develop my critical faculties.'

'I want to get confident.'

One important area of change seems to be in beginning to value and understand how to use existing attributes. Examples might include a student realizing her charm and enthusiasm encourages others to cooperate, or another beginning to realize what an asset his organisational skills are.

'When I see other people, I think perhaps I am thorough.'

Students who have areas they wish to develop or change are often able to identify activities and experiences which will help them to do so.

'I'd like to experience working on my own and in a group so I can see what's better for me.'

'. . .over the summer I planned to and then read a lot of books, like Orwell, because books like those I just haven't read, and the more words I read the more my vocabulary will extend and I'll be able to express myself better.'

Sometimes the course itself provides the stimulus for change.

'. . .personal skills were not something I thought about until I started the course, they weren't something I needed, but now I've *got* to improve.'

Students' expectations about the likelihood of change seem to influence the extent to which change is perceived. A minority of students do not feel the course is significant in bringing about change.

'Being on the course hasn't changed my life much — it's like walking home — you may go one path one night and a different path another night but it's still going home.'

'You can't plan to develop yourself as a person — you just have experiences which may change you.'

Such individuals tend to refer less to major personal change than do those who are hoping for or expect such change. Others in the sample who have reached the end of their courses, referred to growth in areas which had been an issue for them throughout the course, for example in becoming more able to make approaches to others.

(x) *Accepting responsibilities for self*

In their different reactions to a similar situation a significant factor seems to be how far individuals accept responsibility for it, as opposed to attributing responsibility to others.

'Losing some close friends from the course has actually been a benefit — it's forced me to make contact with others.'

as opposed to:

'I've been lonely since my friends left at the end of the year. It was up to the other students to be friendly to me.'

Clearly you are less likely to make friends if you wait for moves rather than initiating them. However, this is a complex issue. The same student can be extremely accepting of responsibility in some areas and not in others, or even in the same area can vacillate between 'it's up to them' and 'it's up to me'. Is confidence a factor here? Referring back to theme (i), successfully negotiating a challenge can encourage an individual to take more responsibility in similar situations in the future.

'In the future I'd take action earlier.'

(xi)   *Making effective relationships*

The capacity to make effective relationships is of relevance to many of the other themes. It may influence your ability to obtain appropriate feedback or support from others, and, as table 9.1 illustrates, it can be a source of problems and difficulties.

Failure to establish effective relationships can damage the whole student experience, or significant parts of it. Whilst lecturers tend (from the student perspective) to focus mostly on academic issues, the personal issues seem to have a significant impact on course performance. Relationships with others can be a source of distress or of support and stimulation.

'My relationship with my partner has made me feel a lot better about myself.'

Given the importance of feedback and support, failure to establish good relationships with peers can at best be uncomfortable and at worse distressing. Students' perceptions of the same situation can vary enormously, and often they seem unaware of their effect upon each other.

'I wish others would say something in seminars, any reaction is better than silence.'

'A lot of what the people who talk a lot say hasn't been well thought out and isn't worth answering.'

This lack of appreciation by the talkative of their inhibitory effect, and by the quiet of the frustration caused by their lack of response seems to run through many group activities, though sometimes there can be a breakthrough.

'One of the most important things I've learned is when to shut up.'

Relationships figure prominently throughout the monitoring process from initial hopes for the course:

'I'd like to be more confident, assertive, better at talking to people.'

to the final reflections about the course

'The main effects on me have been social.'

How Well Prepared do Students Feel for Employment? What Else Would They Like?

Clearly the above sections indicate that students do develop a wide range of personal skills and qualities which are valuable in employment, though the focus varies between courses and some develop certain PSQ to a higher level than others. Some courses rely heavily on research activities, others on problem solving, others on activities which develop individual autonomy. Our findings seem to support Brennan and McGeevor's high, medium and low scorers in the abilities rated by graduates in their survey, though our work is qualitative rather than quantitative. (Interestingly only the arts students in our sample actually used the term 'critical thinking'.) The situation since their sample graduated in 1982 does seem to have changed with respect to computing, with most of the courses we looked at having opportunity for word-processing or other computing skills.

Students seemed less well prepared in their ability to see how the PSQs they had developed could be useful to employment and in the actual processes of career choice and search. To return to the structured group sessions run to date with five arts courses, students' views on omissions in their courses included:

'Knowledge of up-to-date practices/practical skills and applying knowledge in real situations.'

'Knowing how to job hunt, what jobs are available.'

'Contacts with industry.'

'Experience of work.'

'Direct knowledge of work-related skills.'

'Confidence about work'.

Comments from the in-depth studies of arts students include:

'I find it difficult to sort out what to do after the course.'

'Some people are really worried about what to do after the course.'

'Life isn't real in education, you have so much more to deal with when you leave.'

However, although students may not have felt specifically prepared for life after graduation there was a sense of new options available.

> 'Choice and variety of career options we didn't have before.' (structured group session)

> 'Now there are more options and possibilities, before it was a dead end.' (in-depth study)

Where students have the opportunity to do placements or where their career choice is closely linked to course activities, they tend to be clearer and less anxious about postgraduation opportunities.

Implications for Courses

Clearly students do develop PSQ on their courses, but those which are critical for individuals vary, or the combinations of them vary for each students, and students' starting points at the beginning of courses in terms of existing experience, values and PSQ differ. Given this, course teams can provide a range of experiences, support, and enough flexibility to allow students to identify what they need and enable them to use activities to meet those needs.

The issues raised through our eleven themes should not be seen as prescribing any one correct way to encourage PSQ development. They are, rather, our current view of some of the factors which can influence personal development, and they might help course teams reflect on the nature of the experiences their students encounter. We are not advocating, for example, that difficulties and problems should be deliberately put in the way of students, but rather are indicating that these are a learning resource. We are not advocating particular course structures, but rather intend to point out that course structure has an effect upon the type of experience a student has and therefore upon the opportunity to develop particular ranges of personal skills and qualities.

We feel that obtaining student perceptions of their higher education experience is crucial. It can reveal mismatches between student and staff perceptions and enable staff to reflect upon provision and the reasons for such mismatches. Above all it indicates the personal investment made by students in their courses, their capacity to adapt experiences for their own purposes and the range of experiences which might meet the diverse personal requirements of any group of students.

References

BANNISTER, D. and FRANSELLA, F. (1980) *Inquiring Man*, Krieger.
BOUD, D. (1986) *Implementing Student Self-assessment*, University of New South Wales Higher Education Research and Development Society of Australasia.

BRENNAN, J. and MCGEEVOR, P. (1988) *Graduates at Work (Degree Courses and the Labour Market)*, London, Jessica Kingsley.

WIRRAL METROPOLITAN COLLEGE/TRAINING AGENCY (1990) *Learning Gain in Further Education and Achievement Based Resourcing Project, Bulletin Two*, Birkenhead Wirral Metropolitan College.

Chapter 10

The View of a Recent Graduate

Chris Chadwick

I would like to begin by giving a very quick history of my academic career, because I think it is relevant to supporting some of the things that I have to say a little later on.

I came out of secondary education as a complete idiot. I was every teacher's 'pain in the neck'. I came out with one grade 1 CSE, a couple of grade 2s, and a half a dozen grade 4s. When I got out of secondary education at the age of 16 I was very disillusioned with the whole educational system. Fortunately for me I had a teacher at the sixth form college in Fenton, Stoke on Trent, who persuaded me that maybe I did have the abilities to continue. After much debate and much persuasion from the gentleman concerned, I decided to go back into education and have another bash. In one year I took five CEE or CSE equivalents and passed the five, and encouraged with this momentum I then decided to stay on at the sixth form college and take two 'A' levels, one of which I failed. However, I was determined to keep going so I stayed there for a third year, retook the 'A' level and failed it. Then I thought 'well, the last chance is to ask for a re-mark'. I asked for a re-mark and eight months later they marked it up. In that eight months' period which eventually became a twelve month period I got out of the educational system and I worked on a temporary basis at the North Staffs Royal Infirmary cleaning floors.

That taught me a tremendous amount about what it is to have a nine to five job. But it also taught me a lot about life, working in a hospital and seeing people dying. It really did teach me something about the real world. Of course after eight months I realized that I had passed this 'A' level. I now had two 'A' levels and that meant that I could go on a bit further. But this was a time when I really did struggle because I thought 'well hang on, you're going higher education, degrees and all that sort of thing. There'll be all those boffins there in national health glasses and blue blazers and will you be able to cope?' I decided to go for it; I was not really sure what I wanted to do; I got an idea that perhaps I wanted to be a teacher after all this time in education. However I was not convinced and the college was offering a BA Humanities Degree which was in religious studies and educational studies. The 'A' level that I passed the first time was in religious studies so I thought perhaps that was the one I was most likely to get. So I took the religious studies and educational studies approach, and I think it is fair to say that I emerged from that course a changed person. I think the whole educational experience was as important to me as the qualification I achieved at the end of it. I was one of those people who went in knowing that I would probably struggle and so I was going to get everything out of it that I could even if I did not make it at the end.

One of the most valuable things about that Humanities Degree was the input of the other students. The Humanities Degree had a high percentage of mature students as well as people who had come straight from academic life. They were all from different backgrounds and they were all moving into different areas, so their wealth of experience could be shared with others. The actual content of the course was also designed to bring out the experience of those people. It was very much a seminar-orientated discussion group approach. We were learning by self-development.

Discussion groups were very beneficial to somebody like me. Having to do presentations to a group of people who you knew well and knew the subject probably a lot better than you did was also beneficial. These skills became equally as important as the subject because when I finished my degree, I first of all went into a managing agency for the Youth Training Scheme. During my six months there I learnt a little more about this whole idea of transferable skills and competency in certain skills. I then entered into a period of self employment. Where did I get the computing from? Well, in the second year of my degree all those in the third year had said to me 'Hey, before you get into your third year you must get into wordprocessing, so that when you do your final dissertation at the end of the year you won't have to pay a typist a fortune in order to do it for you.' And literally that is how it happened; it was almost by accident. I started to get involved in what would be a future useful skill in typing up my dissertation at the end of the year, and it became a personal interest. I had learnt a tremendous amount in the two years by voluntarily attending some of the lectures in computing. I then used that knowledge to develop my business. That went fairly successfully. I was earning enough to keep myself alive, I could eat at the table and so on.

However, I was then offered, after an interview, a job with NMW Computers, a computing company which provides a service to stockbrokers in keeping their accounts up-to-date. I found myself moving into computer training. This involved training people in the use of computers and also in general staff development within the company. I have now been working with them for eight months and have become heavily involved in management development programmes for all of the senior managers, middle managers and grade two managers. When I first went on the course just as an observer, I thought to myself 'I've done all this before': talking to people about how to lead a team; how to stand up and make a presentation about the way their department is progressing; how to get a group around a table and thrash out ideas that are associated with a new project and to analyze critically the various suggestions.

All of these things had been a part of my educational development while I was at college. The subjects I studied have not been a tremendous amount of benefit in the job that I am doing now, but the educational and the training side has. Moreover the whole experience of going through the educational system at that level has been very valuable in equipping me with those transferable interpersonal skills necessary in the world of work. It amazes me that so much of what we are doing with our management people is inputting these skills. Therefore I think that the Humanities Degree that I did and the way in which it was structured helped to develop in me some of the skills that I possess now in the job that I am doing.

I think too that the year I took off cleaning floors at the North Staffs Royal Infirmary was beneficial. It was valuable to know what it was like to go in at nine in the morning and come back at five in the afternoon when so much of academic life was unstructured. If I had to talk about changes that I would like to see in the Humanities Degree that I did, I think that further emphasis on the value of the skills would be useful. I developed them, perhaps, because I was not so interested in the academic qualification at the end but recognized the benefits involved in learning such skills as how to make presentations and how to lead discussion groups. You might think they are incidental to the subject but they are actually a very important part of your whole development as an individual and of great assistance in equipping you for your future job.

Part D

Institutional and Curriculum Responses

Chapter 11

A National Perspective

Sir Christopher Ball

There is no conflict in my mind between the humanities and the world of employment. The idea of value is the link between the two worlds and it is the best kind of link. The humanities are centrally concerned with questions of value, with the two senses of the word 'good', i.e. what is worthy and what is excellent. Industry and commerce for their part are also concerned with value, in the quality of their products and their services, 'value-added', 'value for money' and other such concepts. It is a misperception to think that there must be a gulf set between the world of the humanities and the world of employment. The enterprise society and the caring society are two sides of the same coin. I believe that we can't have one without the other, and I want both.

In 1986 Kenneth Baker, the Secretary of State for Education and Science, wrote to the then National Advisory Body for Public Sector Higher Education a letter containing the following sentence. He said, 'We are all united in our aim of providing wider access to a useful and cost-effective higher education.' It is a telling sentence and one I often repeat. I actually drafted that sentence but he signed it! It contains a summary of the policy of the National Advisory Body for the last seven years. It is certainly my own personal agenda for the next seven years.

What is going on in higher education is both conceptually and morally right. 'Wider access' means the replacement of an elite system of higher education with a popular one: a very difficult thing to achieve, a very important thing for an advanced society to achieve and quite a painful process to go through. Almost all our concerns can be taken back to that one observation. We are trying to replace an elite system, without throwing away the good within it, with a popular system of higher education. Everybody knows about the demographic dip, the fact that there is a 30 per cent drop in the number of 18-year olds between the years of 1985 and 1995. The idea that we should try to expand through that trough by providing wider access is a bold undertaking for higher education. To do that we need to attract new students, 'non-traditional' students as they have been called. I prefer to think of them as new students, drawn from the ethnic minorities, from the socioeconomic classes which higher education has repeatedly failed to penetrate, and including a greater proportion of women. We must also seek to attract and admit more handicapped students.

It is primarily the humanities courses that will be able to find ways of bringing these students in. Many of them are not going to have the kind of qualifications that will enable them to start work immediately on engineering or science courses. We know that already and therefore the role of the humanities in developing that wider access, which is the major thrust of government and higher education policy at the moment, is central.

This brings us, of course, to these personal and transferable skills which today have been so much part of our discussion. They have to do, in my view, with communication, with team-work skills, with problem-solving, with confidence in handling numerical and statistical methods, and with a sense of values — knowing how to go about establishing and clarifying values. How does my own humanities course match up to that challenge? Communication skills — yes, I could defend it very well. Team-work — vey poor, we don't teach team-work when we are teaching English at the University of Oxford, but why don't we? We should do something about it. Problem-solving —yes, not bad. Numerical and statistical methods — again a minus. Sense of values — alpha, that of course is what the humanities are all about.

The idea of a useful higher education is one that I find fascinating. I would wish to see a major debate in order to reestablish the idea of useful higher education. For my part I have to confess that I learnt more of the personal transferable skills during my national service in the army than I did at the University of Oxford on the English course there and that has always concerned me as a teacher on that same course.

The good course of higher education would, I think, do three things — and most of them do. First, they attract students. The course that can't attract students is no good and doesn't survive. We all know that. Secondly, they are academically rigorous. Notice that the first judgment is made by the students, but the second is made by the academic staff (and validators) — is the course academically rigorous? Staff must insist on that. But the third thing is what we have been discussing today. All our courses should be enabling, they should enable our students to leave their institutions and go out into the world to win and hold down worthwhile employment or to look for vocational fulfilment depending on what they came to the institution for. Not all our students have come in order to prepare themselves for a life of work — though most have. Some come in order to improve their skills at home or in leisure, and we should recognize that too. The principle is, however, clear: courses should be enabling. More work needs to be done here.

There is no doubt that the employment figures for humanities students constitute a sobering situation for those of us who teach the humanities and are concerned with the humanities. This is particularly a problem for the polytechnics. But there is also concern on the university side. After three years too many people who have studied the kinds of subject I teach are still struggling to reach appropriate and rewarding employment. We must address that question and ask why our courses are not enabling them to achieve what they want to.

We might do that by asking ourselves what the letters BA certify: what do we mean when we give a student at the end of a course a BA? Is it just a quaint tradition that we do not say 'Bachelor of English' or 'Bachelor of Philosophy' or 'Bachelor of History'? The CNAA has very much resisted the tendency to move towards the subject-specific degree titles. What does a BA mean when we set aside the specific disciplinary skills that have been learnt? There is too little debate in higher education on that question and it is very difficult to find an answer. I will offer an answer in order to start the debate. BA means the capacity for independent judgment in complex matters, the capability of independent learning and suitability for positions of responsibility in leadership. If that isn't true, it ought to be. But how do we know and how do we show that we are achieving these things? We cannot merely assert it as I have done. We need long-term employment studies and we need help from the employers to get feedback on our courses. But we have got to make some claims for the BA because if we say that the BA means nothing, then our grounds for continuing are very weak. If claims such as these are adopted, then the debate on personal and transferable skills is of central importance to higher education and to the world of employment.

There is of course very wide interest in these questions and many new initiatives: the Capability scheme of the Royal Society of Arts, the Enterprise scheme of the Training Agency, the interest that has grown in development training both within higher education and outside in industry and further education leading to schemes like the Pegasus scheme which runs at Portsmouth Polytechnic and in the University of Cambridge and at some of the colleges of higher education (I wish it ran at Oxford), the work of various education/industry link-bodies like the Industry Matters forum of the Royal Society of Arts which I chair, the Vactrain scheme at the University of Oxford — and of course today's conference and the year's work that lies behind it.

But those of us who are old-fashioned academics (as I am) are aware of a problem of rigour. These are very elementary skills. Why should higher education offer remedial education, doing the job that the schools should have done? Communication skills, team-work and so on — can't we leave all that to the schools? No, we can't — for two reasons. First, because it is the duty of more advanced levels of education to remedy the deficiencies of the earlier stages, when they appear (as, to an extent, they inevitably do). Secondly, these skills themselves can be acquired at an elementary or highly sophisticated level. The communication skills of David Attenborough, the team-work skills of Michael Brearley, are subtle and complex. But we need to develop a better language to talk about the advanced skills that we should be looking for in higher education. What precisely are the advanced skills of communication? We need to have a language of analysis so that we can help our students to develop a capability of communicating with an audience — and perhaps also not communicating, when they choose not to. We need to have an idea of how you assess these skills and what kind of performance indicators would be appropriate to them. There is a lot of work to be done on this area.

What, finally, is to be done? First, I would say we must review our courses in the light of what we have learnt today and over the past year. Are they useful courses, are they enabling, are they work-related, do they offer work experience? If not, why not? We should ask for advice from our students, and even more from our ex-students, from the employers and perhaps above all from the careers advisers who are in a pivotal position to help us to undertake that review. We could do worse than consider the challenge of the Single European Market and ask ourselves what that means, what it should mean for the courses we teach on. It can hardly mean nothing. I advise students now in public and in private that they should always ask when they are about to apply for a course whether that course has been systematically reviewed and thoroughly reformed during the last seven years, and if it has not that they should apply elsewhere — regardless of the reputation of the institution.

Secondly, to employers I would say this: recruit more widely, recruit more discriminatingly than perhaps you all have been content to do in the past. I would condemn the facile use of a graduate's subject, and even more the prejudicial use of a graduate's institution, as a proxy for quality and appropriateness. Do not say (as some do): 'we only recruit from the universities' or 'we only recruit people who have been on computer courses'. Look more deeply, be more discriminating and you will serve your own ends better. I welcome the Prudential's lead in moving to recruit within the polytechnic sector as well as from universities. It comes not a day too soon. I would say to employers that they should take note of initiation schemes for graduates. Here is an area where the employers could turn to higher education and ask us to help them.

I would also ask employers to offer training schemes as a regular item of what they offer their employees — very much in the same way that they offer pension schemes. Perhaps I could put that in the form of advice. I would advise any student, any child of mine, that unless the employer's commitment to training is at least as strong as the employer's commitment to the pension scheme they should look elsewhere for work because training in the future is going to be quite as important as pension schemes (and perhaps more so) and I suspect it needs to be funded in the same way.

Thirdly, we need to coordinate all the agencies interested in development education in higher education. We need to codify the role and nature of development education in higher education. We have heard from Kenneth Wilson, from David Bradshaw and from David Watson. I find all that work particularly impressive and it needs to be brought together. Here is a task for the CNAA and perhaps for the Prudential too: to take the lead so that the good work of today and earlier days will not be wasted.

Chairman, I started and I finish with Kenneth Baker's sentence: 'We are all united in our aim of providing wider access to a useful and cost-effective higher education.' That is the agenda, that is my agenda, that should be the agenda of everyone in this room. The usefulness debate is central to the future of higher education: it is particularly pertinent to the humanities, but, of course, it applies in other subjects too. Both employers and humanities teachers must come together as they have done today to develop the idea of a useful higher education. The value of this conference is as much in the year's work that preceded it as in what has been said today by government ministers and by others. It is a many-voiced debate: all voices must be heard, for listening skills are important. But today's conference has, I hope, made a substantial contribution to that debate. Tomorrow's work must be to carry that forward. The solution for those who are fearful of political interference — I am not one of that group, I see no threat — is to take the initiative. I hope we will do so: all of us: together.

Note

Sir Christopher Ball has, since this presentation, chaired an enquiry into higher education under the auspices of the Royal Society of Arts. The publication presenting the findings, *More Means Different* is available from the RSA.

Chapter 12

Humanities and Employment — The Institutional Perspective

David Watson

My brief is to talk about perceptions in the institutions of the issues relating to humanities and employment and I want to divide my remarks into three sections. I want to talk first about institutional *sensitivities* to the issue of humanities and employment; secondly, about *reactions* within institutions — what we have done in response to these sensitivities and various external stimuli; and thirdly, about institutional *obligations* — what we think we should be doing and perhaps have not yet succeeded in doing.

Institutional Sensitivity

Should We Be In The Business?

The issue of employment and employability of humanities and social science graduates is one about which institutions are extraordinarily sensitive, especially in the public sector. College principals and directors are avid readers of material like my first illustration. This is a table published in *The Independent*. Peter Wilby took university and polytechnic statistics on destinations of graduates and carried out an analysis which justifies, he claims, the hypothesis that polytechnic students have an edge in the hunt for jobs. The evidence is that of twenty-six subject groups fourteen indicate that the polytechnic graduates are in permanent employment quicker. However, your discerning Director or Principal will also notice that the groups towards the bottom of the table (and 'humanities' in particular) produce exactly the opposite result.

My second illustration is far more indicative of a widespread prejudice.

> 'Sir, — Much as I admired the clarity of Melanie Philips's article on Latin and the curriculum, the fact remains that one may be extremely "well educated" (Latin, Greek, literature, history, philosophy etc) and yet most of us have to work for a living.

> I have a degree in humanities which, as a course, was far more relevant than Latin and has proved to be about as useful as a criminal record as far as employment is concerned.

Who wants to be the most civilised person down at the DHSS?

Yours faithfully,

Paul Thompson

Albert Park,
Montpelier,
Bristol.

(*The Guardian*, 2 November 1987. Reproduced with kind permission of *The Guardian*.)

This is a recent letter to *The Guardian* contributing to the debate about the usefulness of Latin, from a humanities graduate. I think that it speaks for itself.

There is a public relations problem here that the public sector in particular has to get over. So from the point of view of institutional sensitivity there is first of all a major question to be answered. Should the public sector be in the business at all? This question is asked at several levels. I remember an influential speech by Lord Annan in the House of Lords during the Education Debate in 1984 for which he prepared himself by reading a selection of polytechnic prospectuses. One of his questions came out as a headline in the *Times Educational Supplement*, which was read very carefully in my institution: 'Should anthropology be taught at Oxford Polytechnic?' The case was being made that the polytechnics historically had misread the brief that they were given by Crosland and the original architects of the binary system and that they should not be providing courses in humanities and social sciences to the extent that they are.

There are lower level reflections of the same prejudice. There is a cultural view, represented for example by Tom Sharpe's *Wilt*, that assumes that the contribution of humanities in the polytechnic is best represented by engineers reading *Lord of the Flies* in a Nissen hut on Friday afternoons. So first of all we have to answer the question: should we be in the business? I feel strongly that we should.

Performance Indicators and Planning

Internally both sectors of higher education are waking up to several characteristics of performance indicators. One feature they have begun to appreciate is that virtually every set of performance indicators so far devised is flawed for the purposes to which it has been put. Consequently much of the debate about performance indicators is dragged down into a condition which statisticians call 'data war', as institutions and central government argue about what are appropriate indicators to measure our success, for example, in putting humanities graduates into socially productive positions. A second feature of the debate about performance indicators is an increasing awareness that central government is going to use performance indicators whatever the state of the art at the time. There will be an irresistible drive to justify as scientifically as possible what may have been decided for political or other motives. So we

Table 12.1: *'Poly students have an edge in hunt for jobs'* (Source: *The Independent,*
15 October 1987)

| Subject | Employment rates of polytechnic and university graduates 1986 | | | |
	Unemployed universities	Unemployed polytechnics	Permanent employed universities	Permanent employed polytechnics
Pharmacy/pharmacology	2.2	2.0	88.8	96.3
Chemical engineering	7.9	30.6*	75.1	60.2*
Civil engineering	7.6	13.3	78.1	78.6
Electrical/electronic engineering	6.9	10.8	79.3	82.7
Mechanical engineering	7.4	13.3	81.1	79.3
Production engineering	3.1	10.5	77.9	80.4
General engineering	5.8	14.1	79.9	75.5
Building	2.5	5.3	91.1	92.3
Biological sciences	14.7	19.4	47.0	54.0
Maths/stats/computing	7.6	9.1	71.0	82.5
Physics	11.8	21.0*	52.0	56.5*
Chemistry	10.2	17.6	47.1	49.6
Business/management	9.7	11.8	83.5	84.7
Accountancy/finance	3.6	6.7	89.2	87.2
Economics	10.5	24.0	76.8	61.0
Psychology	18.8	28.3	52.1	50.6
Sociology	17.6	28.8	37.7	54.4
Architecture/planning	4.7	5.7	68.9	74.4
English	18.3	31.7	47.1	40.8
Foreign languages	14.3	20.9	55.0	52.7
Humanities	17.3	31.6	50.7	42.3
Art/design	13.2	20.9	65.2	65.3
Drama	27.6	20.9	43.6	51.4
Music	8.3	7.5*	33.7	22.4*

Note: Overseas graduates leaving the UK, graduates not available for employment and
those whose destinations were unknown are excluded from the analysis. Graduates in
short-term employment (jobs which they expected to continue for less that three months)
are included with those unemployed at 31 December 1986.
* indicates that percentages are based on total of fewer than 150 graduates and must,
   therefore, be treated with particular caution.

Reproduced with kind permission of *The Independent*

have to take the question of employment statistics as a performance indicator
extremely seriously.[1]

Institutional Reactions

What kind of reactions have polytechnics and colleges evidenced as a consequence of those sensitivities? Broadly I think they have chosen two roads.

The High Road

Along the high road a number of arguments can be put forward: arguments
about education for its own sake, as well as arguments about the enduring

Table 12.2: Views of employers, final year and first year students

Item no.	Item	Rank Order of Mean Ratings		
		Stage 1	Year 3	Employers
1	More than one major field of study	10	5	11
2	Wide range of options in Stage I	9	8	14
3	Flexibility and adaptability of programmes	8	9	9
4	Contribution of coursework to degree assessment	7	11	5
5	Opportunity for interdisciplinary study	6	4	8
6	Regular and frequent coursework deadlines	5	7	1
7	Opportunity to acquire computing related skills	1	1	1
8	Opportunity to combine arts, sciences, social sciences and professional disciplines	12	9	13
9	Independent study required for project dissertation and module	2	2	4
10	Regular and frequent feedback on progress	11	12	6
11	Termly examinations	14	14	12
12	Personal control over programmes of study	4	6	7
13	Opportunity to enhance numeracy by taking maths and statistics modules	3	3	3
14	Close contact with tutors in negotiating programmes of study	13	13	10

Shows the rank-orderings of mean ratings of importance of the sixteen Features of Degree Courses included as Subscale 2 of the rating scale ('Employability Importance'). Rank orderings are given separately for Stage 1, Year 3 and Employers.

qualities and values associated with scholarship and study in the humanities. Institutions have also begun to talk much more systematically about what humanities students learn and about the characteristic skills and capabilities that are developed as a consequence of study of those subjects.

We ought not to assume that industry is uniformly cynical about either of these arguments. However, we must be careful that we are talking the same language about personal transferable skills. If you look at David Bradshaw's paper on 'Transferable intellectual and personal skills' (Bradshaw, 1985) you will note that we can't assume that there is a 100 per cent coincidence between what we and potential employers mean by personal transferable skills. It is vitally important that we talk across the divide about our mutual objectives in those areas. One of the key points of controversy highlighted by the Bradshaw article is over what is meant by the 'clarification of values'. We can put up that phrase as a kind of totem but it will mean very different things in different contexts, and we should help our students to be sensitive to this fact.

Institutions then are beginning to look carefully at articulating the arguments for education for its own sake and articulating the arguments about personal transferable skills in a way such that a dialogue becomes possible. At Oxford, for example, a recent research project took the Modular Course, identified its main characteristics and undertook a survey of the reactions of 150 selected employers in the Roget *Dictionary of Graduate Opportunities*

(Lindsay, 1984). We simultaneously tested our first year and third year students to identify what they thought were the most important features of their degrees. My next illustration is a summary table which occurs towards the end of the report bringing together the views of the employers with those of final year and first year students. What is interesting is the high coincidence of agreement at the top of the list, and the nature of these areas of agreement. The agreement between students and employers occurs very largely on items of course content. Employers like students to be numerate, for example. There are, however, also some quite interesting divergences. Employers also rate reasonably highly aspects of the manner in which students have studied — whether they have been forced to work in groups, that is whether they have been required to communicate with each other in ways that they are going to have to develop when they are in an industrial or a commercial situation. Employers turned out to value things like the contribution of assessed coursework much more highly. Similarly, regular and frequent feedback on progress is welcomed. It is clear that employers feed that kind of view back into what they expect of higher education. Students should be able to assess their progress and see where they are going.

So we have an obligation to begin a constructive dialogue about what goes into our courses and about how our students themselves conceptualize what they are doing on those courses in order to help them to talk to potential employers. That is the high road.

The Low Road

It is also possible for us to march down the low road. I think that if we become obsessed with some aspects of performance indicators we will actually do ourselves considerable disservice. The low road in these terms consists crudely of playing the performance indicators game. Institutions with large humanities programmes have by now almost all played what might be called the *supplementary survey card*. Here is our own contribution, which I am sure Colin Pedley and other colleagues from Oxford will be glad to elaborate. Humanities departments are especially frustrated by low returns on the national first destinations survey. So many institutions have returned to their graduates, for example, a year after, or three years after graduation. The Oxford Survey falls into line with what has been learned elsewhere (for example at Kingston). If you do go back to your graduates after a reasonable period of time you will increase the number of them found to be in permanent full-time employment and give the lie to the assumption (which has incidentally been presumed by the DES in some of their recent work) that the 'unknown' category conceals unemployment. You can feel very warm and very good when you get the results of this kind of survey. There are, however, problems. First of all, in constructing and undertaking the supplementary survey you have no control group. Many of these exercises have been conducted purely from the perspective of humanities departments and the results have not been tracked against the performance of other graduates. The second problem is potentially more serious. *Eventual* success may well mean that we have left humanities graduates with hurdles that they have had to take time overcoming.

Table 12.3: *Humanities Students Graduating July 1986 — Analysis of First Destination Returns*

	FT/Perm %	PT/ST %	Training %	Unavailable %	Unemployed %	Unknown %
A	Oxford Polytechnic Modular BA 1986 (100% = 236)					
	47	11	14	5	5	18
B	Oxford Polytechnic Humanities Department (100% = 175)					
B1	December 1986 (response = 80%)					
	45	10	17	5	3	20
B2	September 1987 (response = 59%)					
	36	3	14	1	2	44
B3	December 1986 + September 1986 (combined response = 87%)					
	53	7	17	3	6	14
C	Oxford Polytechnic Humanities Department — Analysis by Field					
C1	English Field (response = 92%)					
	59	6	20	3	3	9
C2	History Field (response 80%)					
	48	4	12	4	12	20
C3	History of Art Field (response 84%)					
	47	14	16	2	5	16
D	Comparative Analysis of Surveys					
D1	Responding in December 86 but not in September 87 (43 returns)					
	53	9	14	7	16	
D2	Responding in September 87 but not in December 86 (10 returns)					
	70	10	10	0	10	
D3	Responding in December 86 and in September 87 (64 returns)					
Dec	50	20	27	3	0	
Sept	66	5	23	2	4	

The fact that they are employed two, three years after graduation in satisfying jobs is not necessarily a measure of *our* success. It may be that they could have become employed in satisfying jobs earlier if we had taken various other steps in designing their higher education experience.

Either of those two roads — the high road or the low road — is taken largely I think for external consumption or PR reasons. Picking up the challenges that we were given this morning I think we have some actions to take internally as well, and my final section is about institutional obligations.

Institutional Obligations

Generally I think that our obligations fall into three areas, which I shall try to illustrate as far as possible from experience at Oxford Polytechnic.

Course Design

First of all we have a series of obligations which relate to course design. We had some indications from our two keynote speakers that humanities degrees need to build bridges between the traditional humanities subjects and other subjects. Here I think we should play to one of the strengths of the public sector. Combined studies and modular degrees make up almost 50 per cent of course registrations. The public sector has been something of a pioneer in both these developments.

Modular and combined studies approaches bring various directly relevant advantages. They cause students to be self-conscious about what they are trying to achieve in each of the disciplines if they are studying more than one. They give students opportunities to take options outside their main disciplines. The Oxford Polytechnic Modular Course has at the moment about 27,000 registrations on individual units each year (about 2400 FTE, of which approximately 310 are in humanities subjects). At the end of course there is scarcely a student who has not taken a basic computing module and is therefore not able to go into an interview with a prospective employer knowing something about databases and how they are constructed and interrogated. Independent study within the modular or a combined studies framework is another development well underway in various courses of this kind. Independent study may provide us with a vital bridgehead into work experience for those students not fortunate enough to be funded for the four years that a sandwich degree generally takes. At Oxford various fields connected strongly with humanities disciplines, like publishing, have independent study modules which can be used to get the student away from the polytechnic for a term pursuing a project in industry and commerce.

Finally this kind of course also enables us to experiment. Oxford is in fact introducing a careers module into its modular scheme. As a basic module it is set at a first year level even though it can be taken in the advanced stage of the course as one of the options students have at this stage. It is voluntary and it has, of course, been very carefully scrutinized for its academic content. (I think it is important that it *is* voluntary because there are some philosophical problems about making preparation for careers compulsory parts of courses like this. There ought at least to be a conscience clause when course designers are looking in that direction.) We hope to have some information by the end of the year about how the first forty-five students who are enrolled on the module have in fact used it and we hope to develop information over the next two or three years about how they reflect back on it after they have begun their careers.

Pulling these aspects of course design and their potential together I think the key is *negotiated study*. To echo one of our chairman's phrases earlier, humanities degrees have suffered in the past from being monolithic, from being offered on a take-it-or-leave-it basis, and from having the curriculum laid out in front of students in the way that they never engage with critically. The key is to give responsibility to students, and to allow them to select and to change a flexible programme. Only in this way will they be helped to articulate effectively what their curriculum has consisted of and the skills they have absorbed.

Evaluation

A second obligation, that follows directly, is that of the institutions to evaluate; especially to evaluate in some of these experimental areas. If we do modify course aims, if we do build personal transferable skills of various kinds into our courses, we must ensure that we meet them. We must build a bridge between the rhetoric of personal transferable skills and their achievement.

Attitudes

Finally, I think that we have the obligation to change some rather entrenched attitudes. This is a highly sensitive point, and one on which a series of seminars like this, as well as an interest group like the institutions of higher education, needs to proceed with care and consideration. The legislation which is now beginning to affect primary and secondary schools and which will shortly reach higher education, refers unambiguously to the function of education in inculcating positive attitudes towards the world of work. I think that we can meet this challenge *and* remain pure, and I will try to explain what I mean. It is very easy for people highly educated in the humanities to dismiss this kind of talk as driving us towards narrow functionalism, and as driving our students towards a critical and essentially uncreative approach to the world of work. We look with dismay, for example, at the hostility that is being expressed about the contribution of some of our subjects to the training of teachers. There appears to us to be an emergent obscurantism damaging some of the main traditional concerns of the humanities. The further implication is that several of our disciplines are making students critical of social and economic institutions in ways that are in fact dragging down our economic performance.

This is something which we can, and should, face up to. The best way to face up to it is by returning to the questions of students' own conceptualizations of what their studies are for. We can turn out students who are both critical *and* self-aware. We can only do this by giving them a measure of control over the curriculum and by encouraging them to be articulate about why they are making certain curricular choices and where they are headed. As a sector we have traditionally prided ourselves on a position where we can be accountable to society and the economy on precisely this kind of issue. Humanities disciplines can, and I believe should, prepare students for effective and productive employment.

Afterword: February 1991

Three years and four months after giving this talk on the institutional reaction to the problems posed by the employment market to humanities courses I find myself in another institution (Brighton Polytechnic) with an undergraduate humanities course which has been explicitly designed to focus upon personal transferable skills. This course has also made a virtue of its approach to non-standard entry requirements, leading to a high rate of success in recruiting mature students, and poses particular challenges of interdisciplinary working (CNAA, 1990).

Elsewhere other developments predicted in the sessions of the conference at Stoke-on-Trent have proceeded apace with or without the special stimulus of responding to the requirements of the Education Act of 1988. This was then only referred to (apprehensively) as the GERBIL ('Great Education Reform Bill'). While I retain my uneasiness at the suggestion governments can officially characterize their actions as reforms, let alone calling them 'great', this was also, of course, before the then Secretary of State became the Party Chairman (DES, 1987).

The march of modularity goes on unchecked, and with it the contribution of humanities to a wide range of student courses (see CNAA, 1990, *The Modular Option*). Simultaneously, the potential of humanities courses to assist institutions in their plans for expansion, especially through their considerable success in the market for students on access courses and 'new' students generally has resulted in a dramatic change in their reputation among institutional managers. Indeed, the strong 'market' for courses in humanities and social sciences caused the DES to replace the concept of student choice with the more complex variant of 'informed', student choice; the idea being that if applicants appreciated the salary rewards associated with qualifications in sujbects like engineering and applied sciences they would choose these over the arts, social sciences and humanities. The trouble is that they don't. Finally, the dialogue between course providers and sympathetic industrialists continues. The dominant trope remains that of trait analysis, as in the search for student characteristics which tutors seek to inculcate and employers claim to welcome (Council for Industry and Higher Education, 1990).

Other things have changed. The fragility of the cult of transferable skills has been exposed by a fluctuating market for graduates 'of any discipline'. In the mid-1980s a dramatic increase in jobs advertised in this way was read by educationalists as an affirmation of their success in persuading employers (who mostly turned out to be in accountancy or financial services more genarally) of the validity of their educational reforms. An economic downturn — more recently the recession — has shown how the extent of notification of opportunities in this way is directly correlated with the demand for graduates overall. When the demand is restricted the requirements of the suppliers swiftly reverts to the norm, which in this case means the fixation of employers on graduates in specific disciplines.

These gloomier thoughts do not in any way change my views of institutional sensitivities, reactions and obligations. In an even harsher world than that we were dealing with in the pre-GERBIL days of 1987 the duty and the necessity of tutors and courses *empowering* their students seems even more compelling.

Note

1 NAB Industrial, Commercial and Professional Liaison Group (1984) *Report on Graduate Employment Statistics*, NAB Board 52/84, 13 September, para. 12.

References

BRADSHAW, D. (1985) 'Transferable intellectual and personal skills', *Oxford Review of Education*, 11, 2, pp. 201–16.

COUNCIL FOR INDUSTRY AND HIGHER EDUCATION (1990) *Towards a Partnership: The Humanities for the Working World*, London, CIHE.
COUNCIL FOR NATIONAL ACADEMIC AWARDS, (1990) *The Nature and Structure of Humanities Provision in the Polytechnics and Colleges*, London, CNAA, pp. xii–xiii.
DES (1987) *Higher Education: Meeting the Challenge*, Cmnd 114, London, HMSO.
LINDSAY, R.O. *et al.* (1984) *The Value of a Modular Degree*, Oxford, Oxford Polytechnic.

Chapter 13

Curriculum Development and the Role of the Tutor

Kenneth Wilson

For many years higher education has seemed to be tested by standards appropriate to research institutes, where the quality, style and professionalism of the teaching has been of less concern than the quantity of valuable research results and publication. We now see a situation where the vitality of the teaching, the capacity of the tutor to enhance the range of learning opportunities of the student, and the ability to assess and mark intelligently for the student's benefit, will be of at least equal importance, if not more so. The decision to separate the funding of research and teaching underlines the crucial importance of teaching, not merely the need to evaluate the usefulness of the research.

Thus my brief is to consider curriculum matters, skills training, staff development, even, I think, the perception of ourselves and our role in higher education so that we may meet, and meet effectively, the needs of employers. What I have to say falls under six headings, so I shall be brief with dealing with each of them.

First, there is the question of our own perception of ourselves and what it is that we provide for the community at large. One might say that we provide skills, and in particular we would want to say that we provided skills which were in short supply and great demand. But such a view, even if extended to the matter of transferable skills, to which I shall allude later, is far too limited to do justice to the responsibility we have. Society, if I may use that term, does not simply look to higher education anymore than it does to the education system as a whole, to provide services or fill niches in the nation's economic programme; on the contrary, society expects us to provide educated persons, capable of moral perception, generous judgment, shrewd imagination, who are of loyal and courageous disposition, etc. This is so taken for granted that it is hardly ever mentioned. It is true nevertheless. We do not want accountants, doctors, teachers, scientists, economists and mathematicians; or at least we do not want people who are simply good accountants, scientists, technologists, in the sense that they are the receptacles of information and knowledge. We want people who are so educated as to be capable of accepting responsibility for the science, economics and technology which they know. Environmental issues, community matters, personal qualities are all matters of concern to an institution which wishes to convince employers that its students are people that they would wish to employ. The question for us is not simply how many physicists have you produced with an upper second, but how good is the quality of the student that you produce? And how do you know? And what are you doing with regard to the curriculum and its delivery to improve the quality? These matters cannot be taken for granted; they need to be discussed. Many a manager's meeting in industry will take account of them. Do we? And in what forum?

Secondly, students need to know themselves if they are to have the confidence necessary to take responsibility for the knowledge and skills that they acquire. Now it is clear that students change in the course of their time in higher education. All of us in higher education will have had that great pleasure which comes from seeing the change which is brought about by the experience of our educational programme between our first meeting with student X and his/her graduation three or four years later. But this change may be very deceptive if it is taken for maturity: it may or may not be so. Of course, maturity may be a relative term, we could discuss what we meant by it for hours. However, some points can be made regarding our organization, management and perception of our role which are relevant.

For example, lectures are not the best places in which to establish a personal relationship, at any rate between a tutor and a student. Yet in too many contexts, pressure of work reduces the range of interaction between tutor and student to that which is centred on the lecture situation. What could be done in developing learning and teaching strategies, for example, to bring about a greater depth and continuity of experience between tutor and taught? I am in no way referring to the possibility of a renewed paternalism, simply a sense that a higher education institution should take seriously the personal exploration which is appropriately involved in any enquiry or study, and that, therefore, attention should be given to the importance of a student's growing knowledge of him/her self. Moreover, this is not an afterthought which can be covered by a counselling service, or handed over and assumed to be undertaken by the chance involvement of external agencies. On the contrary, in a proper and important sense of the word, it is a curriculum matter. It is certainly something which a good employer will expect of us. It is also a matter for staff development, not only for a selected few, but for the majority of our colleagues.

Thirdly, there is the matter of references. We have all read too many which have much in common with poor road accident reports or book reviews. One wonders whether the person was actually at the scene of the accident or the reviewer has read the book. But what steps do we take to help colleagues to produce helpful, sensitive, honest and judicious references? If we have such little knowledge of the student, and too little knowledge of the overall pattern, styles, delivery and purpose of the course in general, and have taken such little effort to find out anything about students, so as to be able to offer no more than insignificant insight into character, personality or experience, beyond that which has been assessed by the examination system, it is hardly surprising if neither students nor employers think that we are able to perform the service they expect of us. Fourthly, transferable skills are a key feature, or should be, of any educational process. After all, little of what we in fact learn, or at any rate are examined upon, will survive to be useful in later stages of our career. One could mention the relevance of the organization of complex and sophisticated material and its rendering in an essay in brief, cogent and readable style. One justifies history, for example, by pointing to the relevance of this skill to the writing of civil service reports. But oral presentation is at least as important in most professional contexts as capacity for the written word. Group assessment, self-teaching, an ability to learn from experience, an ability and willingness to produce brief oral or written response in new situations, all are significant in assessing a student's grasp of an issue. What account do we take of these in the teaching and learning process, let alone for the most part in the assessment of a student's performance? While a knowledge of medieval field patterns, the authorship of the book of Isaiah or the development of Gerald Manley Hopkins' prosody may not of themselves be employed by us in argument, at any rate with regard to their more technical aspects, the ability to read extensively, select the relevant material, and to shape it in clear, direct, persuasive and cogent manner is valuable. And I stress the persuasive: bland logic is no substitute for cogent rhetoric — both are essential if we are to see the facts straight and be motivated to take account of them.

Now, of course, our students will only be helped to attend to the appropriate manner of argument in any case, for a particular purpose, be it in literature, history or theology, if we as tutors are passionate about our subject. We have no right to teach it if we are not. But somehow we have to offer a style of learning to our students which enables them both to gain the ability to generalize the skills they are acquiring, and to gain a knowledge of the particular discipline. It would be a help if all of us knew what employers wanted, so that our teaching, assessment patterns and content were planned with regard to them. This, in my view, is not compromising our professional concern as historian or philosopher, since it is an equal concern of ours to enable a student so to imbibe the insights of the disciplines we profess as to want to maintain contact with them in his/her own professional concern. A manager who is not aware of the relevance of historical enquiry or cultural difference to the development of planning strategies and the making and implementing of decisions, will be likely to be a less effective manager than one who is. But the point is, we need both: and this means that we need to draw attention to both in our tutoring of students.

Fifthly, few of our students will have the luxury again of operating in a very specialist context, at any rate specialist in the sense that mathematical logic, for example, is the be all and end all of existence. Of course, few of us in higher education will for the future, it is well to remember, be able to identify ourselves exclusively with our subjects; after all, skills in committee, in public speaking, in economic awareness and cash generation, become increasing features of academic life. Interdisciplinary skills, with the need not so much to know about, but to take account of other approaches to a problem will be at a premium. That is so for our students too. This is not news, of course; it is history. We are aware of this fact and it figures in one way or another in most courses. For example, a history course will have in it both economics and political philosophy, maybe, therefore, even some statistics; a literature course may have within it both literary theory, linguistics and some philosophy. And we would not call these combined degrees because we understand that these approaches are all involved in getting at the central matters for study. What I am aware of, however, is that all too frequently students themselves are not familiar with, because they have not identified, or had identified for them, the varieties of argument, styles of approach, linguistic structures which they have employed. And in order to demonstrate the flexibility implicit within the opportunities for study which they have, we need more self-consciously and critically to draw attention to them. For example, a good theology course will involve the study of language, textual criticism, historical enquiry, philosophy, literary theory, the study of other cultural traditions, etc.; hardly a narrow range of skills or insights. The same could, and should, be said of other disciplines. Their assessment and our ability to structure the whole range into students' and employers' consciousness is both a curriculum and a staff development matter. Puzzlement about learning, an intellectually coherent approach to it, a critical, consistent and continuously critical evaluation of it, and the promotion of these things in relation to student performance, are all, of course, parts of good primary school practice. We could do worse than listen from time to time to the best of what happens there.

Sixthly, it is not a one-way process. What I have said so far concerns us in higher education; things we are doing, but which we would do better by dealing with them consciously; things we need to ask ourselves or because they are so obvious we assume are taking place when they are not. But there are things we need to get into perspective. The higher education system is not a space between school and employment for some 14 per cent of 18-year-olds, as if the schools had some pupils who are handled by the higher education half-backs and then passed to the employers who score the tries. Indeed, when you think about it, that is hardly a good account of the modern game of rugby, if indeed it ever was. That being the case, we need to look at what could be the best model on which to base an understanding of the higher education system and employers. We might make a start by recognizing that all higher education institutions are employers, and all employers educational environments, that all courses are vocational to a degree, and that all those in employment in industry require to reflect initially from time to time on their work. In fact, the distinction between theory (higher education) and practice (industry) is false. We might then affirm that both are serving society at large and not simply one another, and that in order for both to have their own distinctive contribution to make, neither must be domesticated by the other.

Thus in our case since we are employers this role must include the needs of our own institutions to employ some graduates of vigorous academic potential and critical sensitivity, whose whole purpose and intention is to pursue truth, to enquire for its own sake, and to inspire similar aspirations in others. As employers it is important, indeed vital, for our society that this purpose of higher education remains alongside all the others. On the other hand, employers too offer educational environments with educational and developmental needs, some of which need to be undertaken by themselves. I know that, of course, this is the case for many employers. By such reconceptualization of our roles with regard to our constituencies we may develop further a need to collaborate which offers constructive ways forward. It could, and I personally think this would be a vital way forward, end up with much greater flexibility of employment between industry, industry/finance and higher education: not simply with those technical staff such as economists and information technologists, but with other areas of the curriculum where skill, intelligence and ability to argue cogently are seen to be interchangeable. This flow of talent in both directions would maintain and develop what is already under way. As staff development it would be very helpful; as a form of interaction between two structures it could renew our understanding of one another; it could change all our attitudes.

My final point before I conclude, is to draw attention to how rapidly things change. Some twenty years ago I used to meet regularly with a group of employers on the future of our society. At that time, 1968 and all that, there was such anxiety about the quality of student coming from higher education into industry, and above all their attitudes to work and colleagueship, that there were strong moves to recruit directly from school and to stamp the house style early on the adolescent personality. Why wait until the universities, colleges and polytechnics had ruined what otherwise might have been a very satisfactory employee? Why not take them and train them yourself, through your own programme, and only make use of outside educational structures for the technical bits you could not do yourself. The humanities, of course, at that time, were not so much criticized for their irrelevance, as for their capacity to politically destabilize naive and impressionable students. What we now have is a profound awareness on the part of industry for the most part, that it depends upon an educated and adaptable workforce. Given the modest proposals for the expansion of higher education, matched against the growing demands of industry for staff, we must attend carefully to the issues we find raised for us by employers, or in order to ensure their own survival as the downturn in the demographic curve continues to the mid-nineties they may well have to return to recruiting directly from school. The financial incentive to a pupil may well make us look less attractive. A joint approach to the needs of society, however, will demonstrate how coincident are the needs of higher education and employers, and how vital that coincidence is to the future well-being of our society.

In conclusion, we are concerned with the quality of the student, not simply the grasp of a subject; we are concerned with the range of applicability of the skills the student has; we are concerned with the student's knowledge of him/herself and his/her adaptability; we are concerned as tutors and institutions to enable students to learn for themselves; we are concerned with our capacity as institutions and tutors to deliver these things and to demonstrate and evaluate our performance in so doing; we are concerned to reconceptualize the relation of higher education and employment in order to retain the opportunity together to meet the needs of our rapidly changing society. We know that the need is there: the question is, can we meet it? I see no reason why not, and there is some evidence that it is beginning to happen. Indeed, I would say beginning was an understatement; in some contexts we are already moving to the second phase of development. Of course, to further develop what has already begun can be the most difficult thing.

Chapter 14

The Pegasus Initiative: A Case Study in Developing Transferable Skills

Peter Findlay

Introduction

The Pegasus project is an independent educational initiative which works together with higher education institutions on a national basis.[1] Founded in 1985 and funded primarily by public and private sector employer sponsors[2] its central aim is to support academic institutions in providing students with the personal skills necessary for an effective transition from full-time study to employment. The initiative therefore seeks to introduce integrated personal and career development work in the curriculum of higher education courses. Pegasus offers participating institutions a well defined, but flexible, course delivery mechanism for the development of students' transferable skills. This includes arrangements for start-up funding, access to a resource bank of teaching materials, and a staff training programme, all of which will help academic departments to develop courses for the enhancement of what might be broadly characterized as 'transition learning' or 'work-place readiness'. From its beginnings, the initiative has been very much an educational partnership between employers and academic departments, often with an institution's careers service playing the intermediary role. Representatives of participating employers help to frame the policy which guides the programme, through their participation on the Pegasus management committees at national and local level; they have given essential support both through direct sponsorship and through the secondment of company staff who have helped to administer and deliver the programme. Responsibility for designing, planning, organizing and delivering the Pegasus programme remains firmly at the academic base, however, with staff from departments drawing on the central bank of materials, but also developing their own discipline-related approaches. It is generally the case that the developmental approach in the initiative has been very open and flexible; different institutions use it in different ways. In some the Pegasus elements are offered as a 'stand-alone', non-assessed option; in others they are integrated into courses, and assessed as modules; in others again the Pegasus course is offered centrally as a 'bolt-on' element supplementing careers education. The courses differ in length from a single term's option to an extended programme running over several years. An important characteristic feature of the whole initiative is that it is supportive and facilitative rather than prescript-ive, and recognizes that the motive force for development and change in this area has to come from inside academic institutions, which will each wish to change and adapt in different ways and at a different pace. Nevertheless, Pegasus has been guided by a number of key principles and a central develop-mental model. What are the main features of this model?

The Pegasus Development Model — Aims and Processes

An important common feature of the Pegasus work in different institutions has been the encouragement given to collaborative curriculum design. The initiative explicitly aims to bring together as partners in course design the academic staff, the careers service, student counsellors and educational develop-ment officers and representatives from industry. The work on planning a Pegasus programme has proved to be of great value in itself, in stimulating this four-way discussion and in opening up new perspectives and relationships between these different agents in the educational process.

In the context of that planning activity, the initiative proposes some key aims and objectives in relation to the process and content of the course to be offered. Pegasus is about learning transferable skills, and in terms of processes, the intention is to offer a programme which is very much 'student-centred' (although not simply leaving things to the individual student!). For if one aim of the whole initiative is to increase the students' self-confidence and self-management skills, it is clearly essential that those participating in it should be able to make an active contribution to the various parts of the course, its development, and its evaluation. With this in mind, a large amount of Pegasus work is based on group activity. This can range from simulations and business games to team competitions or task-related projects. Group work of this sort has proved to be a most valuable learning framework which can underpin a number of transferable skills through such activities as: personal task respons-ibility and organization; participation in the group strategy and planning; communications skills; reporting skills; personal and group self-assessment. Through activities of this kind, students can learn the value of exercises (such as 'brain-storming' or nominal group technique) which emphasize collective understanding and decision-making rather than individual performance.

Another rather different aspect which is important in the learning process of the programme is explicit ongoing self-assessment. It is intended that students should become more aware of their own patterns of motivation, of the values and attitudes which will eventually help to shape their personal career develop-ment. This requires strategies for reflection and summation, such as the work-diary, the personal profile, or careful 'debriefing' after active involvement in simulation exercises. More systematically, some Pegasus programmes have used psychometric tests or personal/attitudinal questionnaires such as the Meyers-Briggs Type Indicator to help students to build up a personal frame-work of self-understanding.

Both of these emphases are part of a 'learning through experience' ap-proach, which is perhaps the key educational principle underlying Pegasus programmes. In accord with this, the initiative also encourages institutions to run intensive residential weekends for students on the course. It has been found — as with the CRAC Insight into Management courses — that students often find it enormously valuable to get away from the study routine and focus more sharply on self development in this sort of framework. Similarly, Pegasus encourages the provision of work experience for all students who participate in the programme.

In describing a pattern of curriculum development such as the Pegasus model, it is very difficult to separate the learning objectives from the learning process, the 'content' from the 'form' of the activity. Pegasus as a concept contains both a particular approach to learning, as outlined above, and a framework for the acquisition of particular skills and knowledge relevant to graduate employment. This identity of aims and methods is clearly signalled by the positioning of 'transferable skills' at the heart of the programme: it seeks both to help the student to *understand* the concept of these skills and why they are important to future employment, and to allow the student to *acquire* transferable skills through specific learning activities within the context of the programme. The backbone of the Pegasus curriculum is built around the development of specific transferable skills. Of these the most important are:

Self-assessment

Students are asked to reflect on their own particular individual approach to learning, on their characteristic contributory role in group work, on their range of existing skills and aptitudes. They are expected to make a frank appraisal of their own strengths and limitations in each of these contexts, and to think of ways in which they can develop personally by building on the one and confronting and overcoming the other. They are asked to relate this self-assessment to the determination of career choice and direction. In all these ways the students are confronted with the need to find a personal strategy for self-development.

Problem-solving and Decision-making

Students participate in exercises and activities which require a structured approach to a problem, working towards a decision through the collection and assessment of information.

Planning

An understanding of the principles of time management, team management, and project design, execution and evaluation.

Communication

Deciding on the most appropriate form of communication, whether written or oral, graphic or computer-generated. Learning to speak to a large group effectively, to chair a meeting, to negotiate an agreed decision, and to present, explain, defend or sell.

Teamwork

Forming, leading and participating in a team.

Transition to Employment

In addition to this central focus on transferable skills, there is a part of the programme which addresses in a more explicit way the question of the transition into employment, and which is perhaps more directly related to the advice and support conventionally given by careers services in institutions. But it does constitute a more tailored and in-depth approach to 'transition learning' than the careers service is usually able to offer to courses on its own. This part of the programme would be placed in the second or third year of a course, and will often involve collaboration and teaching contributions from careers advisers. It would usually include the following components of study activity:

(i)   understanding the debate about future patterns of work, and in particular the impact of information technology on the employment market;

(ii)   understanding the information resource base for graduate job selection;

(iii) exploring in more depth career routes of specific interest to the students' area of study;

(iv)   relating the students' personal interests, values and achievements to the available range of occupations;

(v)   decision making in relation to career choice;

(vi)   job application (through simulation exercises), including the preparation of an effective CV, understanding the selection and interview process, and taking part in practice group selection exercises and individual interviews.

The Model in Practice: Portsmouth Polytechnic

Portsmouth Polytechnic entered the Pegasus scheme in 1986 and since then Pegasus programmes, or integral course elements derived directly from the Pegasus model, have been offered in departments across all the main Faculty areas, with the exception of Engineering (where similar work had already been introduced). Pegasus proved to be of particular interest to the Business School (where its approach to learning effective self-management was immediately attractive to students of economics and accounting, and even of business studies); and to the Faculty of Humanities and Social Sciences, where the broadly 'generalist' qualification of graduates and the pressurized employment market of the mid-eighties indicated the need for a curriculum development strategy which would allow humanities students to develop their personal skills and enter a competitive job market well prepared.

Work on the development of the programme was supported in a variety of different ways. Central administrative direction and some support for the teaching programmes was provided for by the secondment of managers from British Telecom to the Polytechnic Careers Service over a number of years; the Royal Navy offered the Polytechnic free use of its local training facilities for residential weekend courses; academic staff from departments were given time for course development through the staff development programme, and were advised and supported in this by the Educational Development Unit; staff in the Careers Service joined in the planning of the programme and contributed to the teaching of some components.

Staff were encouraged not to accept the model in an 'off-the-peg' version, but to modify and adapt the various approaches and exercises to the needs of students in their own disciplinary area. The result is that there are now eight distinct Pegasus courses running in the Polytechnic, each with their own particular character and emphasis, but all drawing on similar materials, and indeed on the expertise and interests of other colleagues involved. Each Pegasus course consists of a core of group workshop sessions modified and developed in the light of student feedback. This now represents a sum total of 122 hours of teaching materials related to transferable skills development which have been prepared, recorded and annotated and thus forms a resource generally available to staff in the Polytechnic. Course developers can also draw upon a series of learning modules for use in the programme which have been published by Pegasus at national level.[3]

Pegasus Course Offered to Students in the School of Languages and Area Studies, 1989–90

The course covered four terms, embracing the central and final years of the students' academic study. Thirty students from across the range of degree courses offered in the School of Languages attended the programme. The sessions lasted two hours, and were led by two members of staff from the Department, supported by a colleague from British Telecom.

Autumn Term

This term was divided into two parts. The first half was deliberately devoted to 'setting the scene' and introducing the idea of transferable skills development with some clear examples relating to group dynamics and decision-taking. In the second half of the term the focus shifts to employment related issues.

Spring Term

This term's work concentrated in more detail on the definition and development of transferable skills. Practical exercises and group discussion are central to the programme in all these sessions. Particular skills worked on are communication skills, consultation, negotiation and diplomacy, time management and personal organization.

Summer Term

For these Pegasus students from the School of Languages, the summer term was spent on an extended project of five weeks' duration. The students were divided into four groups of seven-eight students. They were set the task of preparing a presentation, to be made to employers, on the theme of 'Preparing for 1992'. A range of documentation and material (some of it in French or German), and database access was available to each student group through the Polytechnic's European Documentation Centre. Students had to delegate tasks, gather information, prepare their report and decide how to present it. In the final week, each group made its presentation to the rest of the class. All the presentations were recorded on video and discussed after playback. In the debriefing on this exercise, students were asked to identify the range of skills used in the project, and to assess the contributions of members of the group to the process which led to the final presentation.

Autumn Term — Final Year

Job search, applications and interview

The final component of the programme involved students in a six-week long exercise relating to job choice and the application process. This was partly based on a series of presentations and exercises, but the main emphasis was on a simulation of the real application process (which some of the students were already beginning for real). Students were asked to apply for jobs chosen from a range of real advertisements relevant to their subject area, and then their applications were assessed, and interviews relating to the application were conducted by invited managers.

The Pegasus course as a whole concluded with the completion of the Pegasus profile by each individual student, discussion of the profile with course tutors, and an evaluation of the programme by the students.

There are two important common principles which we have tried to follow in developing Pegasus courses at Portsmouth. The first of these is the 'disembedding' of transferable skills from the mainstream curriculum. It is a commonplace in discussions of the employment-related competences of new graduates that many HE courses develop transferable skills in their students as part and parcel of their normal studies (for instance through the preparation, delivery and discussion of a paper in a seminar). It is the case, however, that in many subject areas, perhaps particularly in those such as the humanities and social sciences, which are not directly vocational, the students do not realize or recognize that they are acquiring such skills (in the seminar example they might be listed as, planning and time management, information gathering, analysis, formulation of an argument or case, writing up, presenting, understanding the audience, responding to questions, summarizing etc.). Part of the objective of every Pegasus course is to introduce the students to the conceptual framework of transferable skills, to apply that framework to their own specific pattern of study, and to allow the greater understanding which hopefully results to inform their consequent work within their main course of studies. The second, related principle is that of 'explicit contextualization'. What is meant here is helping the student to understand, in broad terms, the larger context within which their course of study operates. It is recognized that our society and our national job market will be substantially affected by such developments as the Single European Market, the growing importance of the environmentalist lobby, the fifth generation of computers — do students know about these changes and are they given the opportunity to reflect on how the design of their own studies fits into this changing picture? Putting it at its simplest, these two governing ideas in the Pegasus 'experience' should allow a student to look at their studies 'from the outside', and to gain a better understanding of their academic work as a pattern of particular skills and competences which are vocationally relevant and useful, and which they can go on to develop in relation to a rapidly changing economy.

Problems and Issues

Drawing on the experience at Portsmouth, it may be useful at this point to indicate some of the difficulties which may lie in the path of those wishing to offer a Pegasus-type course programme and to highlight some of the strategic issues which have been raised in the developmental process.

(i) *Externally funded or internally driven?*
Although Pegasus is a national initiative, it is run on a tightly constrained budget with only one full-time post — the national Director. It is highly dependent upon employer sponsorship for survival at national level. The contribution which can be made to institutions from this level in terms of direct funding for programmes is therefore likely to be small. The real value of Pegasus at a national level is in an advisory capacity, and as a facilitating mechanism for the early stages an institutional programme through access to staff development and advice on course design and course materials.

This means that, unlike the Enterprise in Higher Education (EHE) initiative with which it has some common features, Pegasus cannot offer substantial financial support for curriculum innovation. Its signal advantages, however, are that it is not a selective or competitive initiative, but responds to the actual level of institutional interest. Thus for some institutions it can offer a more flexible and gradualist approach to the introduction of the transferable concept, and does not have the prescriptive and universalizing character sometimes found in EHE.

As with EHE, though, it is very important that Pegasus gains the support of institutional or at least faculty management. Institutional acceptance of the programme depends crucially on a widening of perception about what is legitimately included within the higher education curriculum. This is true of the teaching methods used, but is probably even more applicable to the course content and its assessment. It has to be recognized that for many staff, and often for understandable reasons, a Pegasus course will be felt to be at best an additional luxury and at worst a peripheral distraction to the main programme of academic study. A clear commitment from the top can make a great deal of difference in this vulnerable situation.

(ii) *Staff resources and training*

As with many new initiatives, Pegasus has shown itself able to win over sceptics, but only when they can get involved. At Portsmouth, the early years of the programme were supported in the main by the dedication of a few willing enthusiasts, but as it has extended across the institution there has been a need for a more specific targeting of resource, and a systematic staff development programme which would help staff in those departments newly embarked on development to learn about the Pegasus curricular approach. The further Pegasus extends across the institution, the more necessary it is to integrate it into the general strategic planning for development.

(iii) *'Bolt-on' or 'integrated'?*

The availability of resources for the central coordination of common parts of the programme has proved to be important for its development, as has the sharing of course materials and tutor notes for particular course units. There are sufficient common elements in the different course programmes to provide an argument for a single all-purpose 'add-on' Pegasus module for all students, and clearly this could be an asset when seen from a resource angle. Against this, as has been argued above, there are substantial benefits in terms of the attraction to students in having some level of discipline-related work in the course.

Equally, many staff feel that the Pegasus element will only have a powerful appeal to students when it is more fully integrated into the mainstream of institutional provision (as an accredited module, perhaps, or as a course option). There are also those who believe that, as a sort of educational catalyst, Pegasus should eventually disappear as transferable skills work, the assessment of competences and the integration of careers guidance become an integral part of all courses. The danger here, of course, is that the 'disembedding' effect will be lost, and explicit work on skills development disappear.

Evaluation and Achievements

We have been able to make an initial evaluation of the impact of the Pegasus programme at Portsmouth, and there has recently been an independently conducted evaluative survey commissioned at national level.[4] Some of the most important outcomes of these two surveys are summarized here.

Institutions and Staff

Staff responses from institutions indicated that many of the expected benefits to the institution from participation in Pegasus had been realized. These included: greater staff involvement with the introduction of work related to transferable skills; an increased awareness of and responsiveness to employers, needs and interest; a greater collaboration between services to students seeking employment; a greater interest in how general approaches to teaching and learning might change. Asked what were the essential prerequisites for delivering a successful Pegasus programme, staff responded (as might be expected!) that they needed: time; a development strategy; staff training; top management and departmental support; pump-priming funding; good teaching materials; a fair amount of self-reliance.

At Portsmouth we asked staff whether participation in Pegasus had changed the way that they taught their other courses, and in what way. A number mentioned that they now place more emphasis on group work and active participation by students, giving them more scope for self-direction in their learning. While some staff commented on the struggle it was to persuade their colleagues of the value of Pegasus, others commented on the way in which it was influencing departmental policy decisions, particularly the design of new courses.

Another commented that the existence of the Pegasus course permanently raised questions in the department about how to incorporate its elements into other courses, and encouraged staff to use similar group-based approaches to their teaching. One staff member commented that a more lively, positive, self-assured, competent year group had been reported to him by colleagues after the students had completed the Pegasus course. Looking at other perceived benefits to students, staff believed that some students had gained in self-confidence, better organization of work and self-direction, and there was a widespread view that students gained a more realistic and focused approach to career decision making.

Student Outcomes

Students who had participated in Pegasus courses generally responded very positively. The majority of those questioned joined the programme because they wanted to develop their personal skills; they had found the Pegasus sessions worthwhile and stimulating. Many of the respondents felt that they had gained real insight into new ways of working, and were more confident in areas relevant to their mainstream academic studies, such as time management and organization. An impression of the student response can be gained in a representative selection from the extensive comments on the course offered by students at Portsmouth:

> I am grateful for having been given the chance to participate in the Pegasus programme and am strongly in favour of making it compulsory for all students. Most students are very uninformed about the world of work and its demands, and so it is a shock to them when they graduate.

First time I've learned through playing games.

Pegasus made me believe that I was in with a chance and really helped me to get a job (after two interviews).

Pegasus helped me to identify what I actually can do and gave me an idea of the range of possible options; as a result I have embarked upon a career about which I knew nothing before the Pegasus course.

Pegasus didn't help me to choose my career, but it helped me to see what I wanted from a career.

It helped me to evaluate what was important for me and therefore helped me to feel my work has value and significance.

The residential weekend was brilliant fun. It helped me to learn to work in a team and uncovered strengths and weaknesses I didn't realize I had. It was also good to see how various groups interacted (or didn't!).

These achievements point to real and potential benefits which can follow upon the introduction of a Pegasus programme. Course development which focuses on transferable skills in this way must inevitably throw up questions which are part of a much wider policy debate about the thrust of higher education and its relationship to the world of work. Staff who have participated in the delivery of the programme often feel that they have gained through a closer collaboration with colleagues in the careers service and with employers; they also value the opportunity to experiment within the Pegasus framework with new approaches to teaching and learning. The most striking successes and the most important supporters of the initiative, though, are those students and graduates who believe that they have really benefited personally — that the Pegasus course has given them a new self-awareness, allowed them to develop in new ways, or directly helped them in gaining satisfying employment. At Portsmouth, these students have most commonly been from the Faculty of Humanities and Social Sciences. Through the work that they do on the Pegasus course, many of them are helped to make a positive and realistic assessment of their own particular personal qualities and skills, to appreciate more fully the intellectual training which their academic courses have given them and to understand how these assets can best be realized in their working lives.

Notes

1 The national Pegasus project was given launch funding by the DES and the British Institute of Management. Since 1987 it has been associated with the Understanding Industry Trust. The national Pegasus Management Committee is chaired by Sir Christopher Ball. The Pegasus National Director, from whom further information may be obtained regarding involvement in Pegasus either as a sponsor or as participating institution, is Mr Bob Johnson, Pegasus National Director, 29 Templar Road, Oxford, OX2 8LR.
2 Current sponsors include: Digital Equipment, IBM, British Petroleum, British Rail, Esso, Legal and General, British Rail and the Post Office.

3　These modules cover: presentation skills; communication skills; managing time; managing change; developing assertiveness; developing team skills; leadership skills; project management.

　　　A Pegasus Profile to assist in the analysis and recording of student's personal achievements and skills is also available. Work is proceeding on a database for materials developed in Pegasus courses on which newly participant institutions may draw.

4　'Personal Competencies in Higher Education — the Pegasus and similar Initiatives', 1989, report by Angela Brew, Director of the Portsmouth Polytechnic Educational Development Units; 'Pegasus Evaluation Report' 1991, for the Pegasus National Executive Director, by Digby Associates Bewdley, Worcs.

Chapter 15

Arts Graduates and Employment — A Careers Adviser's Perspective

Patricia Pearce

Many arts graduates complain of feeling confused particularly during their final year at college. Much of this confusion stems from the fact that they think they are on non-vocational courses; that they lack direction because their courses 'do not lead anywhere'. While on the surface this may appear to be the case, a deeper inspection finds that all degree courses allow for the development of many and various skills all of which, to a greater or lesser extent, are in demand by employers of graduates.

Despite this, many undergraduates and indeed postgraduates equate their degrees with knowledge rather than skills, whereas it is to be hoped that the process of higher education is *inter alia* about acquiring both in some measure. This is not to set hares running about education versus training but rather to assert *pace* Newman: 'If a liberal education be good, it must necessarily be useful'.

Careers advisers have rarely needed persuading that 'learning in higher education must lead to a higher order state of mind' as Ronald Barnett has stated in *The Idea of Higher Education*. However, their interface with recruiters of graduates has constantly brought home to them the need for graduates to be able to articulate the justification of their particular career choice. Most students do not appreciate the level of detail expected of them.

The study carried out by Brunel University in 1987 called *Expectations of Higher Education*' concluded:

> non-academic characteristics were important to employers in select-ing graduates. If most used academic qualifications in pre-selection and in screening recruits, the final decision about which candidates to employ was made on the basis of non-academic criteria. Whilst aca-demic qualifications target employers to a given level of ability, non-academic qualities which the employers want may override academic qualifications.

The fundamental aim of careers services in higher education is to help students understand the process of career choice and to develop their capacities to determine and execute immediate and later career decisions. In order to achieve this aim, careers advisers have therefore to help students clarify their skills, abilities, interests and values; help them to understand the range of opportunities available; help them relate the assessment of themselves to occupations; help them learn how to choose between alternative courses of action, and how to plan and execute a strategy to achieve their career goals including, if necessary, the acquisition of new skills.

The process of careers education may be said therefore to consist of:

— Self awareness: where the student is given the opportunity to explore the kind of person he or she has become or is in the process of becoming. This inevitably entails a chance not only to develop skills and interests but also to begin to test out values and clarify them. And the skills development will inevitably include intellectual, practical, sometimes technical and certainly personal skills. Only via processes and tasks leading to self awareness can students begin to evaluate what might be satisfactory for them in the world of work. As Joseph Conrad said in *Heart of Darkness*: 'I don't like work. . .no man does. . .but I like what is in work. . .the chance to find yourself. Your own reality. . . for yourself, not for others. . .what no other man can ever know'.

However, self awareness rarely takes place in a vacuum and goes hand in hand with:

— Opportunity awareness: where the student has the chance to understand and explore how the world of work is structured and what range of opportunities exist for both employment and further study. This exploration can then feed the knowledge of self and contribute not only to skills development but also to clarify values and interests, and thus help decide what might be satisfactory or unsatisfactory goals for the student.
— Decision learning: this process enables the student to gain insight into prioritizing actions in such a way as to optimize his/her chances of satisfaction. Again, in career decision-making it involves integrating what they know of themselves with what they know of the world of work in order to take action.
— Transition learning: this area of learning prepares students for coping with environments outside the world of education and enables the student to amalgamate self awareness, opportunity awareness and decision learning and proceed realistically with taking action. All this is the process of careers education. A possible conceptualization of the relationship between the four tasks of careers education *pace* Watts (1977) is thus:

| SELF AWARENESS | OPPORTUNITY AWARENESS |

| DECISION LEARNING |

| TRANSITION LEARNING |

This is a diagrammatic representation and does not properly take into account that in most people there is a constant feedback process taking place.

It will be seen from the preceding paragraphs that project learning, work-based learning, work placements and vacation work, more emphasis on student-centred learning, modularization and the assessment of prior experiential learning all have a vital part to play in contributing to the students' view of themselves, particularly in relation to employment. Although, therefore, the process of career decision-making is more complex than simply an analysis of one's skills, the fact that many arts graduates are not clear as to what their skills might be has led many careers advisers to introduce the concept of transferable skills in their work with students and academic staff in an attempt to develop the students' self-awareness. Certainly personal skills development programmes such as Pegasus and Enterprise in Higher Education have been enormously valuable in putting the concept of transferable skills centre stage. Skills which hitherto have been held to be implicit in arts degree courses such as communication skills, analytical and synthesizing skills, creativity, group skills, investigative skills, problem-solving, reasoning, skills of critique etc. can now be developed more explicitly within the course, apart from any other skills developed in an extra-curricular way. The case for articulating these skills more explicitly seems all the more important as it would appear that although skills clarification is not the only major criterion in this genre of decision-making, it nevertheless is a powerful clarifier, enabling students to proceed with values and interests clarification and at the same time imbuing them with an increased sense of confidence.

Putting the concept of transferable skills more noticeably on the agenda has not only affected the work of many careers services but is also effecting a quiet revolution in curriculum design and delivery as well as in academic staff development. Many of the skills which higher education has always purported to develop and which the world of employment need, are now being incorporated into modules added on to courses. These include for example: assertiveness training, self-presentation, numeracy, communication skills, etc. Gradually, however, it is being appreciated that to realize fully the course's objectives, such skills must be embedded in the curriculum. It is this realization which has given rise to lively debates concerning not only academic staff development but how and whether it is possible to deliver all of the major skills without rescrutinizing course design, methodology of curriculum delivery and attendant resourcing issues. It is good to see, therefore, that these issues have not only given rise to debate but also have produced an increase in short courses for academic staff covering these topics. What is becoming clearer to many tutors is the effect on students who have moved from a position of not being clear where their skills and therefore their futures lie to one of being surer of how to analyze what they have learned; they become more motivated to do better in their studies and become more confident as people. Such a process, therefore, not only enhances their vocational aims but also their academic ones. A vivid example of this occurred at the Polytechnic of Central London where a group of students studying French as part of a BA Modern Languages whom many staff felt to be less than highly motivated suddenly seemed to be writing essays of better quality and meeting deadlines more promptly. This followed a short series of exercises with the careers adviser on how to analyze their degree course and extra-curricular activities in terms of transferable skills. This was an example of a 'bolt-on' series. In the following academic year, a tutor in getting a class of undergraduates to research and analyze the work of a modern French poet was able to build into the curriculum other such skills as organization, team work, working to tight deadlines and creative skills. These were encouraged by setting up a group project involving videotaping a dramatized version of one of the poems. The exercise not only rehearsed the skills but had a noticeable energizing effect on the students who tackled the rest of their academic work with increased vigour.

Work-based and project-orientated learning is now much in vogue but in the past has been more usually associated with business/management studies or with technological and applied science subjects. Now it is becoming clearer that in arts subjects, too, what is taught and how the course is structured can powerfully boost not only the intellectual message but also develop personal as well as other skills.

Ronald Barnett in his *The Idea of Higher Education* writes, 'A practice can only be tolerated in higher education provided that it is susceptible to examination, evaluation and if necessary repudiation.' Thus the debate about skills teaching and learning necessarily now includes not only whether humanities courses should be associated with skills development and if so, how, but also whether and how they might be evaluated and assessed. Ultimately, not only is assessment essential to preserve academic rigour but it also helps students appreciate the importance of the process of learning as distinct from the content. Whatever the difficulties associated with skills assessment, careers advisers can state empirically that it is those students whose intellectual horizons have been widened and who have a greater consciousness of their ensuing range of skills as well as knowledge who are then able to optimize their chances of choosing and finding satisfactory employment and even of deciding on further study. From the students' point of view this is a highly desirable outcome; from the employers' of arts graduates point of view it is also desirable since they are searching out those who can transfer their learning to unfamiliar circumstances.

It is, therefore, more important than ever for careers advisers and academic staff to work closely together in the interests of students not simply because the former are in possession of much occupational and employer intelligence but because they constantly witness the transition of students from education to employment and are aware via the process of careers education of many of the educational, psychological and philosophical issues to be tackled. Equally academic staff bring a wealth of tutoring and creative course design expertise to curriculum development. All of these skills must be harnessed in the interests of students' intellectual and personal development and in the interests of the wider society to which they have such a large contribution to make.

References

BARNETT, R. (1990) *The Idea of Higher Education*, Milton Keynes, SRHE/Open University Press.

WATTS, A.G. (1977) 'Careers education in higher education: Principles and practice', *British Journal of Guidance and Counselling*, 5, 2, July.

Part E

Conclusion

Chapter 16

Making the Connections: Humanities, Skills, Employment

Heather Eggins

The need to search out effective ways of providing the country's arts gradu-ates with the skills they require is made more urgent by the constantly grow-ing popularity of these subjects. The expansion of access to higher education, and the encouragement being given to mature candidates to enter the system, has brought about a natural growth in student numbers in the arts areas. Figures for 1990/91 released by the Universities Funding Council indicate an expansion of 10.1 per cent in humanities, the largest growth area. Those who enter higher education in later years often do not possess the numerate and scientific basis of knowledge which would enable them to study science and technology subjects to degree level; they frequently, however, are well-read and have pursued interests in literature, history and the social sciences that any well-stocked local library can supply. Hence they can come, in their 30s and 40s to study arts subjects with an excellent grounding. Indeed the number of mature students with few previous paper qualifications that attain first class honours degrees is impressive.

A notable part of the present expansion of access is the rise in the number of women seeking higher education. Shifts in marital patterns, along with changes in academic and career expectations for women, are among the factors which are likely to make this more than a passing phenomenon. Women are particularly interested in the humanities: indeed, an overall figure of 2:1 has been indicated for the ratio of women to men on humanities courses (DES *Statistical Bulletin* 10/91). The trend then is for a growth in arts graduates as the UK moves towards mass higher education.

There is a further factor which emphasizes this trend. The cohort of 'A' level, 18-year-old candidates continues to show overall growth, despite the demographic downturn in this age group, but the growth is markedly uneven in pattern. There is a decline in the numbers for 1991 of those taking math-ematics and science subjects, and a steady growth in arts and humanities. English 'A' level, for instance, had 5000 more candidates (79,137 as against 74,182 in 1990); mathematics, on the other hand, lost almost 5000 candidates (75,006 as against 79,748 in 1990); French, German and Spanish candidates all increased by at least 10 per cent. David Hart, General Secretary of the National Association of Head Teachers, commented 'The decrease in 'A' level entries for maths and sciences is deeply worrying, not least in terms of this country's economic and industrial needs' (Hart, 1991).

It is clear that with the numbers of scientists likely to continue shrinking steadily over the next decade it is even more vital to give serious consideration to how the expanding numbers of arts graduates can be prepared for employment. The Standing Conference on English in Public Sector Higher Education (SCEPSHE) decided, as an aid to tackling the question 'How far down the skills and competences route is it possible to go without losing sight of content?' which had been posed in a CNAA Briefing Paper[1] that they would undertake a survey (Gee, 1990) of past students' opinions. Recent graduates who completed their degrees in 1985 and 1987 were asked whether they made use of skills related to their undergraduate studies in their current employment, and, if so, what they were.

The findings chime well with the views of the industrialists given in earlier chapters.

(i)   There appears to be no correlation between class of degree and level of income. Indeed, the report notes that 'it is noticeable how several of those achieving a pass or third class degree write their large salaries in *very* large print'. This tallies with Helen Perkins' view that what employers are seeking is 'a reasonable level of academic ability and then the personal skills and personality that are likely to make the individual a successful recruit and potential successful senior manager'.

(ii)   The range of jobs taken up by the sample of graduates is instructive. The largest categories are teaching and lecturing, administration and operational management, and buying, marketing and selling. A good number are employed in four further categories: media, including journalism; social work, medical work and the security services; financial work; and information and library work. Personnel, management services and creative and entertainment work follow behind, all with significant numbers. What is interesting is that smaller groups of arts graduates are moving into areas perceived as scientific in the public mind: scientific R and D development, engineering R and D development, scientific engineering service and environmental planning. Although the numbers are not high they represent 5 per cent of the sample — not inconsiderable if a genuine indicator of national take-up rates. Perhaps the shortage of science and technology graduates is already creating openings for humanities. Peter McManus testifies in his piece to the fact that this has always been the case, particularly in industries in expansionist mode.

When one turns to examine the employers that the graduates work for, a similar wide range is seen. Unsurprisingly schools, further education, polytechnics and universities account for some 20 per cent, the public sector 28.2 per cent, and the media industry 13.9 per cent. What is of interest is the involvement of humanities graduates in the financial sector (6.6 per cent), in commerce (13.9 per cent) and in industries not immediately obvious as employers of humanities graduates (10.5 per cent). These included chemical and pharmaceutical industries, engineering, manufacturing industry, building, agriculture, fisheries and food industries. The author points out that both engineering and design (the categories attracting single numbers) have lengthy courses of training which have the effect of shutting out humanities and other graduates from access. One can also argue that the engineering industry has suffered in the past from a lack of the infusion of those skills such as communication commonly found in humanities graduates.

(iii)　When asked whether they used skills related to their undergraduate studies in their employment, the past students responded positively. Their perception of the skills developed in their course and transferred to their employment are to a large extent compatible with those listed by the employers featured in earlier chapters, for example, Prudential Corporation, British Rail, National Westminster Bank. They also echo the findings of other researchers. There are some nice touches, for example:

self-skills
'everything you learn relates to what you teach' (teacher)
'I "abused" the freedom of study at Poly, but it taught me how to motivate myself — vital as I tend to work alone and set my own time-frames' (Development Officer)

group skills
'presentation of material in team meetings akin to seminars' (probation officer).

specific skill
'computer systems require logic and reason, as well as a certain amount of creativity' (business analyst)

job-specific skills
'techniques learnt in literary criticism useful for reading and understanding legislation: skills of time management, self-motivation always useful' (trainee solicitor)

The ability of the young graduates to analyze what skills they now use which they acquired during their undergraduate studies gives heartening credence to their maturity of outlook. It is pleasing to find that a high percentage of those interviewed considered that their present post offered good career prospects (84 per cent). Perhaps this fact alone indicates that humanities graduates and their skills are indeed making satisfactory connections with their employment.

However, much remains to be done, not least further work on the definition of the skills that the students develop on their courses, and on their assessment. Mrs Margaret Smart, Chief Inspector, HMI, writes:

There is an increasing tendency to look to 'transferable skills' for some kind of common element. This may well be a useful way forward, but what is rarely found is a clear definition of how these skills are developed and assessed within and across modules. It is, of course, very difficult to define and assess progress in, say, communication skills in a first year German module, a second year psychology module and a third year history module. Can there be agreed criteria for analysis and synthesis within and across modules? (personal communication, DES)

These problems are further explored in a recent DES publication (DES, 1991) which calls for considerable work to be done on the assessment of modules inculcating skills within humanities degrees.

The necessity to be able to define what exactly students have learned in terms of 'learning outcomes' on their courses is currently being addressed by a project being undertaken by the Unit for the Development of Adult Continuing Education (UDACE), soon to be merged into the Further Education Unit (FEU) of the DES. This project aims to develop descriptions of learning outcomes in five subject areas in higher education, one of which, English, is in the humanities. Their aims are two-fold: to reword existing course description to describe the learning outcomes expected by the course provider; and to examine in detail the aims, objectives and actual outcomes of the chosen courses, and the expectations of students, staff and employers. The findings will thus take further the thrust of this book.

In February 1991 UDACE published an interim consultative paper *What Can Graduates Do?* which charts the progress of the project. Interestingly the learning outcomes reported for English are the least satisfactory of the subjects under consideration. The consultative paper, under discussion by the CNAA Committee for Humanities, produced some of the same anxieties expressed by Margaret Smart:

> If physics, let us say, identified twenty-five learning outcomes and English thirty-six, and some of these are given the same name (for example, communications skills, personal skills, problem-solving skills) there is no reason to suppose that the competencies in the two subjects will be the same. Indeed, the type of problem-solving in physics, with its tendency to abstract from the detail and to generalize, will be very different from the problem-solving involved in English, where particular attention is given to detail. (CNAA, 1991)

Concern was also expressed that the UDACE project aimed to break down learning aims into 'small and explicit statements':

> Much of what is to be gained by deep study of any subject is necessarily inexplicit, a sensibility and sensitivity to the matter of the subject which is acquired naturally through immersion in the subject. This is particularly marked in a subject like English. The atomistic and explicit nature of the statements called for by UDACE abstracts from that tacit knowledge which is crucial to human practice.

One can argue, indeed, that even if one attempts to list the abilities developed by the discipline of English they are by their very nature subtle and immaterial. They arguably include, recognizing the place of the study of poetry within the curriculum:

(i) a continual awareness of the beauty of *form*;
(ii) an insight into levels of meaning, and ranges of significancies; a recognition of types of ambiguity;

(iii) a grasp of the ways in which language and the shapes of language carry meaning;

(iv) an understanding of tone, and of the reverberations of words and phrases that gather symbolic meaning;

(v) an appreciation of logic and rhetorical discourse;

(vi) a knowledge of people as they are, for example, Chaucer, and the ability to 'read' people;

(vii) the ability to make imaginative leaps in thinking.

On the one hand, then, one is faced with the problem of defining and re-cognizing what has been learned in that the outcomes are unlikely to be clearly perceived in precisely the same way by others, and on the other with the problem of assessing those outcomes which by their nature are necessarily inexplicit.

Research into how students learn and how their approaches to learning can be made more efficient is currently being studied in a CNAA development project being undertaken at Oxford Polytechnic. It is becoming increasingly evident that when students are trained to analyze their own learning approaches and grasp what skills they are themselves developing, then their overall academic performance improves. The introduction of personal skills profiles in a number of institutions is a testament to this hope.

All these developments are naturally having an impact on the curricula. A growing number of new syllabuses have now been validated which prepare students for the world of work in various ways. Two such examples are the degree in history and politics at Huddersfield Polytechnic and that in humanities at Staffordshire Polytechnic. An interesting aspect of these courses is the inclusion of opportunities for the students to develop further their grasp of information technology training and numeracy skills, as well as sharpening up communication skills. The humanities degree at Staffordshire, for instance, offers basic training in such skills as desk top publishing which are of clear benefit to graduates interested in the wide range of job opportunities in ed-iting and publishing. Courses such as these have proved to be highly popular: competition is fierce to gain a place. Indeed, there is growing evidence that those traditional university single honours courses are coming under increasing pressure from student and employer alike. A particular case is the traditional modern languages degree which concentrates on literature, in marked contrast to modern language degrees in polytechnics which also deal with the economic and political context of the countries whose language is studied. Likewise, modular courses, already well rooted in polytechnics, are being established in universities.

Institutions which had taken part in the CNAA 'Humanities and Em-ployment' initiative were invited to comment on how the initiative had affected their thinking with regard to their humanities courses.

The following quotations give a flavour of the responses:

> The seminars catalyzed a number of initiatives already coming to the fore and focused debate in helpful and specific ways. While the debate effectively raised staff consciousness, considerable agreement about

the need to address the skilling of students in relation to the labour market led to a greater emphasis generally in the revised course provision on student centred learning and, more specifically, the inclusion of modules in learning skills including numeracy and computer literacy and the introduction of work placements. (*The Polytechnic, Wolverhampton*)

The Course Committee resolved to invite the Careers Advisory Service to provide a series of seminars and workshops for personal tutors, designed to build their confidence and expertise in preparing their students for making informed decisions about their choice of work. (*Nottingham Polytechnic*)

Following the presentation of the Pegasus programme by a team from Portsmouth Polytechnic at the 'Humanities and Employment' conference, the Faculty of Human Sciences at Kingston Polytechnic decided to introduce the programme onto all its courses. (*Kingston Polytechnic*)

The seminar had some impact on staff morale: it made those concerned with developing employment-related skills among their students feel less isolated, and gave them the impression that what they were doing was taken seriously and valued by some of those in high places. (*Portsmouth Polytechnic*)

In addition to organizing 'Careers Events' for humanities students, we hope to bring back former students to give current undergraduates the benefit of their experience in the world of work and to encourage as many students as possible not to leave decisions about career opportunities until late in the final year or after graduation. (*Bristol Polytechnic*)

The range of responses is broad, but each impacts either directly on the educational experience offered to the student or on the staff involved in the delivery of the courses.

The discussions on learning outcomes are similarly bringing about a changed approach to the curriculum. Already some courses list projected outcomes including skills developed during each unit. However, the difficulties noted by CNAA and HMI remain in that course designers can find themselves making claims for skills which are resistant to assessment, particularly if they are of a subtle, highly sophisticated nature. Yet despite these problems, which are being grappled with, there is no doubt that institutions are making the connections between humanities courses and employment in ways that have not been attempted previously.

The message of this book, then, is clear. Research findings such as those alluded to by David Bradshaw, Chris Boys and Stina Lyons point towards the establishment of new knowledge on what skills students develop and how they develop them. Allied to this is a slow but surely developing dialogue between industry and higher education. The barriers of their different languages are being removed, assisted by such initiatives as that of CNAA, and by the Pegasus and EHE schemes. The awareness of students who are learning what to demand from the courses they are considering in humanities, coupled with the recognition by institutions that resources are well worth putting in place to enable staff to deliver these new approaches, is affecting the system. Evidence from courses such as that cited by Patricia Pearce indicates that the right approaches can have a marked effect on student performance and provide incentives for others who are concerned to maximise the student's abilities.

The message is that no single set of disciplines can provide *all* that society needs, but the growth of multidisciplinary programmes of study combined with the provision of numeracy and information technology packages does much to prepare a student for entry into employment. The humanities degree remains, as the Council for Industry and Higher Education (1990) pronounces 'a first-class preparation for working life'. It can be said, indeed to enhance the whole of life.

The increasing demand for qualified human resources will draw on all the Arts graduates we produce. The new approaches that will be needed by industry might well be satisfied by the skills engendered in our graduates:

The logical linear approach has to be substituted by lateral creative and most of all — holistic thinking. (Siegel, 1991)

It is hoped that the humanities graduate workforce of the twenty-first century will be enabled by their courses to contribute fully to society, and to continue in lifelong learning. Indeed, already Massachusetts Institute of Technology offers courses throughout the life-span of their students, already paid for. Perhaps the future of our higher education system might be mass and continual provision of higher education to our students and ourselves, to establish and maintain 'the tuning up of the mind' which is, in essence, higher education.

Note

1   CNAA (1990) *Humanities and Employment: The CNAA Initiative*, Briefing Paper 1, January.

References

CNAA COMMITTEE FOR HUMANITIES (1991) response to UDACE, London, CNAA.
COUNCIL FOR INDUSTRY AND HIGHER EDUCATION (1990) *Towards a Partnership: The Humanities for the Working World*, London, CHIE, p. 8.
DES (1991) *Higher Education in the Polytechnics and Colleges: Humanities and Social Sciences*, London, HMSO.
GEE, R. (1990) *Humanities and Employment: A SCEPSHE Survey*, London, SCEPSHE.
HART, D. (1991) *The Guardian*, 15 August.
SIEGEL, M.R. (1991) *Developing Leaders*, 7th Management Symposium for Women, Zurich, October.
UNIT FOR THE DEVELOPMENT OF ADULT AND CONTINUING EDUCATION (1991) *What Can Graduates Do?*, Consultative Document, London, UDACE.

Notes on Contributors

Sir Christopher Ball is currently Director of the Royal Society of Arts 'Learning Pays' project, and directed the earlier enquiry into higher education which resulted in the publication of *More Means Different* (1990) London RSA. He has also been, at various times, Warden of Keble College, Oxford and Chairman of the National Advisory Body.

Chris J. Boys has been concerned with research into employment and competences in work undertaken at Uxbridge University, and at CNAA. He now works for The National Council for Vocational Qualifications.

David Bradshaw OBE, an educational consultant, is Deputy Director of the Royal Society of Arts 'Learning Pays' project 1990–92, and formerly Principal of Doncaster Metropolitan Institute of Higher Education 1976–1989.

Christopher Chadwick was Training Officer with NMW Computers plc, Nantwich and is now Director of Mouldtech 2000 Ltd, a manufacturer of synthetic moulds for the pottery industry.

Professor Geoffrey Channon is Dean of the Faculty of Humanities, Health and Social Science, Bristol Polytechnic, and Chairman of the Steering Group on Humanities and Employment.

Sir Brian Corby is Chairman of Prudential Corporation plc and currently President of the CBI.

Sue Drew and **Roger N. Payne** work on the PSQ Project at Sheffield City Polytechnic.

Peter Findlay is Head of Academic Development and Review at Portsmouth Polytechnic and a member of the National Pegasus Board.

Eva Stina Lyon is Principal Lecturer in Sociology at South Bank Polytechnic. She has been involved in a major project on 'Higher Education and the Labour Market'.

Peter McManus was Head of Interactive Systems IBM UK Ltd and is now Head Director of Technical Strategy and Plans OEM IBM Europe.

Kelvin Moore was Senior Manager, Career Development Unit, National Westminster Bank and is now Senior Manager, Business Strategies Group, National Westminster Bank.

Patricia Pearce is Head of the Careers Service, Polytechnic of Central London, Chair of the Association of Graduate Careers Advisory Services Statistics Committee, and editor of 'First Destination Statistics for Polytechnic Graduates'.

Helen Perkins is Chairman of the Association of Graduate Recruiters and is Head of Management Development (Europe) for Price Waterhouse.

Professor David Watson was Deputy Director (Academic Affairs), Oxford Polytechnic and is now Director, Brighton Polytechnic.

Kenneth Wilson is Principal of Westminster College, Oxford.

Colin Wheeler is Infrastructure Services Engineer, York and a British Rail Contact Officer for universities and polytechnics.

Index